Robert Sténuit was a student of politics in Brussels, but left university to become a professional diver. He first heard of the *Girona* in 1958 while working in Vigo Bay, after which he devoted as much time as he could to both academic and practical research in the history and adventures of the ship. *Treasures of the Armada* is the result of that research. Mr Sténuit has also written *Les Epaves de l'Or*, an account of the expedition to look for another sunken Spanish galleon which took place in Vigo Bay in 1954.

D0522278

TREASURES OF THE ARMADA

Robert Sténuit

Translated by Francine Barker

CARDINAL edition published in 1974
by Sphere Books Ltd
30/32 Gray's Inn Road, London WC1X 8JL

First published in Great Britain
by David & Charles (Publishers) Ltd 1972

This book is set in Intertype Lectura

Printed in Great Britain by Cox & Wyman Ltd,
London, Reading and Fakenham

ISBN 0 351 18326 4

CONTENTS

PART II: GOLD UNDER THE SEAWEED

To dream is easy. To make a dream come true is not easy. A dreamer will not succeed alone. True, he drives the practical people with him toward a goal, but he would never reach that goal if the same practical people were not physically pushing him toward it.

Money, hardware, backbreaking work, enthusiasm, confidence were the things I absolutely needed if I were to succeed in taking back from the sea the treasure of the *Girona*. All these things, a Maecenas has given me. Henri Delauze, the Maecenas, has dived many times to 32,000 feet in the French bathyscaph (of which he was 'Chef de Laboratoire'). With the diving systems, the suits, the breathing apparatus which he and his company have engineered, he has dived down to 1,100 feet. Arriving there took him half of his life, but today under the seven seas his divers are opening a new field to the off-shore oil industry. To achieve just that, Henri Delauze has built the right organisation: COMEX, Compagnie Maritime d'Expertises, originally of Marseilles, now of the whole world. It has become the number one company in the field of deep diving and under-water engineering, and today Henri Delauze, President of COMEX, has thought fit to put back to the service of undersea archeology the tool and the fortune from his under-sea businesses.

Without the divers of COMEX, without COMEX, without Henri Delauze, there would have been no treasure and no book.

Robert Sténuit

LIST OF ILLUSTRATIONS

LIST OF ILLUSTRATIONS

Happiness is a childhood dream
fulfilled in adulthood.

Freud

Prologue

The galleass rolled from side to side in a welter of foam. Suddenly, looming in the night, 'Breakers ahead!' The first man on his feet leapt to the prow. With one blow of his axe he cut through the ropes that retained the cable. The anchor dropped.

Too late. The watch-keepers, who were desperately trying to heave in, saw a huge black and white mass hurtling towards the ship's side. With a cracking that seemed to herald the end of the world, the *Girona* gutted herself on the rocks, spilling out her cannon, her coffers, her innards. Into the breaking waves she cast one thousand three hundred sick men, many of them too exhausted to struggle.

One thousand three hundred men; including Don Alonzo Martinez de Leiva, Knight of Santiago and Commander of Alcuescar, the bravest captain of them all, favourite of Philip II, and commander designate of the Felicissima Armada, in the event of the death of Medina Sidonia; including sixty sons of the most noble families in all Spain, specially entrusted to Don Alonzo and anxious to serve under none other; including a young hidalgo, whose last thought as he choked on salt water must have sped toward Spain. Before setting out to conquer England, he must have spent his last night ashore with his betrothed. In the morning, his horse was already saddled, when she slipped a ring on his finger, a keepsake, specially commissioned from the best goldsmith. Left and right the swell tossed his body. Crabs and conger eels gnawed away his flesh. The ring slipped from his bony finger, and rolled away, with the contents of his pockets, down into a crevice. Storms heaped sand on to it, lumps of rock and lobster shells, slowly cemented together by the rust from the oxidising cannon balls.

After 400 years, deep in the dust of archives, I reconstructed the story. Under 30 ft of icy water I found the site of the wreck and with four team mates explored every cranny. We broke up the concretion, lifted huge boulders, sifted every grain of sand. Right at the bottom, beside a two escudo piece from Toledo and a few pieces of eight, we found the ring, given, to the music of the lark's song, by that tearful, red-eyed fiancée.

On the boat, the ring shone softly in the Irish sun. Out of all the treasures of the Armada, this is the most beautiful, the most moving. The setting is a tiny hand holding a heart and an open belt clasp. Engraved in the gold, I read these words: '*No tengo mas que dar te.*' 'I have nothing more to give you . . .'

PART I

The Most Fortunate Fleet

Jehovah blew and they were scattered.

(Dutch Commemorative Medal)

I

King Philip's Mission

Reverently I placed the ring in a jam pot in the bow of the boat, strapped a fresh cylinder on my back, gripped the mouthpiece between my teeth, and dived again.

A jungle of brown seaweed covers everything, our measuring lines included. But by now I know every rock and every crevice in the chaotic world of the seabed. Winging my way over that dense foliage I can spot them by a slight protuberance, an imperceptible hollow. Just as hurricanes flatten palm trees in Florida, the ceaseless swell of the Atlantic furls and unfurls the sunken forests. The swell is the sea's pulse. We live by its rhythm. To go forward I must wait for a wave to catapult me. When the movement stops I cling to a rock or to a sea tangle hurled suddenly backwards, its fronds flapping in the current like a flag, while the hose from my regulator, pulling against my clenched teeth, vibrates next to my ears. Then, like so many whips, the thongs of seaweed lash back again, and I am hurtled once more towards the narrow cleft in the rock that I am heading for.

At the end of my last dive I had to leave a silver coin wedged in the rock. This coin intrigues me. It is not a piece of eight, or four, such as we find everywhere. On the half visible face I manage to make out the unexpected words, HILARITAS UNIVERSA. I have brought a hammer and chisel with me this time. Gripping my legs round a rock to steady myself against the swell, I set to work on the calcareous mass that cements the rocks together. I shift one small stone to get at a larger one. I kick that out of the way. Now, sweeping with one hand, I can stir up the sand at the bottom of the cleft. The swell carries it off in thick clouds and reveals a cannon ball in its rust-coloured matrix. The matrix shatters under my hammer, the water turns black. A taste of iron in my mouth. I lift out the cannon ball. Later on I shall mark

17

its exact position on the plan. At last I can slip my crowbar in through the gap. I push long and hard on it. The boulder moves. I grasp it, straddle it, arch myself, take a deep breath and wait for a good roller. I pull with all my might. The boulder rolls out of its hole.

I pick out the coin and rub it between my thumb and fore-finger. A profile appears – a Roman breastplate, straight nose and forehead, a grave look in the eye, a noble beard. On the reverse the arms of Spain in an oval frame. A Neapolitan silver escudo, hardly blackened. Of course! The *Girona* was part of the squadron of Naples, the capital of the Kingdom of the Two Sicilies. It's the ambitious king, the administrator, the spider king, who, from the depths of his palace of San Lorenzo de Escorial, spun that intricate web with which it was his mission to bind the world. It is Philip II, the Prudent, Defender of the Faith, Suppressor of Heresy, by the grace of God, King of Aragon, Castile, León, King of Sardinia and the Two Sicilies, King of Navarre, of Granada, Toledo, Valencia, Galicia, Majorca, Seville, Cordoba, Corcyra, Murcia, Jaen, the Algarve, Algeciras, Gibraltar, the Canary Islands, the East Indies, the West Indies, the Spanish Main, King of Portugal, of Algarva, Brazil, the Azores, the Cape Verde Islands, Ruler of the Guinea, Angola, Mozambique and India settlements, Governor of Aden, Muscat, Ormuz, Java, the Moluccas, the Philippines, Macao, Archduke of Austria, Duke of Milan, of Limburg, Brabant, Luxembourg, Guelders, Marquis of Antwerp, Count of Hapsburg, Burgundy, Tyrol, Barcelona, Flanders, Artois, Hainault, Namur, Holland, Zeeland and Zutphen, Lord of Biscay, Molina, Overijssel, Tournai, Groningen, Utrecht and Friesland, King of Jerusalem, a defeated King.

Numb with cold, my fingers close on the history of Europe. For years I have pursued it, spending hour upon hour in dusty libraries and archives of Britain, Spain, France, Belgium and Holland. At last I have history literally in my grasp, here, under the sea, in the very place where it was made.

I close my eyes and Philip lives again, the man who, in 1588, after twenty years of intrigue and hesitation, launched against England the most powerful expedition, the largest fleet ever seen, 'because such was the mission he had received from God'.

The sun never set on Philip's empire, and never had so scattered an empire depended to such an extent on supremacy at sea. Each year more gold was mined in America than had existed in the whole of Medieval Europe. Special fleets of armed galleons, the *Plata Flotas*, the plate fleets, carried this annual haul back to Cadiz. Pirates of all nations dreamed about it, and so did the sailors of Her Most Gracious Majesty Queen Elizabeth's Royal Navy. Sometimes they did more than dream. If Philip was going to keep the world in his clutches for himself, if he was going to protect the Spanish trade monopoly with the Americas, to continue unhindered transporting from Peru and Mexico to his own coffers the gold necessary to maintain Christ's Army, there was one last rival still to be swallowed, Elizabeth, who obstinately persisted in putting England and her ships in his way.

As early as 1568, this divine mission must have begun to take shape in the mind of His Most Catholic Majesty. That year, one of his ships was leaving Spain with an escort of four *zabras*, taking as pay for the Duke of Alba's troops to Flanders, one million gold ducats. The ship had to make an unscheduled stop at Southampton. Elizabeth stole the gold. Unable to pay his men, Alba found himself in an extremely difficult situation. He retaliated by putting an embargo on all the English merchandise he could lay his hands on in Flanders. Elizabeth replied by seizing every Spanish merchant ship in English waters. Spain then seized all English ships in Spanish ports and sent their crews to the galleys. England arrested the Spanish Ambassador. Negotiations went on for years, but Philip never saw a *maravedis* of it again.

His mission was brought to mind again in 1580. For as long as anyone could remember he and the Pope had been financing and arming Irish rebels. Encouraged by the fact that the Earl of Desmond, leader of the latest uprising, had managed to crush the Lord Deputy's troops at Glenmalure, Philip sent over in support a landing force of several hundred Spaniards and Italians. An English army hurried to the spot, took them all prisoners at Smerwick, and strangled them one by one. There was nothing Philip could do. There had been no formal declaration of war. Spoke Spanish, did they, these soldiers? Strange. Where could they have come from? He, in any case, knew nothing about it.

Action became more pressing still in 1583, when Elizabeth expelled Don Bernardino de Mendoza, the Spanish Ambassador in London, certain ministers having accused him of being rather too deeply involved in Throckmorton's plot to kill the Queen. Philip took offence. He threw all the English in Spain into jail, confiscated their property and put a ban on all trade between the two nations.

During a corn shortage in Spain, in 1585, he gave a specific safe conduct to a group of English merchants and invited them to send a fleet of corn ships over to his northern ports in May. The fleet had hardly arrived when one crew threw overboard some Spanish soldiers who attempted to go on board in disguise. Philip ordered that all ships and cargo be seized and the crews sent to the galleys. But one ship managed to get away, and brought the news to London. It met with an angry reaction. The good faith of the King of Spain was questioned.

And during these last fifteen years, English pirates persisted in plaguing Spanish ports and the Spanish fleet with their plundering expeditions, carried out in the Queen's ships, financed by her, by her ministers and by her courtiers. Vigo, the Cape Verde Islands, Cape St Vincent had all been attacked. A certain adventurer, of humble birth, Francis Drake, was waging his own personal war against the most powerful king in the world. He had sacked most of the West Indies ports at least once. He had pillaged San Juan de Ulla, scoured the Gulf of Mexico and brought down Nombre de Dios, helped by some French pirates and a band of runaway black slaves. In the Isthmus of Panama he had seized the annual haul of gold from Peru, on its way by mule from the Pacific to the Atlantic. On his return Drake explained to the Queen that the booty had been acquired through 'exchanges with the natives'. The Queen passed this on to the Spanish Ambassador, who very nearly exploded with rage.

As the *Golden Hind* rounded America in 1580 by the Straits of Magellan, *El Draque,* the dragon, completed the first round-the-world buccaneering trip, at the expense of galleons looted en route and Spanish ports on the Pacific, where he had arrived unexpectedly. The voyage had lasted two years and ten months. Of the five ships that set out four did not return. Nonetheless there were still silks, spices and purloined gold (much of the silver had been thrown overboard before the return journey because it was too bulky), enough to yield a dividend of 4,700 per cent to the shareholders, over and above

Drake's own cut and Her Majesty's. And still England and Spain were not at war. When the Spanish Ambassador, in the name of his sovereign the King, thus discomfited and robbed, demanded compensation for his ruined merchants and his murdered subjects, and insisted once again that the man responsible be punished, the Queen hesitated. Once again she reckoned up the share of the fabulous booty that lay in her coffers. After a sumptuous banquet, she dubbed the marauder Sir Francis and appointed him Admiral of her navy. Then, the *pirata luterano,* as the Spaniards called him, again put to sea. After looting on the outward passage various ports in Spain, the Canaries and Puerto Rico, he held San Domingo for ransom and pillaged it, laid seige to Cartagena, set fire to St Augustine in Florida, and returned with two hundred cannon in addition to the usual booty.

Philip's divine mission had become very clear indeed when Elizabeth opened the royal purse and lent ships to Don Antonio, the Prior of Ocrato and illegitimate grandson of Manuel i, who had himself crowned King of Portugal, to the throne of which Philip held title by his first marriage. It had become clearer still when Elizabeth started making overtures to the Sheriff of Morocco, suggesting an alliance with him against Spain, his traditional enemy.

Now, Elizabeth signed a treaty with the Dutch. She had garrisons at Flushing and at Brill, and in 1586 her favourite, Robert Dudley, Earl of Leicester, had landed 5,000 foot and 1,000 horse, paid for out of her own funds, to support the rebel heretics of the Seven Provinces, the northern provinces which no governor had managed to bring into line.

On 8 February 1587, the executioner laid down his axe in the great hall of Fotheringay Castle. He stooped down to grasp the auburn hair, then raised his hand high, crying the customary words 'Long live the Queen'; the crowd had shouted in chorus after him. Only then did the headsman realise that all he held in his hand was a wig and a kerchief. Clotted with blood, the head had rolled to the edge of the scaffold. 'And all could see how worry and anxiety had by her forty-fifth year withered and greyed the queen, who in her lifetime had been counted among the most beautiful women in the world.' The head was that of Mary Stuart, Dowager Queen of France, deposed Queen of Scots, and in Philip's view, legitimate heir to the throne of England. Action was now inescapable.

21

The execution deeply shocked the whole of Europe. Political etiquette required that kings and princes be assassinated, preferably poisoned. A public beheading at the hands of the common executioner was considered outrageous by the nobility. It made royal princes subject to the common justice of ordinary men.

By Catholic law, the dead queen had every right to the throne. It so happened that, before her martyr's death, she had disowned her Protestant son, James VI of Scotland (who, notwithstanding, later becames James I of England) and secretly promised her throne to the direct descendant of the sons of Edward III, His Most Catholic Majesty the King of Spain. She had put her wish in writing and sent copies to Philip, the Pope and the Spanish Ambassador in Paris. It was now up to Philip, the Defender of the Faith, he felt, to carry out the sacred mission of freeing the English people from their Protestant yoke – to take the crown that was rightfully his – or rather, as he promised the Pope, to place it on the head of his daughter Isabella Clara Eugenia.

Philip learned of the execution on 23 March 1587, in a dispatch from his Ambassador in Paris, Count Bernardino de Mendoza. He spent the whole of the following week deep in thought; when he emerged from his study he had made his decision to strike

2

The Enterprise of England

The prudent King had drawn up his plan. The Governor of the Spanish Netherlands, Alexander Farnese, Duke of Parma and Piacenza (Spanish documents refer to him variously as Duke, Grand Duke or Prince) was to assemble the army of Flanders at Dunkirk, while at the same time making ready to embark at Nieuport. Meanwhile, Don Alvaro de Bazan, Marquis of Santa Cruz, would, by the spring, have gathered together at Lisbon a fleet strong enough to hold Elizabeth's at bay and destroy it if necessary. The fleet would cover the crossing and protect the Army's line of supply and communication. Once he reached England, having crossed in a flotilla of barges, Parma would be able to count on the Catholic nobility rallying to him and on the combined forces of the Irish and the Scots. The King sent William Semple over with 42,000 escudos to distribute among potential local fifth columns.

For financial support in his crusade, the Defender of the Faith quite naturally turned to Christ's Vicar on Earth, to Pope Sixtus v, who had been urging him to act since the day of his investiture, and who declared himself ready to aid the undertaking of the leading soldier of Catholicism in every possible way (except one, that is, as I discovered very early on in my research).

Pius v had already excommunicated Elizabeth in 1570 in his papal bull *Regnans in Excelsis,* in which the queen was declared a heretic and a persecutor of true religion and was deprived of 'her pretended right to the throne.' Subsequently Gregory xiii had promised plenary absolution to William Parry, the man picked to assassinate Elizabeth, if his mission were successful. The blundering fool failed and got himself arrested, as did at least two more of Rome's hired assassins, both before and after him. Sixtus v had, in his turn, confirmed Philip's hereditary claims to the English throne. Philip repeatedly assured him that he had quite enough crowns as it was, and that the English one would be for his daughter; that his aim was not to enlarge his empire but purely to defend the true faith.

As soon as Philip had drawn up a plan for his military offensive, Sixtus v launched his psychological offensive. He issued a new bull, informing all Christians that Elizabeth was 'a heretic and a schismatic . . . twice excommunicated . . . illegitimate . . . conceived and born of an incestuous adultery'; that she had 'usurped the throne in violation of the law . . .'; that she had committed 'many serious offences, outrages, extortions and breaches of the law against the poor and innocent population of the Two Kingdoms . . .' that she was therefore incapable of governing and not worthy to live. 'Therefore,' the Bull went on, 'his Holiness renews the sentence of excommunication and relieves her once more of all royal rank . . . and releases her subjects from every sort of subjection, oath and other forms of allegiance . . .'

To all who set off on his crusade the Pope granted plenary indulgence, absolution, remission of sins, apostolic blessing, and everything else.

The ready? Ah, yes, ready money – but of course. Count Olivarez, the Spanish Ambassador in Rome, who was besieging the Pope with his demands, had suggested an advance of two million ducats. After close consideration Sixtus had talked vaguely of 200,000 on account plus a further 100,000 when the army landed, another 100,000 in six months and 200,000 a year for the duration of the war. Olivarez had strict instructions not to take charity and he made this clear to the Pope. But Philip, having made his resolution, was prepared to compromise. He reduced his demand to a million and a half ducats. The Pope promised a million.

A promise is a promise, he had sworn to the Ambassador in the names of various saints. 'The day the first Spanish soldier sets foot on English soil, I, Sixtus v, will give the King of Spain one million gold ducats.' An advance? Patience, my son, patience. A loan, meanwhile? Out of the question, what's said is said. And on 8 August the Ambassador, rebuffed yet again, wrote sheepishly to the King 'His Holiness remained intractable *como un diamante* . . . His Holiness would rather have his guts torn from him than money. I am getting nowhere.'

3

The Marquis of Santa Cruz

I have read every single one of the countless missives that were sent out every day via galloping couriers from the Escurial – to get together at Lisbon and Cadiz, as soon as possible, ships, men and provisions from all over the kingdom. To all those in positions of responsibility, Philip had stipulated absolute secrecy. If it was impossible to conceal the enterprise itself, it was possible to maintain a degree of uncertainty around its objective. 'The house must be ablaze,' he wrote, 'before anyone even knows where the lightning will strike.'

But Elizabeth had been expecting that particular lightning to strike her roof for some time. Any lingering doubts that she may have had were soon dispelled by one of Sir Francis Walsyngham's spies, who learnt of the existence of a letter from Philip to the Pope. It was purchased from a Venetian priest who had himself acquired it from one of the Gentlemen of His Holiness's Bedchamber. While the Pope was sleeping the key to his secret closet was abstracted from his purse, the letter found and copied. It was conclusive.

To gain time to get her defences and fleet in better order, Elizabeth loudly protested her desire for peace and got the ex king of Denmark to suggest a meeting to Philip so as to 'avoid a battle'. Philip protested his own heartfelt desire for peace equally loudly and immediately accepted the suggestion of a meeting. Once they had agreed on it in principle, it was decided that it should take place at Bourbourg near Calais. Elizabeth sent a delegation headed by Sir James Croft. Philip ordered Parma to send the chancellor Frederick Perrenot, an old hand in tricky matters of diplomacy.

While the coastal defences of the whole of England, the Isle of Wight, the Thames and approaches to London were hurriedly strengthened, Drake convinced the Queen that the thing to do was to nip the invasion in the bud. She must let him attack Cadiz. That, he felt sure, would be the main centre of the Spanish preparations. The Queen charged him to do it in one written order, and forbade him in another, which she had delivered to Plymouth nine days after he had left. She was careful to keep a copy of it to show Philip, who would be requiring an explanation.

The arrival of *El Draque,* the Dragon of the Apocalypse, spread panic in Cadiz. He captured six good ships and burned eighteen more, including Santa Cruz's personal galleon. He landed more or less where he chose in Portugal, then cruised off Cape St Vincent, where he sunk or captured sixty tuna fishing boats. What was far more serious, though, he burned forty coasting vessels loaded with staves for casks, barrels, hogsheads, butts, pipes and tuns, forty cargo loads of seasoned wood staves, that the Armada would badly need for storing water and wine and keeping provisions. Drake raised the blockade only to go out and meet the *San Felipe,* an enormous Portuguese carrack on her way back from Goa, her holds packed with spices, silks and ivory and her coffers brimming with gold, silver and exotic jewels. He captured her after a brief skirmish, bringing his booty up to a total of £115,000, of which his own share was £17,000 and Her Majesty's £40,000 (in the Queen's written order, the only paragraph that was absolutely clear and unambiguous was the one establishing the Crown's share of the booty). Drake could boast on his return of having 'singed the King of Spain's beard'. He had completely upset preparations for the fleet for months. It was principally because of his action that the Armada would not be ready in 1587.

On other fronts things were going rather better for Spain. That summer, Parma made use of his rear by capturing Sluys from the Dutch, after an epic siege. All the time he was pretending to negotiate, he was having a new canal dug between Sluys and Nieuport to protect his lines of communication from storms and the Sea Beggars. He was having the whole of the forest of Waas cut down to build another 100 troop barges, 40 flyboats and 2 small, 200-ton galleons.

Meanwhile in Paris, Mendoza was plotting day and night, supporting the Holy League and Mary's relatives, the Guises, against Henry III. Daily more divided and bloodless, France would never risk invading Flanders while Parma was fighting in England.

For four years, Santa Cruz had in vain been urging Philip to act. Suddenly, in September 1587, when he was no longer prepared for it, when he no longer believed in it, when he was actually in the Azores escorting the plate fleet, the King wrote to him, 'As soon as you return and the Neapolitan galleys and Andalusian victuallers have joined you, you will sail for the Cape of Margate and the Thames. Your task will be to support Parma. That the enemy will be taken by surprise is assured, and by the Grace of God for whom we toil you will have calm seas and favourable winds.'

Santa Cruz was dumbfounded, protesting that the situation had completely changed. Drake had doubled his forces. The storm had loosened the timbers of many of his ships. It would be utterly reckless. Philip gave him three weeks to make ready – Santa Cruz begged for five. Philip argued that with the Italian reinforcements, the Prince of Parma had 30,000 men ready and waiting in Flanders, and few would be left if action was delayed to the spring. He ordered Santa Cruz to depart. Santa Cruz complained that he had asked for 50 galleons, but had only 13, together with 4 galleasses and 60 old 'tubs' that were not even watertight. He had neither enough armaments nor enough ordnance, and hardly any auxiliary small craft.

Philip, in December, again pressed him to leave immediately, whether the Armada was ready or not, and to rendezvous with Parma. Santa Cruz reported that he was leaving, but that he had word from England that fortifications had been erected all round the coast, militia troops were being recruited, and that already Drake was waiting for them with a strong and well-equipped fleet. Philip had heard so too. Santa Cruz was to wait, carry on preparations, and be ready by 15 February.

Santa Cruz worked on through the winter without a moment's respite, bombarded by letters from the King full of reproaches and curt instructions to make ready his great enterprise. He was galled that the Duke of Parma should have been given precedence over him. The King was told of this, and begged him to state once and for all whether he was willing to sail under those conditions or whether he preferred to remain where he was, in which case he would still have to see to all the necessary preparations.

Don Alonzo de Leiva, Philip's favourite, former Captain General of the galleys of Naples, and former Captain General of the Milanese cavalry, declared publicly that 'it might be a good idea to send someone to Lisbon to spur the old Marquis on'. The King sent the Count of Fuentes to inspect the fleet and the preparations. His Council of War, sensing that the wind was changing, lined itself up behind the King.

Santa Cruz knew that he was the object of intrigue, that he was being slandered at court. He was sixty-two. At the beginning of February he had to take to his bed. By the 9th he was dead. It was said in Lisbon that what had killed him were the King's 'continual and unreasonable demands', that he had died of 'overwork, shame and grief', and that he was 'universally mourned, by captains and soldiers alike — it was in him that all hope of success had been vested'.

4

His Excellency the Duke of Medina Sidonia

The day Philip learned that Santa Cruz was ill, he summoned his secretary and had him write to Don Alonso Perez de Guzman a letter marked 'top secret', in which he commanded him to take over from the Marquis and ordered him to set off immediately. Known like the most prestigious of his illustrious ancestors as *El Bueno*, he was thirty-eight, a Knight of the Golden Fleece, Marquis of Cazaza in Africa, twelfth Señor and fifth Marquis of Sanlucar de Barramaeda, ninth Count of Niebla and seventh Duke of Medina Sidonia. In other words he owned half of Andalusia. 'Short, stocky, with a thin, friendly face . . . rather bow legged . . .', his friends said of him that he was 'the best horseman in Spain, the best at the sport of canes, the best rejaneador . . . that he had killed with his lance the most savage bulls.' At the age of twenty-two, after an engagement lasting six years and by special dispensation from the Pope, he had married Dona Ana de Silva Mendoza, then aged ten and a half. The marriage was consummated that very night; as Medina Sidonia's biographer explains, 'The Duchess's judgment and discretion more than made up for any disadvantage that her age might have had for the marriage.' At the age of thirty-one he was awarded by Philip the Order of the Golden Fleece, the highest order of knighthood, normally restricted to reigning monarchs and princes of the blood royal.

The Duke was not an ambitious man. He liked a peaceful, quiet life and the calm of his orange groves. When he was offered the post of Governor of Milan, he was profuse in his apologies. He couldn't possibly go . . . a matter of his health . . . the health of his wife. So he carried on shooting quail and looking after his vast estates.

The Marquis's illness and the King's letter vexed him deeply. On 16 February, Sidonia took up his pen. 'I must first kiss His Majesty's hands and the royal feet for having deigned to consider me for so great a task ...' To the most powerful king in the world, who was offering him the most glorious post at the head of the most important enterprise of his reign, the Spanish grandee, noblest of all the nobles, continued, 'But my health is not up to such a voyage. . . . On the rare occasions when I have been at sea I have been seasick, and moreover I catch cold easily.'

The head of the most powerful family in all Spain, in lands, privileges and riches, the man whose personal fortune was reputed to be even greater than the King's, went on:

Besides. I am in such dire financial straits that every time I come to Madrid I have to borrow money ... my estate has debts of 900,000 ducats. I should be unable to contribute so much as a *real* to the enterprise. It would not be right for me to accept, for I have no experience of seafaring or of war ... and even if I had, it would mean going into it blind, throwing myself into this expedition totally unprepared, and not knowing the first thing about it ... besides which His Majesty will find a man most fit to serve him in this voyage in the person of the Adelantado Major [governor] of Castile, a man of great experience ... and His Majesty can be confident that the Adelantado will have God's help behind him, for he is a very good Christian. . . . I humbly beg His Majesty not to entrust me with a task of which I should give a bad account, for I know nothing and understand nothing about it. I have not health for the sea and no money to put into it. . . . May God preserve and keep the Most Catholic Person of Your Majesty.

On the 18th the King signed his official appointment. He had him advised of it the same day and commanded him to leave Lisbon – immediately.

It was said in Spain at the time – how accurately I do not know: these are rumours and gossip reported by a Dominican monk, Fray Juan de la Victoria – that the Duchess had urged her husband to refuse the appointment. According to certain of her lady friends, she is supposed to have said, 'Ladies, I know the Duke can keep up appearances in his own house and in places where he is not too well known, but it pains me to think that now he will be shown up for what he is, and will lose his reputation.'

The Duke did not reply to the royal command until the 29th. He was still at home.

... since Your Majesty, notwithstanding my frank admissions, orders me to serve him, my conscience is clear. I shall do so ... may the Lord help your Majesty in your good intentions, and since what is to be done is for Him, I hope that in His goodness He will do so. ... I should appreciate it if Your Majesty could have me informed and instructed on everything that pertains to this expedition and on how to act in all things ... and that a decision should be made as to what needs to be done. I remain Your Majesty's most humble servant ... and I pray Your Majesty to permit Francisco Duarte, who is very experienced in matters of seafaring, to sail with me.

From the King to the Duke, 11 March:

Duke of Medina Sidonia, Cousin, my Captain General of the Ocean Sea and of the coast of Andalusia ... I thank you for the good will with which, setting aside all difficulties, you have decided to depart and serve me in this expedition. ... I am certain that you will enjoy every success ... that there is no reason for you to worry, and if you should die in this expedition I shall take care of your children.

Meticulously, the Duke put his affairs in order, stepped sadly into his carriage and took the road to Lisbon, through his orange groves.

At Lisbon, he states, he found chaos. He had barely arrived before he buried himself in Santa Cruz's papers. He listened to what everyone had to tell him and looked around him. He assembled a general staff. He surrounded himself with sailors, soldiers, artillerymen, strategists, advisors. The picture was gloomy: too few ships, and those too small and in bad condition; too few cannon and those with only half the range of English guns; insufficient powder and shot; shortage of provisions and water; far too few soldiers, experienced mariners or qualified gunners; and not enough money. Some companies were owed sixteen pays, arrears which could not be made up. For the time being, Sidonia did not mention any of this to the King, who, basing his impressions on his correspondence with Santa Cruz, had written to Sidonia on 7 March assuring him that everything was ready at Lisbon, that there was nothing more to be done. 'You will be able,' wrote Philip, 'to embark the infantry before the 20th, and, weather permitting, and with God's help, you should sail on the 14th or 25th at the latest.'

The old Marquis of Santa Cruz had originally asked for 510 ships. It was asking the impossible of Philip, as Philip was asking the impossible of Santa Cruz in ordering him to sail on such short notice.

One way or another, the Marquis had managed to swell the numbers of his fighting fleet, until it mustered 65 ships and 16,500 men. The Duke increased the numbers further still.

On 19 March he went personally to look over the fleet. On the basis of this inspection he informed the King that everyone was ready. There were just one or two carpentry and joinery jobs that needed doing. He was going to have stronger bow and stern castles built, and the decks reinforced to give better protection to the crew in bad weather and in battle. A few ships were too old and would have to be left behind. Cargoes could be better divided between the vessels, the artillery shared out, and the Andalusian fleet still lacked its full complement, and so on. . . . The galleasses would be finished and ready by the end of the week.

Then, from letter to letter, little by little, I watched this optimism fade. The duke paints a blacker picture of a situation that he sees as more and more serious.

> Everyone is either deserting or about to desert . . . the soldiers are barefoot, few of them have clothes . . . there are many who haven't been paid for a year now. There aren't more than 10,000 men left, more like 9,000. . . . We haven't enough seasoned mariners. . . . The money is melting away.

5

'You will sail with 200,000 Ducats'

On 20 March the King dictated a seven-page letter (of particular interest to me) to Sidonia, ordering him to review his troops and embark them, and giving instructions that the Armada should be ready to sail by the end of the month and not a day later. In addition to clothes and relief already provided, Philip gave Sidonia permission to give every member of the expedition two months' pay, 'which will send them all off in good spirits . . . it would be well to give them only one pay before embarking and the other when they are on board in their ships . . . and once they are on board, you will make sure that no one leaves again.'

What followed interested me still more:

> One pay for the entire Armada . . . mariners and soldiers . . . amounts to 116,000 ducats of ten reals a month, two pays to 232,000 ducats. . . . The Paymaster has in his possession 433,878 ducats of ten reals, which leaves 200,000 to take with you in the Armada. You will permit no one to touch this sum for any reason whatsoever, but will make sure that it is taken on board intact.

200,000 ducats! Even spread over ten *capitanas*, there was enough there to make a treasure hunter's mouth water. Being first and foremost an archaeologist, I merely made a mental note of it, and went on reading.

On 26 March the Duke, who was becoming increasingly reticent, wrote again to the King; 'Your Majesty was told that the Armada was ready to leave at two days' notice. When I arrived I found a very different state of affairs.' The Duke's letter crossed one from the King, in which he was adamant in his insistence. 'Seeing that you have now checked with your own eyes that everything is virtually ready, you will embark the infantry, if you have not already done so. ... You will be ready to sail on April 5th, or 6th at the latest and earlier if possible. ...'

In defiance of orders, Medina Sidonia was calmly having every rotten timber replaced, hulls recaulked, and sails and rigging carefully checked and renewed where necessary. So it was not until 2 April that the Captain General informed the King that the general inspection had taken place and that the troops were ready to be embarked. On the question of money, he wrote:

Even if we give our men only two pays, there will be no money left to take along with us, and the mariners are in no mood to be satisfied with so little considering how much they are owed. As it is extremely difficult to get good work from discontented and underpaid men, I beg Your Majesty to be pleased to send us a decent sum, if possible by special courier or riders.

Meanwhile the Duke had received detailed orders:

Since victories are in the hands of God, to give and to take away as he sees fit, and since your cause is so peculiarly His as to assure you of His help and favour, if this is not undeserved by sinfulness, great care must be taken that none is committed in this fleet, and in particular that no blasphemy is uttered, under pain of the most severe punishment to be carried out publicly, in order that the chastisement for having tolerated such blasphemy may not descend upon all.

On receipt of my orders, you will leave immediately for the English Channel. You will sail up the Channel as far as Cape Margate, where you will rendezvous with my nephew, the Duke of Parma and Piacenza, in order to cover his crossing.

You will send him regular reports of your progress. You will prearrange certain meeting points in the event of the Armada's being scattered by a storm, say Vigo, Corunna and the Scilly Islands. Once in the Channel you will not seek battle with Drake, unless you find his forces divided and are able to get the weather gauge of him ... rather, you will sail on in good order to your rendezvous with Parma.

Do not fail to let every man know that the enemy has the advantage in artillery and with his superior firepower will try to fight at long range. The aim of our men must, on the contrary, be to bring the enemy to close quarters and grapple with him.... You will also be sure that following the victory our fleet does not scatter in pursuit of booty ... and you will have to economise as best as you can all the money there is in the Armada.

Once the troops carried by the Armada have been landed, they will be entrusted to Don Alonzo de Leiva, my Captain General of the Milanese Light

Cavalry, who will command them until the arrival of the Duke, my nephew, to whom he will then turn over his command.

[Done at Madrid, April 1st, 1588, I, the King.]

Medina Sidonia replied to the King on 11 April:

I humbly kiss Your Majesty's hands for doing me the honour of placing such trust in me. . . . I will serve him to the fullest extent of my powers, my only bitter regret being that they are not greater, so that I might devote them all to the service of God and Your Majesty. But I put my trust in the Divine Mercy . . . for the conduct of this mission which is so truly His that no one can be doubtful of victory. . . . Once again I must impress on Your Majesty the seriousness of our shortage of money. While I know that Your Majesty will already have given the order, I beseech him yet again to have some sent immediately, if he has not already done so. This alone is holding up our departure. Until it arrives, I have decided to send a special courier to Your Majesty every day for no other purpose than to request it. To conclude, may God preserve and keep Your Most Catholic Majesty. . . .

On 4 April, tired of the Duke's endless promises, the captains, *alfereces*, officers, sergeants and veteran soldiers, who were still waiting vainly for their pay, threatened to go home. Sidonia wrote to the King, that the most experienced and valuable of his men might leave, and that he would be unable to stop them. Again he pleaded for more money.

By the time I got to this letter I too was beginning to beseech His Majesty, 'Come now, Sire, a bit of generosity. Zounds, Sire, you're not going to have me find the wrecks empty!' My wishes were granted in a letter from Philip giving Sidonia 20,000 ducats to cover his personal expenses in the Armada . . . these 20,000 ducats to be deducted from what was left over from the 232,000 set aside for the two pays. But, if Philip had decided to ignore his demands for money and thought to shut him up by a personal favour, the Duke was in no mood to read between the lines. He turned a deaf ear, thanked him kindly and went on to say he was greatly troubled by the shortage of powder, again stressing the need for funds. Still more dispatches flew back and forth, and once more the Duke emphasised:

Departure is proceededing with all possible haste. If the money for which I have sent Your Majesty a special courier, and the Indies galleons which I expect from Cadiz at any moment, were to arrive, I could leave here within a day. . . . But without money the Armada cannot sail.

6

The Most Fortunate Fleet

While the Duke stubbornly continued to wait, the organising and strengthening of the fleet progressed gradually. But each day passed in port meant fresh inroads into the coffers and into the provisions. It was costing the King 30,000 ducats a day simply to keep the fleet in port.

The Captain General had ordered that the oldest provisions be served up first, but the meat that had been salted down in October was green and putrid in April. The biscuits were crawling with worms. And every day the list of deserters grew longer, in spite of the guards. Every day, too, though it had not yet reached catastrophic proportions, the hospitals and the local cemetery became just a little more crowded, thanks to dysentery.

On 25 April, St Mark's day, the sun shone brightly in a deep blue sky. With great pomp the Captain General of the Most Fortunate Armada proceeded to the Cathedral of Lisbon, to take from the High Altar the sacred banner of the crusade.

After which, standard or no standard, Medina Sidonia still went on waiting for his cash. It was not until dawn on 9 May, with all hope gone and every ruse exhausted, that he finally gave the order for departure.

They manned the capstans and weighed anchor. The Tagus was filled with sail.

'Like a town on the march', the ships sailed down towards Belem under their white and red canvas – the red crosses of war against the white of purity. The galleys and launches helped manoeuvre the galleons, their aftercastles gleaming under a new coat of paint. Pennants and flags fluttered at all masts. On the decks corslets, breastplates and morions glistened in the sun. Gold-embroidered doublets and velvet cloaks shimmered on the poops. Gold chains sparkled and white hat feathers quivered gracefully in the wind.

His Excellency the Duke of Medina Sidonia was himself on the *San Martin*, a galleon of 1,000 tons (Spanish), flagship of the squadron of Portugal. With him he had his confessor, his spiritual advisor and sixty servants.

At the mouth of the Tagus the fleet encountered a strong head wind. The harbour pilots shook their heads. Any attempt at crossing the bar was out of the question. The vessels dropped anchor and waited. Men huddled in the lower decks, while the storm sent an icy wind howling through the badly fitted gunports and hatchways. 'December weather', declared the pilots, and the Duke wrote, 'The weather is preventing the Armada from coming out, . . . but as it is God who sends the weather, this must fit in with his designs.'

The Duke took advantage of the delay to draw up his orders to the fleet and have them passed from ship to ship:

> First and foremost, it must be clearly understood by all, from the highest to the lowest, that the principal aim of His Majesty is the service of God. . . . No one, therefore, must sail without confessing and communicating in true repentance for his sins. Similarly, to utter any oath or to take in vain the name of Our Lord, or of Our Lady or of the Saints is forbidden on pain of the most severe punishments and stoppages of wine. . . .
>
> Gambling is a prohibited, forbidden games in particular and especially at night.
>
> It is well known what inconvenience and offence to God is caused by the presence of public or private women. I therefore forbid that any be taken on board.
>
> Every morning, according to custom, the ships' boys will say the morning salutation at the foot of the mainmast, and at vespers they will say the Ave Maria, sometimes the Salve Regina and, on Saturdays at least, the litany as well.
>
> Brawls and other disgraceful activities . . . will be prohibited and no one is to wear a dagger . . . there will be no private feuds. . . .

Each captain had already received detailed sailing instructions. Signals and methods of communication had been agreed for the fleet. A rendezvous point had been fixed. At sea, in battle or in case of fire, every man knew what he had to do. The Duke placed particular emphasis on the importance of cleanliness and personal hygiene. Each squadron had been allotted its quota of the most experienced pilots, Spanish, French, Dutch and English, with a knowledge of the Channel. Each one of them had been given the latest maps and pilot books, which marked all the ports and landmarks, depths, tides, currents and principal shoals from the Scilly Islands to Dover.

Each captain, in turn, did the same on his own ship, allocating to every man his place on board – on the aftercastle, on the main companionway, in the mizzen crow's nest – and his precise role in battle. Monks, valets, barbers and 'other non-combatants' were assigned the duties of stopping leaks and putting out fires.

Once this was done, they waited for a favourable wind, and while they waited nature began to have her way again. The Duke's stringency, a reflection of the King's, had banned all 'public and private' women from the fleet, which meant that the 'camp followers' had to charter themselves a special ship, in which they sailed behind the Armada. This ship does not feature in the official inventory made before the departure from Lisbon, but there are several references to it in contemporary documents. Furthermore, an English list notes the presence of a 'German woman accompanied by her husband, a gunner', on the *San Salvador* (later captured in the Channel half burnt out).

For seventeen days they waited. Still the wind blew from the wrong quarter. They took advantage of the delay to take on beans, rice, and oil in place of the rotten meat that was already being thrown overboard.

Amused idlers swarmed on the shore from which the roadstead 'seemed covered by a forest of masts'. The *San Martin* was one of the tallest galleons in the Armada, and from up on the aftercastle the Duke had an even better view. He had reason to be proud, for none had ever seen a larger fleet or a mightier expedition.

At the time, however, no one ever called the Armada invincible. While planning the fleet in 1586, Santa Cruz had christened it 'Felicissima Armada', literally 'The Most Fortunate War Fleet' or 'The Most Fortunate Fleet'. Sidonia used the same name or called it simply 'the Armada'. English official documents refer to 'The Spanish Armada' or 'The Spanish Fleet'. Never did the King, or the Duke or any squadron commander, officer, councillor, secretary or courtier, any Spanish chronicler or historian of the period, ever describe it as invincible. Philip was too well aware that *Dios da y quita la Victoria como-*

quiere. Who then gave it the name that was ironically to stick for ever? Perhaps a group of drunks brawling round a table in a Lisbon bawdy house? Or some obscure hidalgo raring for a fight? The English pamphleteers, who were the first to put the word 'invincible' into print? Or the Pope, from whom they claimed to have had the adjective?

Meanwhile the Duke sent the King his 'Report of all that is going in this Armada', a detailed, official inventory of ships, troops, and cannon. It lists 130 ships, 65 galleons, or large merchantmen converted into warships, 25 hulks carrying stores and horses, 19 *pataches*, 13 *zabras* (small, swift frigates from the Bay of Biscay), 4 galleys and 4 galleasses, including the *Girona*. At the gunports were 2,431 pieces of ordnance, 1,497 bronze and 934 iron, and there were 123,790 rounds of shot, or roughly 50 per gun. In the ships were 30,696 men (this figure is almost certainly exaggerated by 20 per cent); 8,000 seamen and gunners; 2,100 rowers, convicts, prisoners, slaves (or volunteers) – the *benevoglie* or *buenas boyas*; 19,000 soldiers, musketeers, arquebusiers and pikemen; and 1,545 volunteers, including 200 gentlemen adventurers, noblemen, hidalgos and caballeros along with their valets; German, Irish, English and Scottish captains; ships' surgeons and other non-combatants, and 180 priests and monks, medicants and others.

The Captain General of the Ocean Sea was personally commanding the ten galleons and two *zabras* of the squadron of Portugal. The man who was called 'the Premier Sailor of Spain', Juan Martinez de Recalde, Knight of Santiago, was second-in-command of the Armada, and Captain General of the Biscayan squadron (ten ships and four *pataches*). His personal pennant flew on the *capitana Santa Ana*. A squadron captain general for sixteen years, he had served in the West Indies and in the plate fleets. He had been Santa Cruz's right hand man. He was said to have the heart of a lion.

The fourteen galleons and *naos* of Castile, with the two *pataches* that completed the squadron, were commanded by Don Diego Flores de Valdes. He had twenty years of transatlantic voyaging behind him and was a brilliant sailor, highly regarded as a technician in matters of navigation and nautical construction; but he was said to be an overambitious man, jealous and quarrelsome. Whether or not this was true, he was hated and despised by all and sundry. Philip made him Chief of Staff to the Duke, an appointment that was as mystifying to contemporary observers and to historians as that of Medina Sidonia. In the words of one commentator, 'If Medina Sidonia was incapable of commanding, nobody was willing to take orders from Diego Flores.' He therefore transferred to Sidonia's flagship, the *San Martin* shortly after sailing, and remained in that ship throughout the campaign.

Don Pedro de Valdez, a cousin and sworn enemy of Diego Flores, was Captain General of the Armada of Andalusia, consisting of ten merchantmen and one *patache*. A knight of Santiago and also trained in the plate fleets, he had distinguished himself fighting in Portugal, in the Azores, and at Ferrol, where he was seriously wounded. In the Armada, he had made himself an energetic advocate of long-range artillery.

Another squadron, that of Guipuzcoa, consisting of ten ships and two *pataches,* was commanded by Don Miguel de Oquendo. Known as 'La Gloria de la Armada', Don Miguel was regarded as a fearless hero. A proud and haughty warrior, his exploits were retailed in every port in Spain. He was considered to be the finest sailor in Spain, second only to Recalde.

The squadron of the Levant – this term denoting Barcelona and the Italian ports – numbered ten good ships under the command of Don Martin de Bertendona, a competent sailor and a brave soldier. His squadron included the *rata Sancta Maria Encoronada*, an 820-ton carrack carrying 35 cannon, 335 soldiers, and 84 seamen and officers. It was in this ship that Alonzo de Leiva, together with at least one of his brothers and almost all the noblemen in the expedition, had taken passage. As the leader who would command in the battle once the troops had been landed, Don Alonzo bore the title of Commander in Chief of the Armada.

Stores, reserve arms and ammunition, field artillery and gun carriages; camp, earthwork and seige material; wagons, mules, horses and grooms, were all carried in twenty-five hulks – heavy, unarmed, or only lightly armed merchantmen. Juan Gomez de Medina had received this inglorious command.

Each squadron had a few *pataches*, frigates or *zabras* for reconnoitering and scouting, taking prisoners and carrying orders and pilots from squadron to squadron. In addition, twenty-two of these small ships made up a separate squadron of their own, the squadron of *pataches*, commanded by Don Antonio Hurtado, from his flagship *La Nuestra Señora del Pilar de Saragoza*, a small galleon.

Don Diego Medrano commanded the four galleys of Portugal.

Lastly, Don Hugo de Moncada, in the *capitana San Lorenzo,* led the galleasses of Naples, four huge and formidable engines of war, each bristling with fifty cannons. Great things were expected of them, particularly in calm weather, when their free movement would give them a clear advantage over the English galleons. The four galleasses were the *San Lorenzo* (*capitana*), *Zuñiga* (*patrona*), *Napolitana* and *Girona*. A galleass was a cross between a galley and a galleon, manned by 300 rowers and 3–400 soldiers and sailors. Moncada, a Catalan of very noble birth, was a dyed-in-the-wool galley man, one of that old aristocracy of the sea. In battle he was known to be the bravest of the brave. He was also known to be haughty and lacking in self-control.

7

Don Alonzo Martinez De Leiva

One thing struck me above all others. It was clear that of all the lords gathered at Lisbon, of all the knights and all the great captains, the best loved and the most admired was Don Alonzo Martinez de Leiva. He was constantly referred to, and always it was 'El Buen Alonzo de Leiva,' or 'Don Alonzo himself'. The historian Antonio de Herrera wrote in 1612, *La segunda persona qui vui en el Armada, despues del Duque . . . era Don Alonzo de Leiva*. The Duke would consult 'all the generals *und* Alonzo de Leiva'. He seems to have embodied for his period every noble and military quality. 'As one knew he would', Spaniards said when he excelled in battle, 'as one might have expected from such a leader', when he proved himself indestructible in adversity.

I have failed to find a portrait of him, but chroniclers of the period are unanimous in picturing him as a young cavalier *sans peur et sans reproche*. He could not possibly have been anything but gay, young, handsome, and flamboyant, whether at court or on the battlefield.

Members of the crew later questioned by the English described him as 'tall and slender, of a whitely complexion, of a flaxen and smooth hair, of behaviour mild and temperate, of speech good and deliberate, greatly reverenced not only by his own men but generally of all the whole company'. 'Don Alonzo was a whitely man with an Abram beard', reads the record of the examination of Jorge de Venerey, a Cretan sailor.

He was the King's favourite and the idol of the nobility and people alike. His wife, daughter of the Count of Corunna, had born him many sons.

Don Alonzo had begun his military career as lieutenant to his father, the celebrated Don Sancho. He fought bravely in the War of Grenada and in all the battles of the period. In Italy at the time when Don Juan of Austria was having trouble confronting the Flemish rebels, he took it upon himself to raise a company of young gentlemen adventurers, appointing himself as their captain, Don Diego Hurtade de Mendoza as lieutenant and his brother, Don Sancho, as sergeant major. All of the 400 soldiers in this company were either one-time captains or unemployed ensigns. With this company, its numbers swelled by valets and men who joined along the way, he marched to the Netherlands. There the courage he inspired in his men changed the course of the campaign. The company gained a glorious reputation. The rebels crushed, Don Alonzo made his way back to Italy.

Next becoming Captain General of the Sicilian Galleys, he led them to victory in the conquest of Portugal in 1580. In naval operations he demonstrated the same personal courage and judgment as his father. The King appointed Don Alonzo Captain General of the Milanese cavalry at a salary of 300 escudos a month, but he resigned his commission in 1587 to join the Enterprise of England.

De Leiva then held the distinguished titles of Knight of Santiago and Commander of Alcuescar. He had hoped that he would be the man chosen by the King to lead the Enterprise of England. Soon after arriving in Lisbon, as we have seen, he is said to have started the rumour that Santa Cruz was deliberately creating difficulties and delays because he was jealous and offended at not having been given command of the invasion army as well as the Armada, rather than Parma. Rumours like this and other slanderous gossip broke the old Marquis's heart and almost certainly hastened his death. Don Alonzo, *joven de condicion asaz ferviente,* who really loved and respected the Marquis, must have found his death painful.

De Leiva was naturally included in the General Staff together with Don Francisco de Bobadilla, the Maestro de Campo General, and the other great military leaders.

In June 1587 the King sent De Leiva to Cadiz to inspect the state of the ships, after which he was to go back up to Lisbon to report the progress of preparations there. In July he was patrolling the Algarve coast with a squadron of galleys, and in November we find his name on a list of noblemen receiving an *ayuda e costa.*

44

A little later the Venetian ambassador in Paris, in a report to the Doge, wrote, '. . . Don Alonso de Leiva's name has been mentioned in connection with Armada's high command . . . but he is too reckless . . .'.

If he really did hope to command the Armada, he did not miss it by much. Before the fleet sailed, Sidonia received an envelope from the King, marked 'secret' and, 'to be opened only in the event of the Captain General's death – to be given back to me otherwise, unopened, on return'. Inside was a second envelope addressed to Don Alonzo Martinez de Leiva and inside that, this letter, now in the Archivo General de Simancas:

> . . . I have resolved . . . in consideration of possible eventualities . . . to appoint a man of valour, courage and experience . . . to succeed the Duke. . . . Having complete confidence in you, Don Alonzo Martinez de Leiva, my Captain General of the Milanes' Cavalry, by reason of the importance and quality of your past services and of the fact that you fulfil all the requirements necessary for such a position, I have chosen you. I appoint you henceforth Captain General of the said Armada . . . I, the King. . . .

Don Alonzo entertained the Duke on board the *rata* in Lisbon. Again at Belem he received him in grand style, with musical accompaniment, at his table sumptuously set with silver plate and cutlery and gold-plated candelabra (which I found four centuries later). Sixty sons and nephews of the most noble families in Spain surrounded him, eager for battle and glory. They had deemed it a point of honour to serve under no one but him. No wonder the grandees of the kingdom would have entrusted their heirs, the hopes of their families, to none other than Don Alonzo.

8

'I Have Set Sail at Last . . .'

On 27 May the wind began to shift. Next day the *San Martín* crossed the bar. It took two whole days for the fleet to sail out. On the 30th Sidonia wrote to the King:

> I have set sail at last, and am now looking for the current which I am told will take us North. . . . I did not mean to be the one to have to tell your Majesty how well I have served him in all this, nor about the problems . . . but I humbly beg Your Majesty not to forget my children, my wretched children who I have had to leave behind, with my house and my calm and peaceful life, in order to serve him with the same love and disinterest that I have always shown. Indeed it is high time he made some gesture of thanks, bestowed some honour on those who have left their homes as I have. Once more, with the humility and obedience that I owe to Him, I beg Our Lord to keep him and give him many more years of life. From my galleon, May 30th, three leagues out to sea. The Duke of Medina Sidonia.

The wind was north-north-west, and it wasn't long before it reached gale force, sweeping first the hulks, and then the rest of the fleet southward.

On 1 June they sighted Cape St Vincent, and at this rate they would soon sight Africa. Philip was advised of the situation and took immediate measures: he ordered solemn and continuous processions throughout his kingdoms, with orations, fasts, alms and penances, and many hours of prayer. His Hieronymite monks were relieved of all other duties. In Madrid, Our Lady of Atocha was paraded for three days on end.

And so God was pleased that this delay should be only a short one. The wind shifted and shifted again. The ships had to tack laboriously, beating to windward, until 9 June, when the wind finally veered to south-south-west. They did not sight Cape Finisterre until the 14th, where they expected to meet some victuallers. 'A large part of the provisions have been thrown overboard, being rotten and spoilt,' Medina Sidonia had written in a dispatch to the King. 'They would have been useless, only infecting the men and making them ill. I humbly beg Your Majesty to send victuallers to meet us with provisions, particularly meat and fish.'

They waited in vain. On the 15th the fleet sheltered in the lee of the Sisarga Islands, eight leagues from Corunna. The Duke sent a *patache* into Corunna with orders to requisition all vessels in the port, load them with provisions, and return with them as quickly as possible.

18 June, and still nothing to be seen. Sidonia sent the galleys for news. The *capitana* was getting the same complaint from several ships; in the barrels of unseasoned wood (Drake had burnt all the good, seasoned staves) the water was turning stinking and green. The men who had drunk it had fallen sick with 'gastric fevers'.

'Tomorrow,' wrote the Duke on 18 June, in his daily letter to the King, 'if the wind still holds from south-south-east, I shall sail on, in spite of the serious shortage of provisions. . . .'

Barely had the Captain General handed his letter to the master of a *zabra* to take it to Corunna, when a storm was seen to be threatening. The Duke called the squadron commanders to a council with the most experienced of the mariners. The council decided simply to stay where they were and see how the weather turned out. On 19 June the wind had freshened, the sea was a little rougher. The Duke hurried into Corunna for shelter.

As for the rest, those that were near the *capitana* followed her: thirty-eight ships and a few *pataches* sailing in her wake. Others, being downwind, were unable to get in by nightfall. The remainder, having had no orders or signal, and being too far away to see the Duke's manoeuvre, continued to cruise off the coast.

19 June. From the Duke to the King,

We waited in vain for provisions. In view of the storminess of the weather and the serious shortage of water and supplies, I sailed into Corunna with part of the Armada. The rest remained outside the roadstead when night fell and prevented them from coming in. They will come in tomorrow, God willing, and I will do my utmost to be finished here in two days. I shall water, drop off the contagiously sick, and set sail again forthwith.

A violent storm broke that night, and on the 20th when the Duke awoke, there was not a sail to be seen on the horizon. He was missing over half his fleet. He drank his chocolate, sat down, played thoughtfully with his pen. A tricky situation: the Captain General himself had actually taken shelter *before* the storm, when in his written instructions he had warned all his captains, on pain of death for treason and confiscation of their properties, against leaving the *capitana's* wake to shelter in any Spanish port. He had already had the wit to bring the storm forward a day. He had to make what capital he could out of this, and gloss over the fact that in his haste he had failed to give the fleet any signal, and that, contrary to the King's orders, he had fixed only one rendezvous point for the fleet, in the Scilly Islands, in the event of their being scattered by a storm. He wrote on 19 June:

> I thought that the rest of the Armada would join me in port the next morning, but alas ... storm during the night ... squalls the like of which have never been seen before. ... And it was a stroke of luck that the whole Armada was not caught out to sea, especially the galleys, which would without doubt, have been lost. ... And the fleet would have been wasted getting it together again; in fact it must have been God's will that part of the Armada came in here; like this, the others will know that this is where they are to come to revictual. The weather is already showing signs of improvement, so they should be here in two or three days. ...

On Tuesday, 21 June, a messenger arrived at full gallop from Vivero with the news: 'De Leiva is in our port with ten ships.' The *rata's* rigging was damaged, quite apart from which she had lost four anchors in Sisargas roadstead. A second rider shortly arrived from Gijon, where there were two galleasses 'in bad shape'; one of them was the *Girona*, needing 'both tillers, her rigging and her prow repaired, her decks and hull recaulked, and her soaked biscuit supply [4 cwt] dried out.' That afternoon, although it was still rough, the pinnaces set out in search of the missing ships. They passed Recalde on his way back to the fleet with two galleons and eight other ships.

On the same day Sidonia again wrote to the King:

> Recalde has lost his mainmast. We have taken on fish, meat and bacon, as well as water, and although I am not at all well, I am seeing to everything as

best I can. It distresses me more than Your Majesty can ever know to think, that for all my care, I was nonetheless forced to come in here with most of the Armada still outside, but God be praised. . . . It is thanks to His great mercy that I did come in here. . . . Seamen and soldiers are under close watch . . . no one will desert. . . . Many of the men are sick.

When the Armada first sailed, the King rather optimistically had started to send his letters for Sidonia to Flanders. A royal letter of 26 June in answer to the Duke's letter of the 19th, betrays his feelings at having to lower his sights.

I want to be certain that you will leave port on the appointed day, without fail. . . . I am expecting you to justify the trust I have put in you. . . . I am sending a copy of this letter to Flanders, since you should have left before this reaches you.

These were the harshest words the King ever had for the Duke, and by the very next letter, he had softened again.

Indeed it was the hand of God that guided you into Corunna where it will be easier for the rest of the fleet to join you than it would have been at sea. You will find it easier too to revictual there and to carry out any repairs. . . . Do not be so distressed about it. . . . In addition to the supplies I am sending you biscuit, oil, vinegar, wine and tuna fish in hulks from Lisbon.

Two very fast, oared *pataches* had left for the Scilly Islands to bring back any ships which might have obeyed their official orders and sailed to the rendezvous. But by the 24th the Duke, frantic with worry, was still without news of twenty-three vessels (including two galleasses) carrying between them 8,449 men.

9

An Honourable Agreement, Perhaps?

If the situation really was as bad as the Duke now maintained, it cannot have been encouraging: dysentery and scurvy, damaged ships, leaks, broken masts, lost sails, uneatable provisions, water gone sour because of the unseasoned wood (Drake, always Drake!) and the weather was 'still as bad as December' with:

> showers and continuous squalls seriously hindering the taking on of fresh provisions. . . . I am particularly concerned and troubled by this because it is so extraordinary for the end of June, especially when you consider that everything that is being done here is being done in God's cause, and after all those prayers, too. . . . But no doubt this must, for some reason, fit in better with His cause; and this brings me to tell your Majesty something that I have been putting off for some time.

It is 24 June. From the galleon *San Martin* the Duke writes his King the most amazing letter. It is of prime importance because it is largely on the document that history has judged Medina Sidonia. Some modern historians used words like 'courageous, intelligent, lucid, honest' to describe this letter. It required of its writer, writes Garrett Mattingly, 'moral courage of a kind . . . unusual in that century'. Others, Spanish historians in particular (with the exception of the Duke of Maura) see in it nothing but cowardice, defeatism, an attempt at desertion.

> What I am about to say is not an expression of my own personal wishes. I am not looking for any last minute excuse. Your Majesty is well aware of my determination and zealous desire to serve him . . . but this is what my allegiance to Your Majesty, my duty and my conscience force me to say. . . .

50

The Captain General goes on to recall in detail his initial refusal and misgivings. He paints a blacker picture than ever of the whole saga of the preparations and the events leading up to the present situation — sick crews whose condition can only deteriorate; provisions spoiled and insufficient, barely two months' supplies; the fleet split up and badly damaged, and no way, that he can see, of repairing it or making the necessary replacements without completely depleting the Indies and Flanders. He claims that the fleet is far inferior in strength to the enemy's, asking the King to judge for himself how the enterprise has started off, and when so much depends on its success. Sidonia reminds him of the consequences of failure and repeats again and again, *ad nauseam* such warnings as:

> Inferior forces, inexperienced crews, officers of which not one, I must in all conscience tell Your Majesty, is up to his position . . . and Your Majesty must not let anyone deceive him on this matter. I have observed it myself and know that it is true.
>
> The Prince of Parma's army is also too small, even if we could support them. As things are we can do nothing for them. . . . Is this really the way to go about attacking such a powerful kingdom, and one with so many allies?
>
> I felt it necessary to bring all this to Your Majesty's notice, that he might decide . . . in view of the present situation . . . whether it might not after all be better to try to reach some honourable agreement with the enemy.

Whether Philip choked with rage, or whether he remained icily unmoved, I cannot say. I have found no account that gives the slightest hint of his inner reaction. He replied once more, obstinately,

> My letters of June 26th and July 1st will have already made my intention clear to you, which is not to withdraw from the Enterprise, but to complete what has been started, overcoming all obstacles. . . . You must send me a daily courier and hold yourself in readiness to get under sail the very day you receive orders from me.

A few days earlier, the Duke of Parma, for his part, had sent Philip an equally defeatist communiqué. The landing was beginning to be *aventurado*, he wrote on 30 May. His army had rotted on its feet under the damp and cold campaign tents; the numbers of sick and dead increased every week; they were consuming more provisions and more gold than he could lay his hands on. In short, he too was now suggesting turning the Bourbourg farce into genuine negotiations. (It is most unfair to Sidonia that no one ever considered holding this piece of advice against Parma.)

Alexander Farnese was considered by friends and enemies alike the greatest tactician and finest military leader of the century. But at this stage nothing could move the Defender of the Faith. To encourage Sidonia he at last got around to the question of money. But alas, not in the way the Duke had hoped (nor I – I saw yet another slice of my prospective fortune slipping into the money bags of Galician market gardeners and victuallers).

> You can spend the money you have left on fresh supplies. There can be no better way of using it than providing health for our men . . . and take care this time with the new provisions that they keep properly, and do not let yourself be cheated as you have been in the past. The information you sent me from Lisbon about provisions gave me an entirely false impression, since belied by the facts . . . and the same goes for the water. . . .

Indeed, the taste of fresh meat and vegetables did restore the sailors to health, and ashore the five hundred who were sick were regaining their strength. The Archbishop of Santiago had set up a hospital that was working wonders.

Sidonia wrote:

> I have posted guards at all the landing stages and on all the roads by which the men might try to escape. . . . Water, which has been my biggest worry, is being loaded as carefully as possible. I have twenty-six coopers working day and night to repair the casks that were completely wrecked in the storm. I hope, God willing, that all will be ready for us to sail this Saturday or Sunday. I have continued to give the men fresh meat, but not bread as there is not enough even for the sick. . . . Only nine have died, thanks be to God.

Another letter from the Duke is dated 26 June. Now all is rosy. What has happened is that the King's early letters have arrived, and from their firm tone Sidonia already has a pretty good idea what kind of response his peacemaking suggestions will elicit.

> I kiss Your Majesty's hands for the grace he has shown me in his recent letters. They have brought some consolation for all the worries, and not unfounded ones, I have had as a result of this storm. . . .

That said, the Duke reported that all the ships had returned to the northern ports, with not a single one missing. For the rest, he would supervise the repairs in person, being more anxious than anyone to hasten their departure.

The whole of the Armada had in fact now returned. Alferez Esquivel, who had gone in his pinnace to the Scilly Islands to look for the missing vessels, had found them on the 30th. Nine were at the rendezvous: Don Juan Gomez de Medina's *capitana*, and most of the other hulks, the *Trinidad Valencera*, the Duke of Florence's galleon and the 'women's hulk' (Urca de las Mujeres).

Gomez de Medina was no more enthusiastic than any of the other generals concerning the Duke's unexpected show of initiative. As soon as he got back he wrote personally to the King to say that 'it had simply never crossed my mind that the flagship might have taken shelter in the port, because it would have been so much better, both as far as the King was concerned and for many other reasons, to do otherwise'. Following the Duke's express instructions, he had made for the Scilly Islands. There he had captured a hulk that the English had taken from some merchants. They had waited there several days, when a small boat had spotted them. They had not been able to capture it (it was a merchantman with a cargo of salt which had hurried off to raise the alert). He had exchanged several broadsides with an English squadron come to reconnoitre them. He had captured several small ships and obtained information about the enemy squadrons. Then, when a *patache* arrived from the Duke, he had returned to Corunna.

If Philip read correctly between the lines of this letter, date 6 July, he must have understood something like this: What I did without any difficulty and according to orders with the worst of our ships, the whole of the Armada could have done too. The storm was not as bad as all that. Sailing before the wind rather than against it would have saved all that damage. If Your Majesty's Armada had had a leader it would be in the English Channel by now.

It was personal letters like that from the Duke's subordinates that finally persuaded the King to send his private secretary, Don Andres de Alba, to 'assist him in his work . . . to supervise preparations and attend the council'. From that day forward, miraculously, the problems began to iron themselves out.

On 12 July, the King had sent definite orders:

> It is my wish that you leave port and start your voyage, the day you receive this letter, without so much as an hour's delay, and even if it means leaving some twelve or fifteen ships behind. . .,

On 13 July, the Duke wrote, 'I hope and trust that God will permit me to set sail with the Armada on Saturday the 16th or Sunday at the latest.' On 14 July: 'Everything is ready, but the sea is like a millpond.' On 15 July:

> By the grace of God, excepting contrary orders from Your Majesty, and weather permitting, I hope to be able to sail tomorrow morning or the day after at the latest. . . . To enable every man to take communion and not be deprived of this spiritual and physical benefit, I have ordered all the father confessors in the Armada to land on a small island in the port and have had tent and altars put up for the occasion. And I have given orders that the island be well guarded. It has all gone so well, I am told that more than 8,000 have already taken communion and confessed. This represents such riches, that I rate it the most precious jewel I am taking with me in the whole Armada. Everything is in far better shape than when we left Lisbon and everyone on board is leaving in good spirit.

Then on 19 July, 'since the 16th the Armada has been waiting only for a favourable wind on which to sail out'. And on the 20th, with the weather still uncertain, the Duke summoned a meeting of the Council. He was undecided. Alonzo de Leiva took the floor, advising that they should sail with all possible dispatch. Admirals and pilots were divided in their opinions. They finally agreed to wait until a favourable wind was well established before setting out.

The wind held long enough to get the fleet out of harbour on the 22nd, only to leave it, a few hours later, drifting still within sight of the coast, sails flapping. The wind shifted northward and the Duke talked of returning to Corunna, then it dropped and they anchored three leagues out.

During the night of the 23rd the wind freshened at last from the south-east. The Duke fired a shot as the signal that he was weighing anchor. Two hours later another shot rang out: the *Zuniga*'s rudder hinges were broken and she could no longer steer. The rest of the day was taken up waiting for them to be repaired, as the Duke explained to the King in his letter of 23 July.

After that, silence.

'Drake is Captured!'

On 24 July 1588 Philip received from Galicia the news that he had been waiting for, week after week, for nearly a year: the Armada had disappeared over the horizon.

In his last letter, the Duke had enclosed his 'report of ships, seamen (*gente de mar*), soldiers (*soldados*), admirals, His Majesty's colonels (*maestros de campos*), artillerists, doctors and officers of justice, priests and others ... leaving this port of Corunna on 23rd inst.' There were now 131 ships carrying 24,607 soldiers and seamen; 1,338 generals, colonels, captains and officers; 1,549 volunteers, gentlemen adventurers, artillery officers; about 800 ecclesiastics, valets and servants. The Duke therefore had nearly 28,000 men in his command. This new report was to be confidential, so this inventory of troops can be taken as accurate. The latest delay had lasted thirty-two days, not two as originally announced, but now the crusade really was setting out, stronger, better supplied and better equipped than ever.

Health on board was good and morale was at its highest for the good reason that the men were now eating every day – some days even eating their fill. The daily rations included 1½ lb. of biscuits, 3/10 pint of wine and 2 gal. of water (solely for drinking and cooking). In addition to this they had 6 oz. of bacon and 2 oz. of rice on Sundays and Thursdays, 6 oz. of bone and 3 oz. of beans or dried peas on Mondays and Wednesdays; and on Tuesdays, Fridays and Saturdays, 6 oz. of tuna with oil and vinegar or dried cod or octopus, or failing that 5 sardines and 3 oz. of chick-peas.

If the written orders of Francisco Duarte, the chief victualling officer, were actually obeyed (which seems highly improbable), the rations should have been calculated according to the list of troops aboard and handed to each man in person, in the presence of the ship's clerk, who would make a note of it in his books . . . and if anyone dies or changes ships his ration will be deleted from the lists. . . . And if, on certain days, because of bad weather or shortage of supplies, half rations only are given, or even no rations at all, this will not be made up the following day. . . .

Once the Armada had sailed, people up and down the country in convents, churches and chapels redoubled their prayers.

On the King's orders, Count Olivarez sought another audience with the Pope. The expedition, he told him, was now under way. The expenses were astronomical. And they would get higher. It was the Holy See which had desired that the crusade take place, and it was on the Holy See now that its success would depend. Parma was short of money, the troops were getting restless: it was impossible to wait any longer.

Nothing would move Sixtus v – his word was final – and the Ambassador was forced to take up his pen again on 19 August and report to his sovereign:

I shall not mention the question of money again to His Holiness. It only irritates him. He turns his back on me at the table and chatters away with less sense than a two-year-old. . . . He has neither charity, breeding nor intelligence. His behaviour is generally put down to his anxiety at seeing the time fast approaching when his ducats will be torn from his heart.

Olivarez was speaking the truth. The Pope had declared to the Venetian Ambassador: 'Philip II's ships are worthless. . . . For every step forward in Flanders they take two back.' The story he told the French Ambassador was that '20,000 men had died in the Armada while it was being made ready in Lisbon. . . . 28 ships had been lost through sheer incompetence.' Medina Sidonia was no better 'than a fool'.

For several days the Escurial had no word of the Armada.

The King waited. On 1 August his private secretary came running with a dispatch from Paris. To Philip in his dark retreat, with its spartan furnishing of leather and oak, where he now spent all his time, Ambassador Mendoza wrote that the Armada had been sighted in the English Channel.

Several letters arrived on 3 August. A large Spanish ship had anchored in the bay of La Hougue.

During the days that followed a shower of letters arrived from everywhere. Gunfire was heard in the Channel for a whole day; the Spanish had landed in England; the Armada had been decimated and was fleeing towards the North Sea with Drake in pursuit; Sidonia had taken Drake prisoner. Rumour followed rumour, and Mendoza immediately relayed every one. Occasionally he took the precaution of adding, 'This news has not been confirmed; it would be a mistake to form an opinion too hastily.'

On 7 June a 'reliable' agent wrote to him from Rouen:

> I learn from the skippers of certain fishing barks returning from Newfoundland, who passed the fleets, that there was an encounter between Drake and Medina off the Isle of Wight. The Spanish took the weather gauge from the English and after 24 hours of hellish fighting, they had sunk fifteen English galleons and captured many more, taking countless prisoners. The galleasses were a great success. The same reports are substantial from Dieppe by some other Newfoundland skippers. . . . A Breton fisherman saw it all: it was a galleass that dismasted Drake's ship with the first broadside and sank it with the second.

According to another source, Drake, wounded in the cheek, threw himself into a launch to escape and fled the battle. This time Mendoza sent the news to the Escurial and to Rome, bursting with delight. He sang out victory all over Paris and had a bonfire built in the embassy courtyard.

On 11 August came confirmation that the Armada had reached Calais, and that Parma was there to meet it. As soon as he heard this the King wrote to the Duke, on 18 August:

> Don Bernadino de Mendoza has sent news from Rouen that God has given you victory, that you succeeded in taking the weather gauge from Drake, that you have sunk fifteen enemy ships, including their flagship, and that the rest have fled to Dover. . . . I trust in God that this is so. . . . I assume that you will by now have gone on to meet my nephew the Duke. With the enemy in the grip of fear and our own men in high spirits we can place our hope in God that more victories will follow. . . . By the grace of God I expect a fair outcome in this cause which is so particularly his. . . . I await confirmation of this.

There was more to come. Dispatch after dispatch. The enemy fleet was burning, it was sinking ever faster. The time had come for Mendoza to put his reports in some sort of order:

On 10 August, he reported, the Armada had in fact sunk seventeen enemy ships. It was in the legs that Drake was wounded, by a cannon ball. On 14 August at 'the battel of New-Castle', thirty ships were captured or sunk. On 20 August, forty English ships were sunk, including the English flagship and Drake's. Drake, wounded again, this time in the cheek, had got away in a launch. In short, as a simple piece of mental arithmetic would show, the enemy fleet no longer existed.

And Olivarez learned on 28 August that the Armada was in the Channel, there had been three days of gunfire, victory was theirs. Straightway he obtained a special audience with the Pope. He asked him to say a thanksgiving *Te Deum* and to have the Vatican illuminated. And, while they were on the subject, as Parma's army must by now be in England, how about paying over the first half million of the first instalment?

Sixtus replied that he saw no reason to do any more than he was committed to . . . that he would not be pushed and that he would do nothing until the fate of the Armada was known for certain. . . .

When Olivarez went back with more news of victory to the Vatican – 'Drake is dead or captured' – he was being less truthful and the Pope was even more sceptical. For other reports, highly alarming ones, were reaching Rome from all over Europe. 'Drake is victorious; the Armada is either fleeing or destroyed.'

The King of France, too, had received different reports. And when Mendoza requested an audience at Chartres to ask that a thanksgiving *Te Deum* be sung all over the kingdom, the King informed him of them, personally. The old ambassador was badly out of favour at court. The power of his King, and his direct interference in French internal affairs, which he did not even take the trouble to disguise, had earned him deep and widespread hatred. Henry's only reply to his requests was to hand him a letter from Calais. The Governor, Monsieur Gourdan, had indeed seen the Armada anchoring under the city walls. Their sails and rigging were all in shreds, and during Sunday night English fire-ships had put them to flight. The following morning the well-ordered English fleet had set sail in pursuit. A galleass had run aground at the foot of the castle.

'It is clear,' said Don Bernardino, 'that we have received differing accounts. . . .' He took his leave and returned to Paris. 'What about the bonfire,' asked his second secretary, 'can we light the bonfire?' 'Wait,' said Mendoza.

These vague rumours and fragmented reports went on for another week. The galleass that had run aground was the *San Lorenzo*; the Governor of Calais was willing to return her guns. The La Hougue ship was the *Santa Ana*, Recalde's *capitana*. Mendoza knew that there were 50,000 of the King's ducats on board. He took immediate measures for their safety. A merchant ship from one of the Hansa ports had sailed for hours without seeing a single sail, but in the sea she had sighted hundreds of horses and mules. The English had captured two galleons, the Dutch two more. One English ship had actually been seen sinking. A reconnaissance pinnace sent out by the Duke of Parma had sighted the entire English fleet in flight. De Leiva had just captured the English flagship and fifty other ships. There was confirmation from Antwerp that Drake had had a leg blown off by a cannon ball. The *Ark Royal* had surrendered. More news from Dieppe: the entire English fleet, apart from twenty ships, had been either captured or sunk. It was after a general skirmish off the coast of Scotland on 13 August that Drake had been captured trying to board the *San Martin*. Having annihilated the enemy, the Duke had taken shelter in a Scottish port in order to carry out repairs and take on water. He was just waiting for the right wind to return to the Channel. England was in a state of panic.

All over Europe, the moment they were received, either by letter or via some traveller, these reports were printed, translated, copied. Pamphlets appeared everywhere, each one more tendentious than the last, and basing their stories on one another's.

By now Mendoza was convinced. He lit his bonfire and wrote to Philip that Drake had been taken prisoner by Sidonia while trying to board the *San Martin*. He hadn't actually had confirmation of this from the Duke himself, but everyone said it was so and it seemed to be highly probable.

The news spread from the Escurial to every castle and village in Spain, where families were waiting for word of sons, nephews, husbands. The narrow streets were iluminated and *gaitas*, tambourines and guitars called people to the fiesta. A victory announcement was published in Madrid, and a second edition quickly produced in Seville.

Once more Olivarez called on the Pope. In his pocket he had an exuberant letter from Mendoza. But he looked worried. From the north were coming the most distressing rumours: two Spanish galleons run aground on the coast of Holland, Don Diego Pimentel captured, and a copy of the minutes of his examination circulated. Spanish banners in St Paul's Cathedral. A pamphlet entitled, 'A pack of Spanish lyes' arrived in Rome. Paragraph by paragraph it refuted the victory announcement published in Madrid and Seville on the basis of Mendoza's report.

Philip II finally learned the truth from Parma's letters, which contained a precise account, up until 10 August, of a disaster. The Armada was fatally stricken, demoralised, short of powder, shot and courage. It was fleeing. There was not a hope of a landing in England now. He was going to strike camp and withdraw from Dunkirk.

Since Parma neglected to inform Mendoza of any of this (Mendoza later vilified him, blaming him for the whole disaster), it was from England that the truth first reached the Spanish embassy in Paris. The first news came in a pamphlet, which was translated on arrival, entitled 'Journal of all that passed between the armies of Spain and England, from July 28th to August 11th, 1588', and then in a second document whose very title sent a chill to the old ambassador's heart. It was 'Certain advertisements out of Ireland concerning the losses and distresses happened to the Spanish Navy upon the West coasts of Ireland. . . .'

Out of Ireland! God! Shipwrecks, massacres, disasters, epidemics, famine – the news from Ireland was too dreadful. No, it was impossible! It was English propaganda! And on 29 September Mendoza wrote once more to Philip: 'The fleet has reformed in the Shetlands and Orkneys. It has taken on fresh provisions, and is now heading for the coast of Flanders, reinforced by twelve captured English galleons, and several Dutch.'

When Philip received this report, a bundle of letters from Alexander Farnese had already been lying on his desk for three weeks. They asserted that Parma had struck camp at Dunkirk, that his unpaid troops had mutinied, that the Armada was somewhere between Scotland and Norway. Also on Philip's desk was a journal of Prince d'Ascoli which had been sent from Calais, and dispatches from Juan de Manrique, one of the Duke's men, putting the blame for all the catastrophes, present and future, on Parma, who had been 'nowhere near ready'. The King had on his desk the *diario,* or journal, of Medina Sidonia, in the Duke's own hand, brought to him in a fast *patache* by Don Balthazar de Zuñiga. And before Philip also lay messages from Santander and the northern ports, where the Duke had arrived with a handful of ghost ships, their decks littered with dying men.

These documents still exist, and one can still see in the margin the toll of lost ships totted up day by day in the King's own anxious hand. In the margin of Mendoza's last victorious communiqué Philip has scrawled: 'Nothing of this is true; he really ought to be told.'

Wrote Count Olivarez:

Judging by His Holiness's attitude these last few days one would hardly credit him with the sort of apostolic zeal for the suppression of heresy and the salvation of souls that his position should demand.... When it seemed that victory was ours he softened his tone and was more courteous ... once the truth was known he turned haughty and arrogant ... and treated me like a slave. Anyone would think that our present misfortune had not come about through his fault, and in the service of God. His ill will and that of the cardinals is such that under the circumstances it is positively heretical.

11

The Armada Takes up a Crescent Formation

What had in fact happened?

At four o'clock in the afternoon of Friday, 29 July, land had been sighted from the crow's nest of the *San Martin*. Towards seven o'clock in the evening, when they were three leagues from the Lizard they struck their sails for the Armada to assemble and take up its formation. Sidonia wrote:

> First sight of land was from this galleon. I hoisted at the main the banner bearing the image of Christ crucified with the Virgin to one side of Him and Mary Magdalen to the other. I ordered three shots to be fired, as a signal to every man to make his prayer.

This letter, like those that followed, did not reach the King until the end of September.

Since the 22nd, the Duke had made regular entries in his 'Journal of the Enterprise of England', his *diario*. On 30 July he noted that several smoke signals had been observed on the mainland and that during the night, while they were sailing up the Channel, alarm beacons had been sighted signalling from headland to headland.

At a council of war on 30 July, Oquendo took the floor, arguing that it would be madness to advance any further until they knew whether Farnese was ready. There wasn't another friendly port in front of them where they could wait for him, and if the wind held from the present quarter they wouldn't have another chance to turn back. De Leiva and Pedro de Valdez spoke next. They urged the Duke to attack Plymouth. There, they believed, they would have *El Draque* trapped, his ships isolated and faced with the difficulty of beating out against the wind. But the Duke hesitated and decided against it. After

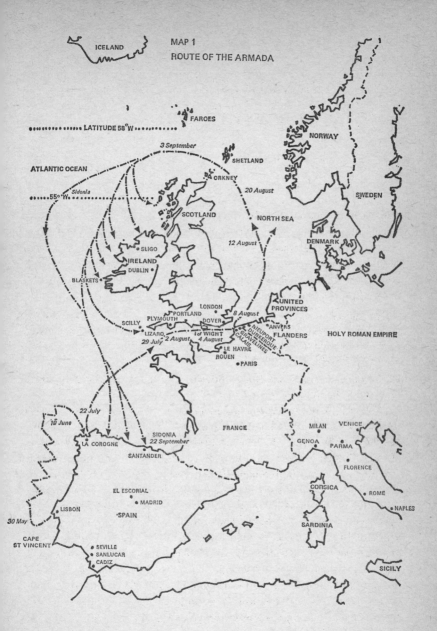

MAP 1

ROUTE OF THE ARMADA

ICELAND

FAROES

•••••••••• LATITUDE 58° W •••••••••

NORWAY

3 September

SHETLAND

ATLANTIC OCEAN

ORKNEY

20 August

••••• 55° W ••••• Sidonia

SWEDEN

SCOTLAND

NORTH SEA

12 August

DENMARK

SLIGO

IRELAND

DUBLIN

BLASKETS

UNITED
PROVINCES

LONDON

PORTLAND

PLYMOUTH   DOVER   8 August

SCILLY   ANVERS

LIZARD   I of WIGHT   NIEUPORT   FLANDERS   HOLY ROMAN EMPIRE
29 July   2 August   4 August   DUNKERQUE
                                  GRAVELINES
                                  CALAIS

LE HAVRE

ROUEN

PARIS

22 July

10 June   FRANCE   MILAN   VENICE

LA COROGNE   SIDONIA   GENOA   PARMA
                22 September
SANTANDER   FLORENCE

EL ESCORIAL   CORSICA
  • MADRID   ROME

LISBON   SPAIN   NAPLES

30 May   SARDINIA

CAPE
ST VINCENT

  • SEVILLE
  • SANLUCAR
  CADIZ   SICILY

the council he sat down at his desk and wrote to the King: 'I propose to sail in good order as far as the Isle of Wight, where I shall stay at anchor until I receive word from the Duke of Parma as to the state of readiness of his fleet and army.' He does not mention the contrary opinions that have been voiced.

That evening they learn from some captured fishermen that there are sixty ships at Plymouth, but that they have started to sail out. Drake had in fact started to beat out of Plymouth on the night of the 29th with the ebb tide. By the afternoon of the 30th most of the galleons were already up with the Eddystone.

That same evening, through the haze of the setting sun, Lord Howard of Effingham, Earl of Nottingham and Lord Admiral of England, had his first glimpse of the largest fleet he had ever seen in his life. It spanned the whole horizon a few leagues to westward and to windward of him.

The *San Martin*'s lookout had sighted white sails picked out by the setting sun and reported a fleet standing out for the open Channel, hard ahead, with the wind abeam. Then as darkness finally fell, the lookout still seemed to have seen a few sails inshore of them.

At moonrise the wind freshened again, blowing from west-south-west. Somewhat perplexed, Sidonia issued orders to heave to, so as not to risk losing the weather gauge to the enemy overnight. The wind then veered to west nor'west.

The first light of dawn revealed eighty ships astern of the Armada, to seaward and to windward of them. This was the main body of the English fleet commanded by Howard and his Vice-Admiral, Sir Francis Drake. Inshore of the Spanish ships were eleven other English vessels, tacking about, sailing upwind to get astern of the Spaniards (they were the last to leave Plymouth and arrived too late to round the van of the Armada). Three of them, three huge galleons, were already exchanging the first broadsides with the Biscayans of Recalde's rearguard.

Stunned by their incredible speed and manoeuvrability, the Spanish gazed paralysed, as the eleven enemy ships, tack after tack, beat up close to the wind, gained the wind and the rear of the Spanish fleet, joining the rest of the English vessels which during the night had made a wide sweep round the front of the Armada.

Howard had been successful. As long as the wind held he would be able to attack how, when and where he chose. He had the added advantage that the best of the Spanish ships, having been placed in the foremost positions, were now right in the rear. 'The advantage of time and place in all martial actions is half a victory, which being lost is irrecoverable.' Drake had written to the Queen in the spring of that year.

The Most Fortunate Fleet had entered the Channel in perfect formation, like an army on the march. Bertendona's squadron of the Levant and the galleasses made up the vanguard. Sidonia was behind with the galleons of Portugal, then the squadron of Castile followed by the hulks, protected to each side by the Andalusian and Guipuscoan squadrons. Recalde and his Biscayans formed the rear-guard. *Pataches* and *zabras* acted as scouts, dispatch carriers and flank guards.

Sidonia had retired to bed late and risen early. From the forecastle of the flagship, the *San Martin*, he gloomily observed the successful junction of the English squadrons less than six miles in his wake.

The Duke ordered a signal to be fired. Promptly every ship came about, shortened or made sail. The vanguard became the starboard wing, on the side nearer France, the rear-guard became the port wing, on the English side. The manoeuvre was complete. With two galleasses at each point the Armada formed a threatening crescent, majestically sweeping across seven miles of horizon. The English were impressed by the perfection of the manoeuvre. It was a classic formation for an army in the field, but disconcerting to encounter at sea. (See plate 5).

The Duke and his council had planned it well in advance. In a letter to the King dated 28 May, the Duke had written:

If Drake is at Plymouth waiting for me to sail past so that he can attack from the rear, while the fleet they have sent against Parma attacks from ahead, I shall be able to confront both at once. Either one of the wings of my crescent, supported by the reinforcement that I will send in and two galleasses covered by four of the largest ships, will easily be able to attack one of the enemy fleets. I, meanwhile, will make a frontal attack on the other fleet, with the capitana, the other galleons and the two other galleasses.

However, contrary to his expressed intentions, and without being threatened by any frontal assault, the Duke had placed two galleasses at each wing of his formation. Contemporary engravings made after Howard's sketches confirm this. Furthermore, according to the plan, enemy ships pursuing the crescent in a following wind, would be able, lest they should lose the weather gauge, to attack only the protruding wings, where Sidonia would have stationed the strongest ships. Any vessels rash enough to penetrate into the middle of the crescent would see it closing in on them and would find themselves the central target of the entire Spanish fire. If the others came to their aid, a general mêlée would arise with the hand to hand combat that the Spanish, outnumbering the English in manpower by five to one, wanted to precipitate as much as the English wanted to avoid it. Such at least was the formation the Duke had hoped to maintain and the results he expected of it.

On the English side Howard and Drake divided their fleet into two columns. Their agreed tactics were to avoid a direct confrontation with such a formidable enemy. If the Spanish showed signs of attacking they would flee, otherwise they would follow at a safe distance, ready to launch a joint attack on any straggler and destroy it in the cross-fire of their long-range culverins. If there were no stragglers, they would try to engage the last ship at the rearmost point, the one, that is, which the others, forced to put back against the wind, would have the greatest difficulty in rescuing. Here it was that the first attempt would be made.

Following the rules of chivalry, unchanged since the Middle Ages, the Lord Admiral of England sent his defiance to the Captain General of the Ocean Sea, using his personal pinnace as a herald of arms. The *Disdain,* commanded by Captain James Bradbury, left the fleet and sped alone towards what he assumed to be the *capitana.* It was in fact the *rata Sancta Maria Encoronada.* When she was within a cable's length of her, the *Disdain* took aim and discharged a minute cannon ball from her small gun into the hull of the enormous carrack.

The gauntlet was down. The pinnace bobbed lightly back over the waves to the fleet, vainly pursued by the *rata*'s fire. Howard of Effingham ordered insignia, pennants and standards to be hoisted. His officers ordered gunports to be opened, guns loaded and fuses recharged. Leading his ships in single file behind his *Ark Royal,* Howard attacked the Spanish vanguard (the right wing). The *rata,* which he

66

still believed to be the *capitana*, turned to meet him, followed by Martin de Bertendona's *Regazona* and the entire squadron of Levant. De Leiva tried to close, but failed. The English ships dodged and the *rata* was too heavy to follow. With the wind abeam, the two ships fired at each other from a distance.

Meanwhile Drake in the *Revenge*, Frobisher in the *Triumph*, and Hawkins in the *Victory* sailed their squadrons towards the rear-guard (the left wing). The first fire thundered from the English ships, the first cannon balls whistled through the air, the first skulls were shattered, the first blood flowed on the decks. The merchant captains of several Biscayans were scared out of their wits: they were all ordinary working men, vine growers, tapsters, tuna fishermen, pressed into the navy and dubbed for the occasion soldiers or sailors. Several captains abandoned their wing positions and fled, ploughing into the main body of the Armada, like sheep into the heart of the flock.

Don Juan Martinez de Recalde, the Armada's second in command, turned about and headed, alone, towards the advancing enemy. Seven ships levelled their fire at him. Don Diego Pimentel, in the *Gran Grin*, hastened to his rescue. For two hours the two of them endured the *fuego horroroso* of the enemy culverins. Bravely they returned the fire, but the enemy ships kept a safe distance of over 300 yards, a wise tactic according to the English, cowardly according to the Spanish. Spanish cannon, demi-cannon and perriers were dangerous at 150 yards, fatal at 80 yards, at 300 yards virtually ineffective. The strength of the Royal Navy lay in her new galleons. They were absolutely the latest thing: they had lower forecastles, rode lower in the water and were narrower and longer than the ships of the first half of the century, which gave them a greater ease of manœuvre and enabled them to carry more guns each side.

Recalde's *San Juan* was now under fire from eight ships. Seven men had been blown to smithereens by English gunfire. Her gunports had already spewed out the blood of thirty-one wounded men. Her mizzen had been hit twice by cannon balls, and her rigging was in bad shape. De Leiva attempted to engage Drake, trying to manœuvre his heavy carrack, but the wind blew him off before he could get alongside.

Now the Duke himself came to his aid. The *San Martin* and the *San Mateo* had turned about and rounded the fleet to westward with the galleons of Portugal. The galleasses were rowing hard. Seeing this, the Lord Admiral broke off the action. 'We durst not adventure to put in among them,' he wrote, 'their fleet being so strong', and added that he thought it wiser to await the arrival of the forty ships still at Plymouth before advancing further. Henry Whyte, a volunteer on the *Mary Rose,* thought his prudence excessive and considered that their first onset had been 'more coldly done than became the value of our nation and the credit of the English navy'. Drake was sufficiently impressed to write, 'As far as we perceive, they are determined to sell their lives with blows.'[1]

On the Spanish side, the personal intervention of the Duke fired the hearts of his men, and even of his generals who had been somewhat reluctant to take up what was essentially a defensive formation, when they had the advantage in numbers. Having got his men out of trouble around one or two o'clock in the afternoon, the Duke tried until five o'clock to engage battle again. He lined his fleet up roughly into four columns and tacked towards the enemy. He was unsuccessful. 'Those enemy ships were so amazingly nimble. . . .'

NOTES

1. The historian Garrett Mattingly makes the unsubstantiated supposition that Recalde intended by his manœuvre and in defiance of orders, to force the Duke to come to his aid, in order to precipitate a general hand to hand mêlée. And that, Mattingly goes on to suppose, is why he ordered his squadron not to follow him.

12

Fire in the Powder Room

The Duke gave up. At a signal from him the Armada, now in total disorder, began to reform into its crescent. In the muddled confusion of ships, the *Santa Catalina,* clumsily steered, rammed the *capitana* of Pedro de Valdez's Andalusians and wrenched off her spritsail yard and bowsprit. Badly unbalanced, the ship lay across the wind. Before there was time to shorten sail, a strong gust brought down her mizzen mast with all its rigging, and her mainyard. The *Nuestra Señora del Rosario,* broken timbers everywhere and her rigging hopelessly entangled, was utterly paralysed.

Valdez fired four shots for help. The Duke stood over to the *Rosario* in answer to his call. Hardly had he gone about when a blinding ball of fire burst into the dusk. A moment later a shattering explosion echoed across the waves, and a heavy red and black cloud mushroomed up above the *San Salvador.* The whole of her poop was ablaze. Once more the *San Martin* went about to bring help.

On board the *Sun Salvador* were the Vice-Admiral of the Guipuscoan squadron and the paymaster-general, Juan de la Huerta, together with a sizeable part of the Armada treasure, 'divided up as a precautionary measure'. When the Duke approached, a terrible spectacle confronted him. The explosion had blown away two decks and the stern castle. The long, regular, piercing howls of men burnt to the bone rose above the roar of the flames and with the wind came the sickening stench of burnt flesh and hair. The whole powder magazine had blown up.

It was almost certainly an accident, although subsequently at least half a dozen versions of the story grew up, all different and all highly coloured, putting the explosion down to sabotage or personal revenge on the part of a gunner, German, Dutch, English or French

69

according to the version, flogged by Captain Priego. It will be recalled that there was actually a German gunner on board with his wife, and this was doubtless the starting point for the most melodramatic account of all, in which the cuckolded husband chose this way of revenging himself on the seducing captain.

A rescue operation soon began. Two pinnaces hooked the prow of the ship to tug her into the wind so that the flames could not blow forward. Rescuers climbed aboard from the *pataches,* to help survivors fight the fire and to take off the wounded. They had a difficult task. A squally wind was coming up and the swell was getting heavier. The decks were slippery with blood, and it was almost impossible to keep one's balance. Dismembered bodies lay in little heaps, arms or a leg ending in a molten foot hung from the shroud ratlines. A charred head rolled from one side of the deck to the other.

Naked bodies, charred bodies, striped with gashes of red, 'giving off a regular rattle', were taken off to the two hospital ships. Some of them, when they were picked up, lost a limb; or their skin fell away; or their flesh, leaving nothing but bones in their rescuers' hands. The number of dead and wounded came to two hundred. According to the Duke's reckoning another fifty were drowned jumping overboard to escape the furnace.

Once the fire was under control the Duke gave two galleasses orders to tow the hull of the *San Salvador* over to the hulks, according to the evening's entry in his *diario.* His final instructions were to 'transfer the coffers without delay on to a seaworthy ship', then (and we must take his word for it) he stood across to the *Rosario.*

During this time Pedro de Valdez's ship had been trailing behind the rest of the Armada under foresail and main topgallants. A gust of wind carried off her unsupported mainmast as well and then she was motionless.

According to his own account, 'The Duke signalled to the whole fleet to heave to and wait while he stood across to the *Rosario* and tried to pass a hawser.' According to an officer of the *San Marcos:* '. . . She fired four shots but no-one went to her rescue. There was a hard wind blowing, a heavy swell, and the English were hard behind. We abandoned her at vespers, following a signal shot from the Duke.'

Jorge Manrique, one of the Duke's men, recorded that: '. . . the

Armada carried on its way leaving her astern in full view of the enemy . . .' and in the words of one of the *Rosario*'s passengers, 'The Duke went on his way, abandoning her to the enemy, who were still following, three miles astern.' Don Pedro de Valdez himself was to later write to the King:

Unable to make the necessary repairs, I sent someone to inform the Duke and fired . . . four shots to signal our distress to the rest of the Armada. . . . The Duke was close enough to see quite clearly what sort of difficulties I was in and to come to my aid . . . but he did nothing of the sort! He seemed to have forgotten that we were servants of Your Majesty and his command! He fired a shot to reform the Armada and sailed on leaving me in distress, and the enemy only a quarter of a league astern of me.

It does indeed seem that the Duke's first reaction was, instinctively, to go to Don Pedro's rescue, but Diego Flores, his Chief of Staff and principal adviser, argued hotly to the effect that night was falling and the weather was deteriorating badly. If the Captain General delayed any longer, by the morning the Armada would be hopelessly scattered and at the mercy of the enemy. It was not right to imperil the entire fleet for the sake of one ship. Medina Sidonia yielded, but not before he sent his personal *patache* over to the *Rosario* to take off the King's treasure and bring it back safely to his own galleon. Boiling with rage, Valdez replied that since he was risking his own life and so many noblemen and hildagos, surely a little bit of gold might be risked too and he sent the *patache* back, empty. He did however allow Fray Bernardo de Gongora to make a getaway in the *patache*, as well as four English Catholics, who would have risked hanging for high treason had they been captured. According to the Duke:

I then ordered Captain Ojedo to go to Don Pedro de Valdez's rescue with his nao and four pataches. . . . I saw them reach the Rosario [it seems that the Duke was the only person who did] and did not leave until I had made quite sure for myself that two other vessels and a galleon had received my orders to accompany them.

Whatever the truth of the matter is, whether the convoy was in fact never sent, whether it was recalled or simply gave up, by nine o'clock Don Pedro was alone on the sea.

The Captain General had listened to the voice of reason. And he had been wrong. For the Castilians there could be no excuse for what he had done. He had abandoned to the enemy a subordinate, a commander who was loved and respected by everyone. In so doing he had forfeited his honour and earned the undying contempt of his captains. The squadron commanders took it as a mortal affront. Not one of them ever spoke to Diego Flores again. The Commander in Chief had also undermined his men's morale. 'If that's the way a *caballero* like that is abandoned, what kind of help can the likes of us expect?' they are said to have asked themselves.

The bitter hatred that Diego Flores felt for his cousin Don Pedro was common knowledge. Only recently the two men had once more violently disagreed in the council. It was openly suggested that Diego Flores had used this as a means of personal revenge.

By that very night angry reproaches had already reached the Duke's ear. Perhaps that was why when he wrote up his *diario* he specifically stated, 'Diego Flores then said to me' and again, 'so, following his advice. . . .'

13

'The Enemy showed Don Pedro more Mercy than we did Ourselves'

At a council meeting that evening the English decided on their battle order. Sidonia might try to shelter in Tor Bay or land on the Isle of Wight, or possibly at Weymouth. Every eventuality should be foreseen. But how could any of these moves be prevented if they restricted themselves to following him rather than blocking his path?

All the squadron commanders were there. At the end of the day none of them had tried to take the two crippled Spanish ships. For sailors who were by tradition pirates rather than military men, the rewards were tempting. But, no, in the interests of the nation such lust for booty must be controlled. Howard brought this up once again in the council. At the end of the meeting the Lord Admiral entrusted Drake with the task of maintaining contact with the Armada, and leading the whole fleet behind the great poop-lantern of the *Revenge*. Howard was in effect doing Drake the remarkable honour of yielding him the position that was properly his own.

When it was dark Drake put out his lantern, headed due north with two of his ships, the *White Bear* and the *Mary Rose,* and disappeared into the night. Once he was out of sight he went about again, due west, and sailed back up the fleet.

Howard was roused and informed that the Vice-Admiral's lantern was nowhere to be seen. Deeply puzzled, he had topgallants hoisted to go and find out what had happened. He pressed on through the night. At daybreak, no Drake.

Dawn on 1 August found Drake and his two accomplices alongside

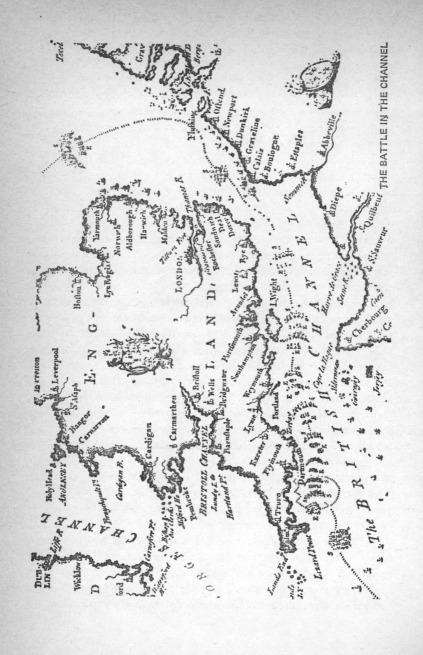

the *Rosario*. He took her without firing a single shot. Don Pedro, hopelessly isolated, had agreed, in exchange for honourable pledges, to surrender his indefensible ship to the three English vessels.

Drake rejoined the fleet in the afternoon with his prize, the Lord Admiral asked for a detailed account of his expedition. Why had he put out the lantern when he had been ordered to keep it alight to guide the rest of the fleet behind him? Why had he not maintained contact with the enemy?

Drake explained that at nightfall they thought they sighted sails to port, between them and the coast, passing to windward of them. He immediately suspected the Spanish of trying to manœuvre round them, to steal the wind and surround the fleet. So, he followed them to see what was afoot. He put the lantern out so that the enemy wouldn't know they were being followed. The enemy ships turned out to be some passing German hulks, Hansa merchantmen, an easy mistake to make ... how odd that no one else saw them! But of course it was very dark. He had come across the *Rosario* by chance, sheer chance.

Sir Martin Frobisher later commented to one of Drake's officers, that Drake had been trying to do them out of their share of the fifteen thousand ducats (*sic*). They would get it back or have his blood. Really, his trickeries were becoming quite intolerable. Drake's booty that day in fact amounted to 55,000 of his Most Catholic Majesty's gold ducats, a ship with forty-six cannon, the ransom of a squadron commander and of several noblemen, and an armful of gold-plated swords with richly encrusted pommels, intended for the English Catholic nobility. He allowed his men to loot cabins and baggage, all except that of Don Pedro (whom Drake entertained royally at his own table, inviting him to watch the remainder of the battle, until Howard pointed out the impropriety of this, quite apart from the potential danger). From the Duke's men, who showed approval of their leader in what they wrote but criticised him sharply in private, this later elicited the comment that 'the enemy showed Don Pedro more mercy than we did ourselves'. Towed to Dartmouth, the *Rosario* was looted from truck to keelson, long before the local magistrates arrived to affix the seals.

That night, 31 July to 1 August, the Captain General of the Ocean Sea slept badly. He had two things on his mind. The points of the

Spanish crescent were too vulnerable, and the rear-guard generally too weak. The first English attack had shown this up, when Sidonia had been forced to send back reinforcements from the van, a lengthy manœuvre and a tricky one against the wind. Clearly it was in the rear that the next blows would come. The Duke turned his quarter moon into a plum, with the hulks as the kernel. Taking advantage of the calmer sea and a light breeze, rear-guard and vanguard linked to form a single rear, strengthened by the galleasses and four galleons of Portugal. There were altogether forty of the best Spanish vessels, under the command of Alonzo de Leiva until Recalde had completed his repairs. The English would now find themselves confronted by a solid wall.

His second problem was that discipline and fighting spirit had been seriously lacking in those ships not commanded by a Grandee of Spain, a nobleman, a hidalgo or a knight. This had been obvious when fifteen ships had fled leaving Recalde virtually stranded. In order to tighten up on discipline the Duke had gallows put up at the yardarms of several *pataches*. Aboard each one he placed a *capitano de campo* (i.e. a military attorney) and a hangman. These *pataches* were to relay to all sergeant majors (provost marshals) written orders for improving conduct. They were to have 'any captain who left his position in the new formation hanged by the neck, publicly dishonoured and deprived of his property'. The Spanish historian, Duro, is profoundly critical of this action, describing it as 'a pointless act of severity, ill adapted either to raise morale or to calm the restiveness'. But Antonio de Herrera says that 'The Armada lacked the discipline vital for manœuvres to be efficiently carried out. . . .'

Towards eleven o'clock the Duke received a message from the *San Salvador* that she was no longer seaworthy and was going down. Sidonia ordered the silver and the crew taken off, and the ship scuttled. He adds in his *diario* that this was done; but it was not. Her captain was badly wounded and the survivors more than anxious to get out of that hellhole. They took off the treasure – whether they took it all or only part of it no one knows – but in any case I made another little mental note on the subject, and later, for greater certainty, transferred it to my little red notebook, Luis de Miranda wrote: '. . . orders were to take off the King's money . . . there were 50,000 or 60,000 ducats on board but only a small amount was removed'. 'There were many on board suffering from wounds and burns whom it was not possible to save,' reported the purser, Pedro Coco Calderon. 'The ship was abandoned in full view of the English,' noted Don Jorge Manrique. 'She was taken by the enemy in full view of the Armada . . .' is a comment in the diary of one of the *Zuñiga*'s crew. When John Hawkins and Lord Thomas Howard climbed aboard the charred wreck, they found fifty wretched men lying on deck horribly burnt and in the most pitiful condition. 'The stink in the ship was so unsavoury and the sight within board so ugly' that they were quickly forced to retire. But there was still some precious shot there and there were even a few barrels of powder left. Having been towed into an English harbour, the *San Salvador,* like the *Rosario* before her, was thoroughly looked over by fishermen and locals, long before any officials arrived on the scene. There is one rather obscure reference in their report to the effect that 'this very night some inkling came unto us that a chest of great weight should be found in the fore-peak of the ship'.

Taking advantage of the lull, supply ships had sailed from the south coast to revictual the English with biscuit, salted meat and sour beer, together with assorted cannon balls and powder 'mixed with a certain amount of sawdust, for they had had to scrape the bottom of the barrels'.

14

De Leiva Enters the Fray

The sea had been quite calm all night. But at dawn on 2 August, a light squall sent a ripple through the huge Burgundy crosses on the *Sancta Maria Encoronada*'s limp sails. This flurry of wind was blowing from the north-east. Was the Armada at last going to be mistress of her tactics?

It must have been God who had ordained that wind for the good of His cause. Alonzo de Leiva lost no time in sending the Captain General a message, begging him to take advantage of it and give battle. He suggested attacking right away with the galleasses to the fore. His messenger, Oquendo's and Recalde's almost collided on the *capitana*'s gangway ladder. They were all bearing the same petition.

Don Alonzo sighted some enemy ships sailing as close to the wind as possible. They were trying to work inshore to get the weather gauge, between the coast and the Armada. His messenger returned with the Duke's orders. They were to attack.

As the two squadrons drew level with Portland Bill, the Armada went about at the tip of the peninsula. With the Levant squadron Bertendona and De Leiva bore down on Howard's flagship. Diego Henriques, Diego Pimentel, Oquendo and Mejia follow with the whole Armada's striking force. The *San Martin* was there too, with the galleons of Portugal. But the English ships moved fast. They beat up close to the wind. To the Spaniards it seemed that they could dodge about at will, that their culverins rang out relentlessly three times as fast as the Spanish guns. Even with the wind in their favour the Spanish failed to grapple and board.

An English ship caught fire, but the blaze was quickly put out. A lucky shot sank one of their smallest vessels, the *Pleasure*. Hugo de Moncada sent his galleasses in against Frobisher's squadron. It was they who worked inshore that morning to steal the new wind.

Howard saw the approaching danger, tried to join Frobisher, but failed. Don Hugo attacked the *Triumph,* which he found at anchor. She was the biggest vessel in either fleet, and flying Sir Martin Frobisher's own pennant. At the approach of the galleasses Frobisher cut his cable, manœuvred round and fired on the rowers, shooting to kill. His cannon balls left gaping holes in the ranks of the galley slaves. Once their ranks were broken and their rowing rhythm lost, the oars became crossed and tangled. Compelled to hoist their sails, the heavy galleasses lost their one advantage, which was their free movement. The *Triumph* and five merchantmen managed to hold them at a distance.

The guns had been thundering away since five o'clock when towards midday the wind suddenly veered southwards, from northeast, to south-west. The land breeze of the morning was replaced by a sea breeze. Drake knew his Channel. Anticipating this change, he had left the battle, and with fifty ships in the wake of the *Revenge* he had sailed out to sea. The Armada in the heat of the chase had scattered once more.

The wind changed and Drake was in position. At full tilt he bore down before the wind. Suddenly he loomed out of a cloud of acrid smoke that had blown like a screen across the sea. The moment he saw Drake approaching, Sidonia recalled his galleasses and centred his attack on Drake. Frobisher was saved. Howard and all the others also took advantage of the situation to overpower isolated Spanish ships. The prime target was the *San Martin.* One after another she suffered the salvoes of the *Ark Royal* and six other enemy ships. The flagship received five hundred hits (according to Medina Sidonia) and lost fifty men. The Duke stood in the aftercastle and with Diego Flore's assistance calmly directed the firing and the manœuvre, which the ship's captain, Marolin de Juan, carried out with the precision of a naval exercise. No enemy ship dared to approach the enormous galleon closely, as she steadily spat fire from her gunports. But Recalde was being closed in on again. His Portuguese galleons had rejoined him at last, and the Duke must go with them to get Recalde out of trouble. So he broke off what was a pretty aimless battle. The Armada took up its plum formation again and sailed on eastward.

From dawn until five o'clock that evening, 'nothing could be heard from the shore but a continuous roll, that kept every man in a state of extreme anxiety'. The two fleets did actually exchange more than 4,000 shots that day, according to the Duke's *diario*, approximately one shot every ten seconds. The action had left the Spanish with fifty dead and more than sixty wounded, though it is not clear whether these figures refer to the whole Armada, or only to the *capitana*. But if the casualty figures on the Spanish side are vague, on the English side they were nonexistent. Captains would conceal deaths among the men in order to go on collecting their pay. The smaller shot had riddled the sails with holes, cut through halyards and stays, and brought down masts and yards. But neither the Protestant roundshot fired at long range out of prudence, nor the Catholic balls fired at long range in desperation, had succeeded in piercing any hulls, nor, in the final analysis, had the balance of power been altered. The two fleets, reforming on the evening of the battle, had spent their powder for nothing.

The action started up again on the morning of 3 August when De Leiva's rear-guard became involved in a hot skirmish with some English vessels. Recalde, with the galleasses bringing up the rear, joined in the action. The enemy seemed to be about to give battle. Once more the gunfire started up, as furiously as the previous day, slowing down only during the course of the day as the guns overheated, and the gunners had to try to cool them down by wrapping them in sheets soaked in vinegar and water.

Finding themselves short of powder and ball, the English finally retired, or, according to the Spaniards, fled. That evening the Duke reckoned that a further 5,000 shots had been fired. Sixty corpses were thrown without ceremony overboard, and the hospital hulks took in a further seventy wounded. Sidonia noted too that he had counted 140 enemy sail that evening. Then, closing his *diario*, he wrote two letters. The first was to the Duke of Parma, to whom he wrote nearly every day, to keep him up to date and to urge him on. The second was to the King. '. . . I intend to take the Isle of Wight and occupy the port. This will be my base when we join forces.' Having done this, he went to bed.

That same night the English were deciding on a change of tactics. They were dividing themselves up into four squadrons, under Howard, Drake, Hawkins and Frobisher.

The first light of dawn on Thursday, 4 August, showed the English two Spanish stragglers in an empty sea. John Hawkins had himself towed towards them. They were the hulk *Santa Ana* (not the *capitana Santa Ana* that Recalde had abandoned because of extensive damage) and one of the galleons of Portugal, the *San Luis*. Lowering their sail, three galleasses immediately set off under oar to their rescue, followed at a distance by several galleons and De Leiva's carrack. The galleasses arrived alone to find themselves surrounded, in an extremely perilous situation, under a hail of iron and lead. The *Girona* lost her poop lantern, the *San Lorenzo* lost her figureheads. The *Zuñiga's* hull was holed at the water level, and she had to move clear, listing badly. Aiming as before into the oars, the enemy fired their shot in among the rowers. And as before the thwarts were soon jammed with bodies (it was impossible to throw them overboard quickly enough because of their chains) and wounded men screaming in agony. There were seven men slaving at each oar, four pulling and three pushing. All it needed was for one man to collapse at the feet of the others, covering the planks with a gory mess of blood and guts, and they were all entangled. And it only needed one oar to stop for those immediately next to it to get caught up too. When one side of the vessel was without a certain number of oars, any manœuvre became impossible. And if they hoisted their sails the galleasses completely lost their mobility. The galleasses demonstrated in the English Channel that, far from combining the advantages of the galley with those of the galleon as had been anticipated, they combined nothing but the disadvantages of both, once they were outclassed in firepower.

Recalde was first to the rescue. Then, as the fleets came abeam of the Isle of Wight, the other galleons joined them. The wind veered from south-south-west to west-south-west. Now, with the wind abeam, the Armada could manœuvre. It was the Feast of St Domingo de Guzman that day and the Duke, a regular worshipper of his, decided to give battle again. He broke out the royal standard and had pennants and banners hoisted at all mast-heads. It seemed as if this time the English were going to let the Spanish get near. Quite soon separate groups here and there began to exchange fire in some confusion. Under fire from the Spanish perriers the 'English flagship' (wrongly identified by the Duke – English documents prove that it was in fact the damaged *Triumph*) was cut off at one moment from the rest of the squadron, and caught on a lee shore, seemed in serious danger. The Duke saw her strike the flag, fire two shots for help and try to get away from the battle towed by her boats. The *San Martín* was ideally placed to dispatch her. The Duke hesitated. That moment was crucial. Alonzo de Leiva offered up a silent prayer. He saw it as their chance to snatch victory. If the flagship had been engaged the rest of the English fleet would have had to come to her aid. At last there would have been some hand to hand fighting.

Still the Duke hesitated. That, at any rate, was what the Spanish captains claimed when they later heaped abuse on him at court. The crack shots had already been ordered to the crow's nests, the arquebusiers had taken their positions, arms loaded and matches already smoking. The boarding parties were at their posts, grappling hooks at the ready.

But the Duke waited, and the English galleon moved off.

She must have slipped away by moving cleverly from an unfavourable local current into a neighbouring countercurrent. She was also helped by nine launches sent in to the rescue under the Duke's very eyes. De Leiva, Oquendo, Recalde and all the generals, indignant with rage, let loose a flood of sarcastic comments. Fray Juan de Victoria later wrote (from hearsay, it is true) that once De Leiva was within hail of the *San Martín*, he hurled across a flood of abuse, of which the least offensive was: 'God's body, His Majesty has given us a man to command us at sea who looks as if he wouldn't know how to walk on dry land.' The friar reported that when Oquendo's ship in turn came abreast of the *San Martín*, Oquendo shouted for the Duke and all his Andalusians to hear: 'Go on then, chickens! Get to your fishing nets, and go fish for tuna if you don't want to fight!' (The monopoly of tuna-fishing rights was a long-standing privilege of the Dukes of Medina Sidonia, as well as being the traditional pursuit of Andalusian sailor-fishermen.) He then shouted to the soldiers on board that the best thing they could do would be to throw the Duke's counsellor, Diego Flores, overboard, after which they might be able to get down to fighting a war. 'The Duke took Oquendo to court for this insult,' continues the good priest. 'He sent the records to the King, who read them and just smiled sadly.'

Elsewhere, amidst general confusion, the battle continued. Both sides were blinded by the acrid black smoke that drifted up in thick clouds. A new wind came up, giving the advantage to the English. The Duke discharged a piece and continued on his course. The rest of the Armada following in good order ... the enemy a long way astern. They were heading now for the Straits of Dover. That day about 3,000 shot had been fired. Two men had been killed on the *San Martín*, and a shot had cut the main throat halyard. Throughout the Armada fifty Spanish bodies were consigned to the waves. There were seventy wounded.

The Spaniards from the North despised the Andalusians as much as the Castilians loathed the Portuguese and the Catalans the Basques. Abused from all sides, Medina Sidonia threatened a few men around him with sentences of death. He wrote up for the King his own account of the day's event.

The capitana and the vice-flagship were gaining on her [*Triumph*] so fast that the rest of the enemy sailed to the rescue. This time we felt quite sure that we would succeed in boarding, the only way we can win a victory.

In the words of Alonso Vanegas of the *San Martín*, who was writing a eulogy of the Duke to which he added something daily: 'We had her almost within musket range when nine launches towed her off, snatching her so swiftly from our grasp, it was quite miraculous.'

So the Duke and his Andalusians were writing up their reports. And meanwhile, instead of lying in the roads of the Isle of Wight, which is what the King had told Sidonia to do, what had been agreed at the council, and also what the Duke had just written to the King that he intended to do, the Armada sailed on up the Channel. If the prevailing winds held, this meant that the fleet was now proceeding without any chance of turning back and without a single port along the way in which to shelter, and it was still not known whether Parma was ready or not.

Why? Sidonia gives not the slightest hint. Very hastily and vaguely he wrote, '... Given that we no longer had the advantage of the weather for our planned attack, the Duke proceeded on his way.' (The Duke consistently refers to himself in the third person.) English records are no more informative. And yet if the Spaniards did not, as planned, sail up the Solent, which is the way into the roads of the Isle of Wight, it can only have been because the English prevented them from doing so. And they must have managed this thanks to their perfect knowledge of the changing winds, and of the complex inter-play of local tidal currents, of eddies, and dangerous shoals.

The success of this manœuvre represented a major victory for Howard. The Armada had not landed or put into port on the south coast of England. The Spanish were, it is true, still making for their rendezvous, and there was still the Thames. But there Howard would have the added reinforcements of John Seymour's ships and the Dover squadron.

15

'The Hellburners of Antwerp!'

Friday, 5 August, the sea was like a mill pond and the fleets, both in good order, drifted slowly two miles apart. On both sides there were broken timbers to be repaired. Carpenters, able seamen and master sailmakers were busy on board. Divers were nailing lead plates to the hulls and inside the flooded holds to stop leaks. Soldiers, rowers and seamen slept.

In his daily letter to Farnese, the Duke asked for supplies of bullets, powder, and 4 lb., 6 lb., and 10 lb. balls, of which they were running short; they also needed more biscuit, and if possible forty or fifty flyboats and small craft, easily manœuvrable, in which Sidonia intended to launch his floating army against the enemy galleons. Farnese had none of these things. Had he had any small seaworthy boats, Justin of Nassau and the Sea Beggars, who were lying in wait for him, would have sunk them immediately they left harbour.

Meanwhile, the English, revictualled by launches from the Cinque Ports, were spending the day loading provisions, powder and shot and augmenting their crews.

At sunset the wind freshened a little and the Armada continued on course to Calais.

At dawn on the 6th, the Duke summoned another meeting of the council. He had decided to anchor at Calais and send word to Farnese to join him there from Dunkirk and Nieuport, these two places, as it seemed to him, not being too far away. The majority of squadron commanders were not at all of the same opinion. The anchorage seemed to them exceedingly dangerous. They were worried about the nearness of the enemy, and most important, they reckoned it impossible that the Flanders army could reach Calais in unarmed, flat-bottomed barges. Recalde and De Leiva advised anchoring further on at Cape Margate, which had several advantages, quite apart from being the place specifically designated in the King's instructions. Oquendo said quite bluntly that if the Armada anchored at Calais 'she was lost'. But the pilots thought that if they went on before the south-west wind, the currents would force the Armada into the North Sea and it would be extremely difficult to get back into the Channel again.

The Duke gave orders to drop two anchors because of the force of the tidal currents. The English fleet anchored too, smartly enough not to lose the weather gauge. The Duke lost no time in sending Captain Heredia to pay a courtesy visit to the Governor of Calais.

In the evening Lord Henry Seymour's squadron and Sir William Wynter's joined Howard. The Armada was surrounded by Howard and Drake to the west, to the north by a section of the fleet anchored between Dover and Sandwich (they were to arrive the following day) and to the east by Justin of Nassau's forty ships, making in all 230 vessels.

Night fell, bringing with it a mood of anxiety. 'We were greatly afraid of a disaster and had a strong premonition that some dastardly trick would be played by that diabolical race of men', wrote Captain Louis de Miranda. The night was quite peaceful however. On Sunday morning the Duke sent his victualling officer ashore for supplies.

Captain Rodrigo Tello arrived back from Dunkirk with a letter from Farnese, promising that in six days everything would be ready for a sortie. Tello himself was less optimistic. The soldiers, he said, had not even begun to embark. The Duke hurriedly sent his secretary to Farnese to urge him to make haste. When the secretary saw for himself the stage things had reached, he estimated that it would be more than a fortnight before the embarkation was completed. Parma replied that embarkation was to begin at once. He ordered his soldiers to embark in 'barges, constructed in such a way that any boarder who jumped onto them immediately landed in the water. Fourteen thousand men were embarked in one day, so tightly crammed that they looked more like sacks of wheat squashed into the holds'.

At sunset the look-outs reported much coming and going by

launches in the English fleet, and sinister-looking preparations going on. The threat was obvious. In that position, lying at anchor, the Armada was the perfect target for an attack by fireships. It was a text-book situation. Captain Serrano was ordered to take up a position to windward of the fleet with eight pinnaces all equipped with grappling irons and butts. If they saw a fireship approaching they were to tow it ashore at right angles to the wind and standing in to the current. All officers in command ordered a double watch and left their ship's boats in the water similarly equipped. No one can have slept much that night.

Soon after midnight a cry rang out, and quickly spread from ship to ship, louder and louder: 'Fireships!' Eight blazing vessels, swiftly propelled by the wind and the tide, were bearing down like a wall of flame on the Armada in lines two pikes' length apart.

Serrano's pinnaces were to be seen rowing hard in the direction of the danger. There was an explosion on board one of the ships, and the cry changed. 'The hellburners of Antwerp! The hellburners of Antwerp!'

That particular cry resurrected old fears. In the siege of Antwerp three years earlier, infernal delayed-action machines drifting on the Scheldt had killed more than a thousand Spaniards. One had wounded Parma himself, who like everyone else had been taken completely by surprise by Frederico Giambelli's diabolical invention. The Italian engineer had had the idea of filling a small boat with gunpowder, then packing the compressed powder round the sides and top, with solid layers of bricks or heavy stones. A well-concealed slow fuse, or occasionally a clockwork timing mechanism, set off the charge. The force of the explosion was devastating, and a rain of falling shrapnel crippled anyone who had not already been knocked out by the blast.

The Duke ordered cables to be cut at once. Oquendo, who was standing by at the time, begged him to withdraw his order and pleaded with him to send more pinnaces with boathooks and grapnels to help Serrano divert the fireships onto the beach, or at least to wait until they had tried. The Duke's idea was to cut their cables, move out of the path of the fireships and then recover their previous positions. Oquendo assured him that such a manoeuvre was utterly impracticable at dead of night, with so many ships so close together and with the wind and current as they were. To no effect. The order went out. Most of the ships cut their cables and hoisted their sails, all at once, and in such confusion that several of them rammed each other and were damaged. Some were seen to be drifting, hopelessly entangled, in the direction of Dunkirk. The fireships, which carried only faggots, pitch and tar, sailed on through the empty roads, their guns overheated by the fire, going off at random, until finally they burned themselves out on the beach. They had not directly inflicted any damage at all.

The *capitana* discharged a piece and reanchored. A few nearby ships did likewise, but at dawn on 8 August, when the Duke looked for his fleet, it was scattered all the way from Calais to Gravelines. Though they had not set light to one single vessel Howard's fireships had succeeded in shattering the Armada's formation and had caused its scattered ships to leave their best anchors at the bottom of the sea. All told, Medina Sidonia had with him two galleons and eight *pataches*. He weighed anchor and stood across to where the main body of his fleet lay.

First light showed the English how the enemy was scattered. At the head of their columns, Drake and Seymour went straight into the attack. They directed their fire first on three detached ships at arquebus range, which they systematically pounded with their overwhelmingly superior firepower. Far away to the north, Spanish admirals and vice-admirals were trying one after another to beat up to windward, and one after another they were caught by the enemy. This battle royal stretched from Calais as far as the eye could see. From 8 a.m. to 3 p.m., with seventeen enemy ships to port and seven to starboard, 'frequently within musket range and sometimes within arquebus range', Medina Sidonia stood at his post without a moment's respite, receiving and returning broadside after broadside, 'as furiously as one might imagine' ... 'That evening the gunners were exhausted, having stuck to their guns and not taken a morsel to eat.' So wrote Captain Vanegas and Pedro Coco Calderon.

16

From Calais to Gravelines

During the night of 7–8 August, the *capitana San Lorenzo* collided with the *rata* in all the confusion. The two ships managed to disentangle themselves, but in the course of the manœuvre the galleass's rudder fouled itself on a cable (probably belonging to one of the anchors that had been abandoned) and both gudgeons were snapped clean off. Don Hugo was rudderless. Dawn found him all alone. With the enemy closing fast, he tried to row into Calais and shelter under the guns of the castle, by arrangement with the Governor, while he repaired the damages. But Don Hugo had no French pilot. He was crossing the bar in a heavy swell when the galleass was swept onto a shoal. The ebbing tide soon caused her to heel over with her starboard battery pointing to the sky and her port battery leaning hard over into the sea. The *capitana* of the galleasses was 'the finest ship in the Armada', an incomparable prize. She was almost certainly carrying more gold and more silver plate than any other vessel except the *San Martin*. Forgetting the plans that had been decided on at the previous day's council, the Lord Admiral – who ought to have led the first attack on the scattered enemy fleet, before Drake, second in charge, and Seymour third – lay to with his entire squadron and sent his officers 'to have their pillage of her'. Though unable to use his cannon, Moncada put up a manly resistance. His arquebusiers went up to the castles and gave the first English boats a hot reception. His small calibre perriers and esmerils, loaded with small shot, beat back fifteen longboats crammed with musketeers. But Don Hugo fell, both eyes blown away by a musket ball. The first to get away were the galley slaves, Turkish and Berber convicts. They swam ashore, followed by Italian artillery-men and sailors. Two captains, Luis Macian and Francisco de Torres were fatally wounded. Man by man the defenders were shot down, until the last survivors hung a white handkerchief on a rapier and surrendered the ship to the English.

Fifty men lay dead in the English boats, awash with blood slopping about in the bottom. The 200 uninjured assailants scaled the sides of the galleasses and rushed in after the booty. The chapel of St Lawrence was sacked, just like the cabins: the baggage was gutted. Officers and men squabbled over 'fourteen coffers of the most noble spoils'. They divided up between themselves the treasure of the squadron of Naples. (22,000 of the King's gold ducats, according to the historians Ubaldino and Steinitz – 50,000 ducats according to Lediard.) Candlesticks, silver and gold plate, crystal, the officers' jewels, including Don Hugo de Moncada's Malta cross, his gold chains, and his insignia of the Order of Santiago. They stripped the sailors and tore chains and jewels from the dead men. None of the loot ever left the pockets into which it was stuffed. Officially, '. . . there was no treasure on board at all, other than a very few things . . .', according to the account of Captain Richard Thomson, one of the pillagers.

The Governor of Calais sent out his cousin and a few other gentlemen in a boat to congratulate the victors on their success, to assure them that he wholeheartedly agreed to their taking their hard-won booty, and to remind them that the vessel herself, with her guns, was lying aground on a stretch of coastline that falls under his jurisdiction, and that they were therefore his by right. It would be quite out of order for them to try to tow her away, and besides the castle cannon are levelled directly on her. Thomson answered politely and hastened back to his pillage. Then, '. . . some of our rude men . . . fell to spoiling the Frenchmen, taking away their rings and jewels . . .'

Furious, the Governor's cousin went ashore and made straight for the castle. The Calais cannon opened fire and the English lost another twenty men killed or drowned, in a matter of minutes. They beat a hasty retreat, leaving the ship and her guns for Monsieur Gourdan. But they did carry off three captains, in the hope of some ransom money. Howard and his squadron then returned to the battle.

While most of the Armada were struggling against a strong northwest wind that was driving them on to the Dunkirk banks, off Gravelines eleven ships were bearing for hours the brunt of the fire of more than 100 enemy ships. Throughout the whole day barely forty Spanish vessels managed to position themselves to fire. The cannonade had begun at 8 a.m. The more manœuvrable English galleons sailed swiftly past, their decks empty, only a pike's length from the Spanish carracks and great ships, their decks packed with soldiers whose courage was useless. The English would fire one broadside, circle to come in and fire the other, and then come in again, reloading three times in the time it took the Spanish or Italians to load once. It was not until three o'clock in the afternoon that the main body of the Armada arrived to help. The English hurriedly retired, not being over-anxious to engage in too equal a fight. Outnumbering the Spanish by one hundred to eleven, they had neither sunk nor captured a single ship. Neither had they allowed the enemy to board, although he had tried to do so a dozen times or more. The *capitana,* one of the eleven, had been 'the shield for the whole Armada,' said the Duke, 'allowing it to extricate itself from the danger.'

The *San Martín* had been holed all over. She had received 107 direct hits, 'enough to bring down a mountain', wrote Alonzo Vanegas. Her divers worked until nightfall to stop the leaks with pitch, tow and lead plates. The English shot had dismounted three guns, pierced her aftercastle, killed twelve men and wounded 120.

The *San Marco*'s pumps could hardly keep down the water. It was rising hopelessly fast, too, in the bilges of the *San Juan de Sicilia.* The *Neustra Señora de Begona* had suffered badly. The *San Felipe* was listing to port. The *San Mateo* and the Biscayan *San Juan* were straggling, their decks awash with blood, and leaving a red wake. They had both received the successive broadsides of a whole English firing line. Their hulls were riddled with holes, their rigging was torn to shreds, their sails were like sieves. The *Maria Juan,* her decks awash, sent out repeated distress signals. Suddenly she sank like a stone, taking down 300 men, all hanging in her tops and in the rat-lines.

The cannonade had cost the Spanish in all 600 men killed and 800 wounded. The wounded were taken off in *pataches* to the hospital ships as soon as the enemy retired. The English had not lost a ship, nor more than twenty men.

17

'Only God Could Save Us!'

At dusk the long hammering of the cannonade died down, but as silence fell over the water, a new danger loomed. Over on the horizon, to the east-north-east, surf was breaking on the Zeeland Banks in heavy rollers, dirty and foaming. The north-west wind was freshening.

'Not a man among us slept that night,' wrote Fray de la Torre. 'All we could do was wait for the moment when we would be hurled into the shoals.'

On the morning of 9 August rain was falling. The Duke wrote that he tried to get the Armada to take up its battle formation again, but that at least twenty of his captains ignored the signal and ran on eastwards instead of lying to and awaiting the enemy. The *capitana* had in company three galleasses, Recalde's galleons, De Leiva's squadron and two other vessels. In all, 109 English ships were vissible, standing in the eye of the wind, but some way off. The swell was rising, the wind blowing fresh from the northwest. Sailing as closehauled as they could, the Spanish ships, driven by the wind and the current, were drifting helplessly into the Zeeland Banks. Already the sea about them was brown with roiled-up sand. They had left their bower anchors behind at Calais and the kedges would never hold in the shifting sand bottom.

The Duke was no longer capable of any reaction. At dawn, it is said, when he was within hail of Oquendo, he had shouted across from the forecastle, in full hearing of two crews, 'Señor Oquendo, Señor Oquendo, we are lost! What are we to do?' Don Miguel shouted back angrily that he should ask Diego Flores . . . as for me, I intend to fight and die like a man.' It was the view of the pilots that 'in the present situation not a ship could be saved except by a miracle. . . . They would all run aground on the shoals and be pounded to pieces by the surf. It was only a matter of hours. . . .' The English must have shared this view. They turned back and beat windward to get away from the Armada and from the trap into which it was being pushed. As the minutes passed, the leadsmen's cries grew more alarmed. The *Trinidad Escala* had six fathoms of water under her keel, the *patrona* of the galleasses less than five. 'It was the most fearful day in the world, for every man had lost all hope and waited only for death,' wrote Luis de Miranda.

'The Duke's officers,' wrote Calderon, 'gathered round him, beseeching him with tears in their eyes to take a pinnace and save himself and the Holy Banner from certain capture. The Duke refused and sent them back to their posts. . . .' But later it was put about at court that Sidonia had 'offered a pilot 5,000 ducats to get him ashore safely in his pinnace, but the pilot refused . . .'

The men on the ships most immediately threatened, confessed, took communion and prepared to die. Then at the very last minute, the leadsmen standing in the chains of the *capitana*, which drew four fathoms, had called six. 'It pleased God to change the wind to west-southwest enabled the Armada to sail full North, without one ship having been damaged,' wrote Calderon.

The miracle had happened. Now the Armada was standing away into deep water, its sails filled by a fair breeze. At eleven o'clock the ships started to reform. That evening Sidonia wrote in his *diario*, 'Only God could save us.'

Not all, however, were saved. The Captain General had to leave to the Dutch two crippled ships, the *San Mateo* and the *San Felipe*.

The Lord Admiral summoned his council. They reckoned up their losses. Hawkins reported little damage and Fenner only slight losses. The council considered their reserves of powder, which like their reserves of match and fuse, shot, victuals and beer were virtually exhausted. Howard decided to send Seymour's and Wynter's squadrons to cruise off the Thames so as to block Parma if he risked coming out. Meanwhile the main body of the fleet, on empty stomachs and with their cannon reduced to impotence, would follow the Armada and prevent them from making a landing or even putting in along the east coast, or in Scotland, if that seemed to be their intention.

The Captain General, too, was holding a council, having summoned all the generals and Alonzo do Leiva to the flagship.

On balance, things looked black. The Duke lingered over the score: eight ships lost, including some of the best, and all the others damaged and making water. Almost all were short of shot. One man in five was dead, wounded or sick. And then there was the wind that was stopping them going back into the Channel for the rendezvous that they had failed to make. And still Parma was not ready. Would it not be wiser to go back via the North Sea? What did everyone think?

De Leiva gave his views:

> You all know how I have given battle. I have now no more than thirty cannon ball, my ship is riddled with small shot, and pierced in several places. She is taking in water badly. But I do not consider any of this sufficient reason not to do my duty. I am not in favour of entering the North Sea.

Recalde suggested that they cruise locally for a few days, until the wind changed, and then return to Calais. An Andalusian captain declared that the time had passed for demonstrations of personal bravery. What they must consider now was what would be in the best interests of His Majesty. What if the enemy were to press hard upon them for three days, what would they do without any ammunition? De Leiva rejoined with a proposal that they sail to Norway for fresh supplies. The Duke objected to all these views. If the whole Armada spent the winter in enemy waters, and the English fleet was not destroyed, the coast of Spain would be without any defence. In the end all were agreed that they should return to the Channel as soon as the weather permitted. In his *diario* the Duke (who did not keep a record of council discussions) translated this as, 'The Council then unanimously agreed to return to the Channel, weather permitting. And if not, to go back to Spain via the North Sea. . . .' Then, making sure that he was covered, he continued:

> In matters of warfare I have in all things bowed to the opinion of Don Francisco de Bobadilla, a man of considerable experience, both at sea and on land, and in everything connected with the fleet and the sea. I have always bowed, too, to the opinion of Diego Flores de Valdez, the veteran amongst us, and to that of the two advisers appointed by His Majesty who were on the capitana.

On 10 August a steady sou'wester was blowing. They passed Dogger Bank on the 11th. On the 12th the English closed several times, but withdrew again as soon as the rearguard turned to face them. Howard feared that Sidonia might be seeking an anchorage where he could make good his defects and return to the battle. When he saw that the Armada had passed the Firth of Forth without showing any sign of attempting a landing, he realised that Sidonia was fleeing. The enemy fleet was returning to Spain by the northern route. (See plate v.)

Towards midday the Lord Admiral of England turned for home, leaving behind a pinnace and a caravel to shadow the enemy as far as the Orkneys and Shetlands.

The rendezvous had been missed. Philip's dream was turning to dust.

18

750 Leagues of Stormy Seas

That same day the Duke made the retreat official by handing out sailing orders to each ship's captain for the return of the fleet to Spain. The English later found a copy on a ship wrecked off the Irish coast.

> The course that is to be followed first is to the north-northeast, up to the latitude of $61\frac{1}{2}°$; you will take great care lest you fall upon the Island of Ireland, for fear of the harm that may befall you upon that coast. Then parting from these islands and rounding the Cape in $61\frac{1}{2}°$ you will run west-southwest until you are in latitude $58°$ and then southwest until $53°$; then south-southeast to Cape Finisterre and so you will procure your entrance into Corunna.

Purser Coco Calderon's reply to two captains who were uneasy about this circumnavigation, was that 'The return journey will indeed be one of the most difficult and arduous ever, for we shall have to sail round England, Scotland and Ireland through 750 leagues of stormy seas, virtually unknown to us. . . .' He might have added that no one had a chart or sailing directions for the route to be covered and that few of the pilots had ever been there before. And he was unaware of the fact that the charts of Ireland that some of the pilots had in their heads were dangerously inaccurate.

On the 13th rations were cut to half a pound of biscuits each, a pint of water and half a pint of wine. Most of the barrels had the worm in them (Drake again!); the staves had shrunk and warped, and the water had leaked, leaving only a couple of inches of slime at the bottom. The wine had soured in the butts.

The Duke ordered all horses and mules to be thrown overboard, in order not to have to water them. There were many hungry men who

LA FELI
CISSIMA AR=
MADA QVE ELREY
DON FELIPE NVESTRO
Señor mandó juntar enel puerto
dela Ciudad de Lisboa enel
Reyno de Portu-
gal.

El Año de mil y quinientosy
ohcenta y ocho.

Fr.suis. A. Jacques Goullain fils Dr. fru Guille: lequel fist lachat de mey. en sa ville Religehonne. 1598

HECHA POR
Pedro de Paz
Salas.

1 Frontispiece of the *General Inventory of the Most Fortunate Fleet*, printed
in Lisbon in 1588 for Pedro de Paz Salas

❧ S V M A R I O ❧
GENERAL DE TODA
EL ARMADA.

	Numero d'Nauios	Toneladas	Géte d'guerra.	Géte d'mar.	Numero d'todos.	Pieças de artilleria.	Peloteria	Poluora	Plomo quintales.	Cuerda tales.
¶ Armada de Galeones de Portugal.	12.	7.737.	3.330.	1.293.	4.623.	347.	18.450.	789.	186.	150
¶ Armada de Vizcaya de que es General Iuan Martinez de Ricalde.	14	6.567.	1.937.	863.	2.800.	238.	11.900.	477.	140.	87
¶ Galeones de la Armada de Castilla.	16	8714	2.458.	1.719.	4171.	384.	23.040.	710.	290.	309
¶ Armada de naues del Andaluzia.	11.	8.762.	2.325.	780.	3.105.	240.	10.200.	415.	63.	119
¶ Armada de naos de la Prouincia de Guipuscua.	14	6.991.	1992.	616.	2.608.	247.	12.150.	518.	139.	109
¶ Armada de naos leuantiscas.	10.	7.705.	2.780.	767.	3523.	280.	14000.	584.	177.	141
¶ Armada de Vrcas.	23.	10271.	3121.	608.	3729.	384.	19.200.	258.	142.	215
¶ Pataches y zabras.	22.	1.221.	479.	574.	1.093.	91.	4550.	66.	20.	13
¶ Galeaças de Napoles.	4.		873.	468.	1.341.	200.	10.000.	498.	61.	88
¶ Galeras.	4			362.	362.	20.	1.200.	60.	20.	20.
	130	57.868	19295.	8050.	27365.	2.431.	123790.	4575.	1.232.	1.151

Gente de remo.

En las Galeaças.	1.200.
En las Galeras.	888.
	2.088.

De mas de la dicha poluora se
lleua de respecto para si se ofre
ciere alguna bateria 600. qs.   600.

Por manera que ay en la dicha armada, segun parece por este sumario, ciento y treynta nauios, que tienen cinquenta y siete mil ochocientas y sessenta y ocho toneladas, y dezinueue mil dozientos y nouenta y cinco soldados de Infanteria, y ocho mil y cinquenta y dos hombres de mar, que todos hazen, veyntisiete mil trezientas y setenta y cinco personas, y dos mil y ochenta remeros, y dos mil y quatrocientas y treynta y vna pieças de artilleria, las mil quatrocientas y nouenta y siete de bronze, de todas suertes en que ay muchos cañones, y medios cañones, culebrinas, y medias culebrinas, y cañones pedreros, y las noucientas y treynta y quatro restantes de hierro colado de todos caliuos, y ciento y veyntitres mil cien to y nouenta balas para ellas, y cinco mil ciento y setenta y cinco quintales de poluora, y mil y dozientos y treynta y ocho de plomo, y mil ciento y cinquenta y vn quintales de cuerda: y los generos de los nauios son en esta manera.

A 9

2 In the summary of the Inventory: 10 squadrons, 130 ships, 30,000 men

3 (*top*) The *Gente de Guerra*: sixteenth-century Spanish captains, pikemen and arquebusiers, from an engraving by Theodore de Bry

4 (*above*) Detail from an engraving by John Pine, showing one of the Armada's four genuine galleasses. Could it be the *Girona*?

5 The Armada in the crescent formation that it adopted in the Channel, with two galleasses at each point. The English, having sailed round them to both sides, have succeeded in taking the wind. The Lord Admiral of England has sent his pinnace, the *Disdain*, to bear his personal challenge to the Captain General, the Duke of Medina Sidonia. This engraving was made by John Pine in 1739 from a set of tapestries made for the Lord Admiral, Lord Howard of Effingham, by Francis Speirrig. Speirrig had used Cornelis de Vroom's designs made from Howard's own sketches

6 and 7 The *San Salvador* was destroyed by fire following an explosion, the English subsequently captured two vessels, both of which had already been damaged. Otherwise they wisely avoided boarding, preferring to take advantage of the longer range of their artillery and the greater mobility of their new galleons

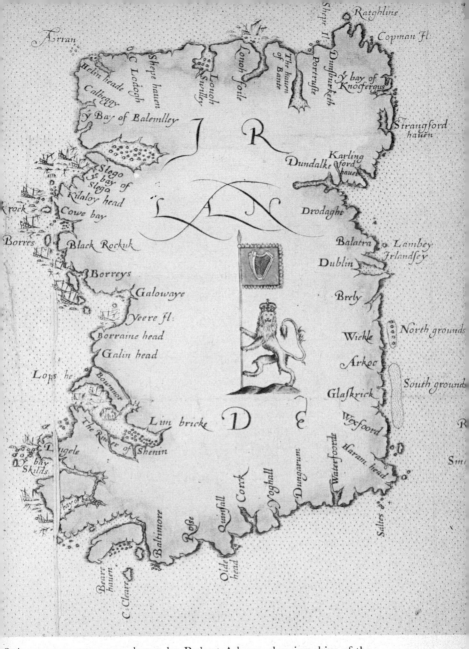

8 A contemporary map drawn by Robert Adams, showing ships of the
Armada wrecked on the Irish coast. The only one not marked is the
Girona – she was the last to go down

9 (*left*) Alonzo Martinez de Leiva sailed in a Genoese carrack, the *rata Sancta Maria Encoronada*, taking with him all the young men of gentle birth in the fleet: from an engraving by Breughel

10 The ship ran aground in Blacksod Bay, which lies in the background of this photograph. Don Alonzo led all his men, carrying their valuables and small arms, safely ashore. They fortified themselves in Fahy Castle (Doona)

would have been only too happy to eat horse flesh, but orders were orders.

The first to desert had been some pressganged Dutch sailors who had gone over to the enemy. Then, once the English fleet was out of sight, the captains of two merchantmen chartered in the Hansa ports sailed off home by night.

On 15 August, the Feast of the Assumption, three Scottish fishing boats were captured and their seamen held to serve as pilots.

Freezing fog on the 17th made it impossible to see from one ship to another. 'In latitude 62° it is not warm. I am shivering, for I left my coat behind on Pedro de Valdez's ship when by a miracle I managed to escape,' wrote de Gongora. It was very cold indeed for August. The negroes were the first to succumb and then it was the Andalusians and Sicilians who were suffering the most. Many men died of cold, for they were practically naked having sold what coverings they had for food or gambled them away. When the fog lifted there were several ships missing. The fleet did not wait for them. Then the wind changed. . . . 'We have decided to avoid the Norway Channel. Instead we shall sail between the Scottish Isles to shorten our journey, and also because we are suffering from a serious shortage of supplies,' wrote Sidonia to King Philip. In fact their course lay between Fair Isle and the Orkneys.

On 20 August having rounded the Orkneys without mishap, the Duke sent Don Balthazar de Zuñiga on ahead in a fast *patache* to bring the King news of the disaster and to take him his *diario*.

Sick and morose, the Duke shut himself away from the rest of the world, handing over the command to Bobadilla, for many would have refused by now to take orders from Diego Flores. On 3 September, abeam of the Hebrides, he wrote to the King in an attempt to justify his failure.

It has pleased God to ordain things otherwise than we had hoped. This enterprise was fervently commended to Him, so it must be that what has happened was the right thing for Him and for Your Majesty. . . . The Armada was in such bad shape, that I considered the best way I could serve Your Majesty was by saving what was left of it, though it meant risking it in this long journey in such a latitude. Our best ships had no shot, and we had already seen how little could be expected of the rest. The Queen's fleet had shown itself vastly superior in battle, in tactics, in the range of its artillery, and in its

97

manœuvrability. So following the advice of the generals and of Your Majesty's appointed advisers, we set off on this course. We were driven to it also by the weather. The wind held first from the south then later from the south-west [the Duke seems to forget that the enemy sailed back to England on the same wind]. Since the 21st we have had four nights of storms, and seventeen ships have disappeared out of sight, including De Leiva's and Recalde's as well as some other important ones. . . . Today at latitude 58° we counted 95 ships. . . . 3,000 of the men are sick, not counting the large number wounded, and many are dying.

Elsewhere, on the other ships, the situation was worse. Scurvied or doubled up with typhoid or food poisoning, the men '. . . were dying of a fine and malignant pestilence, and if any man fell sick only a miracle could save him'. Their stomachs empty and their throats dry, the sick lay one on top of another across sodden mattresses. In the bottom of the ships a fetid liquid stinking of excrement and vomit slopped about, floating with dead cockroaches and drowned, bloated rats. Rain and waves came through the gaping planks in the decks, streaming between the timbers and pouring out of the smashed gun-ports.

The *San Martin*, under the skilful guidance of her chief pilot, took only fifteen days to cover the 1,500-miles return journey. For a ship 'whose mainmast was so badly damaged that it could no longer carry its canvas' this was not bad going. The heavy weather conditions made it impossible to take any astrolabe measurement of the height of the sun at midday, or even to see the North Star at night. The pilots were navigating by guesswork, not knowing where the current was taking them, and at the whim of the squalls, which often turned into storms. One such storm blew up on the 16th, 'the day we all thought to die'.

The Duke had enjoined everyone to avoid Ireland, 'for fear of the harm that may befall you upon that coast'. But for many captains, shortage of supplies left no alternative. Whatever risk, they had to find food and drink and this meant that they had to land. Others, because of mistakes by their pilots, found cliffs suddenly looming across their bows where they had been expecting only the open seas.

19

The Return of the Armada

Tossed by the play of wind and waves, the bones of the old ships groaned pitifully. The ribs warped, splitting the sides and cracking the caulking. Day and night the steady creaking of the pumps never stopped.

By 18 September only sixty ships remained in the *capitana*'s wake. Then such a storm blew up that the Duke was left with a company of eleven.

On the 21st the *San Martin* sighted land one league away. It was Santander.

The galleon sailed up to the harbour bar, but had to wait until the following day's tide to enter. The Duke boarded the first launch to arrive and went ashore as fast as he could. 'I am so ill after twenty-five days of dysentery and fever that I am quite weakened and utterly indisposed,' he wrote. The Captain General was abandoning his fleet, his ship, his crew and his sick men. He was leaving behind, too, the Holy Banner that he had solemnly sworn, on the altar of Lisbon Cathedral, to defend with his life and personally return to the King. Shortly afterwards the wind freshened and carried the *San Martin* on. Diego Flores put her into Laredo.

Sidonia wrote to the King:

The trials and miseries that we have suffered cannot be described. On one of the ships that put in here the crew had gone for fourteen days without a drop of water. On the capitana 180 died of disease, and the rest of the crew are seriously afflicted with contagious diseases and typhoid in particular. So many of my servants have died that I am left with only two. May the Lord be praised for all that he has ordained. . . . And now we are in even worse danger, for in a week nothing will be left of our meagre remains of biscuit and wine. May it please Your Majesty to send some money as soon as possible.

We have not a maravedis between us. Oquendo has all the treasure with him ... 55,000 escudos. ... As for myself I have neither the health nor the head to cope with anything at all.

During the next few weeks sixty-five vessels put into the northern Spanish ports. One sank in harbour as soon as it arrived, another blew up, yet another ran aground at Laredo, because there was not a man on board with enough strength left to lower the sails or to cast anchor. Most of the ships were beyond repair. They were broken up for timber and firewood.

The Duke had set himself up in some comfort ashore, sufficiently far away from the men who were still on board, suffering variously from bronchitis, typhoid or dysentery. By 27 September he found himself so weak that he could neither hold a pen nor even move. He had to dictate this letter to the King's secretary:

My health is not restored. I am good for nothing ... and as for seafaring, never, for any reason whatsoever, or in any way at all, will I involve myself in it again, if it costs me my head. Even that would be preferable to me than failing properly to fulfil a mission about which I neither know nor understand anything and in which I am forced to turn for advice to men whose designs I know not. ...

And he ended by begging the King, in the name of God, to be pleased to permit him to return home to San Lucar forthwith and without a moment's delay. Meanwhile, aboard their ships, Oquendo and Recalde were dying.

Medina Sidonia had returned 'white haired, having set out with a shock of raven black hair'. Shame and sickness had reduced him utterly. He passed whole days delirious with fever. Philip realised this. He wrote to him:

I am distressed to learn that your ill health continues and since you say that it is necessary for your convalescence that you return to your estate to recover and regain your strength, since you are so insistent about it, I will agree to it as soon as you have made arrangements for the care of the sick ... and you will leave orders that as soon as he arrives Alonzo de Leiva is to be appointed Commander in Chief ... and you will make sure that everyone knows help is on the way and that any who tries to escape meanwhile will be severely punished. And you will make sure, too, that I am kept daily informed of developments.

The King was indeed kept informed. On 23 November Juan de Cardona reported:

> On every ship three or four men die each day. For 26 days the men have eaten nothing but mouldy chickpeas, with half a pint of water a day. Most of the men are naked or in rags and soaked to the skin, day and night. . . . The ships they are living in are filled with stench and wretchedness . . . 1,000 sick men in Santander alone. . . . Of our 18,000 soldiers, there are 5,000 alive now in our Galician ports.

De Leiva still had not returned, so it was Don Garcia de Villejo who took over from the Duke in Santander. On 30 September he wrote that the Duke had left that day, saying that he had no instructions to give. The state in which Sidonia left things compelled Garcia to tell the King what he thought of all this. Don Garcia did not mince his words, and he concluded: 'The Armada has ceased to exist'.

As soon as he had the royal permission safely in his pocket, the Duke had himself taken to his carriage. The leather blinds were pulled and he headed south with his men and 'twelve mules loaded with silver and ducats'. Insults and abuse followed him wherever he went. He was flagrantly reviled and greatly dishonoured. Children stoned him at Medina de Campo and at Salamanca.

There were after all 9,000 dead, 60 ships had been lost, and 1,400 million reals scattered to the winds. The whole of Spain was in mourning, Philip had to issue a special edict limiting the period of mourning to thirty days and restricting it to the immediate families of the men who had been lost. What was needed was someone to blame, a scapegoat. The finger pointed to one man above all others, a man hated equally by all and sundry; Deigo Flores, of course. As the Duke was no longer good for anything, it was Flores who had been given the task of organising rescue operations in all northern ports and taking everything in hand. Just as soon as someone was found to replace him, he was dragged from Santander to Burgos castle, and there he was imprisoned. He stayed there fifteen months.

Sententious historians, particularly Spanish ones, have attributed any number of highly inspired historic pronouncements to the King on hearing the awful truth. In fact Philip said nothing. He shut himself away with his confessor. It was gossiped that he never got over it, nor ever regained his health; that he seldom went out again; that from that moment on he began to talk to himself. If none ever pierced the secrets of his soul, the front which Philip chose to present to the world appears in his letter of 13 October.

> Most Reverend Archbishop of our Council, we all know how unpredictable the sea is; the fate of the Armada bears witness to this ... and we know, too, how we are bound to render thanks to God for all that He is pleased to do and for His mercy. I have therefore rendered up thanks to Him, for when one considers the storms and perils that this Armada encountered it would have been reasonable to have feared for it a fate worse than the one it met. I attributed this to your prayers and special orations, which can nevertheless now be discontinued.

The victorious English seamen had also returned. 'Most of our sailors are now seriously ill and some die every day. It is a veritable epidemic. It is reckoned that men newly recruited are infected the first day and dead by the second. Which means that many of our ships no longer have enough men even to weigh anchor. ... Whole crews sicken each day,' wrote Hawkins to Burghley.

Typhus, scurvy, furunculosis, blood-poisoning, scabies, vermin, dysentery – officers and men alike put it all down to the 'bad beer'. The beer was sour indeed, and as Howard had once said, 'for my own part I know not which way to deal with the mariners to make them rest content with sour beer'. Neither can the diseases have been unconnected with conditions on board.

On the 18th Elizabeth received the following letter from Drake: 'We left the Spanish army so far to the north that they will no longer be able to make it back either to Scotland or to England. ... Three days later a heavy storm ... must have done them the greatest damage. ...' Immediately the miserly Queen gave orders effectively to disband everyone, return the freighted ships and send her detailed accounts with all vouchers. Her privy councillors had the greatest difficulty in persuading her that the danger was not yet averted. As Howard wrote, it was still possible that the Armada would reform in Norway, Denmark or the Orkneys and return to rendezvous with Parma. To please the Queen the Lord Treasurer suggested that it might be possible now to economise on the pay of those who had been killed in battle or discharged, and to use this money to pay the others what they were owed. With great firmness, John Hawkins reminded him that in all justice and equity the dead men's pay belonged to their widows and their dependents.

As soon as news reached London that the Armada had rounded the Orkneys, the Queen prevailed. Crews were demobilised, but without pay. They were to be seen wandering the streets of Margate, Dover, Harwich and Rochester, starving, penniless and begging. They slept in the gutters, or after Howard had taken things in hand, on the bare earth in barns and hotels. It was the Lord Admiral who wrote, 'It would grieve any man's heart to see them that have served so valiantly to die so miserably.' It was he too who paid them, out of his own pocket.

20

'But Where is De Leiva?'

Half the Armada had not returned. In every palace in Spain a husband was awaited, a son or a nephew. Day and night families scanned the horizon in every Galician, Asturian and Biscayan port. Envoys ran to meet every ship they sighted, inquiring anxiously, 'Don Alonzo? Where is Don Alonzo?' The answer was always the same. The *rata* had been lost from sight 'following a very heavy storm, that lasted from two o'clock in the afternoon until ten o'clock the next morning'.

This was the storm of 10 September, one that had also wrought havoc on the Irish mainland. That day, according to a letter of Edward Whyte's, 'there blew a most extreme wind and cruel storm, the like thereof has not been seen or heard a long time'. This storm and that of 20 September cost the life of nearly 3,000 Spaniards.

Philip learned nothing more of De Leiva from the copy he received in the Escurial of 'Certain advertisements out of Ireland concerning the losses and distresses happened to the Spanish Navy upon the West Coast of Ireland. . .' In twelve quarto pages he found only one reference. Emmanuel Fremoza, a seaman off the *San Juan* of Portugal, captured and questioned in Ireland, had apparently given some rather confused information which was summed up as follows:

> But he saith, there was a great Prince, an Italian, that was a Chief Man in a great Argosy, very well furnished, who, before their coming to the English Coast, did very often banquet the Duke and the other great men of the Navy. This Argosy was called the Ratte. He saith he did not perceive if this ship were in this fleet, the day before, the said tempest or not . . . but he saith, this being a famous ship, it was often demanded if she were in their company, and it was answered that she was.

It was around 58° N that De Leiva had lost contact with the fleet. With her poorly repaired mainstays his ship could no longer carry even half her canvas. The storm reopened old wounds. Through the holes in her hull, patched up with lead and tow after the battle, and through the gaps between her timbers, she was taking more water than the crew could pump out, though they worked day and night. Alonzo de Leiva had personally supervised the victualling, and though there was rationing on board, no one was starving. They were resisting sickness better than crews elsewhere in the fleet. They were, however, running short of fresh water.

Don Alonzo considered that his carrack would never reach Spain, so he set sail for the coast, counting on the Irishmen aboard to get him safely into port and to make sure he got help from the Catholic princes. Maurice Fitzgerald, son of the 'late arch-traitor Fitzmaurice' as the English called him (in other words, the hero of the Resistance), was on board, as were several Irish pilots, various monks and shavelings, and the Bishop of Killaloe. Maurice Fitzgerald never saw his homeland again; he died forty leagues out at sea.

On 17 September the *Santa Maria Encoronada* entered Blacksod Bay, north of Achill Island (County Mayo) and found an anchorage northwest of Fahy. There with due ceremony Fitzgerald's remains were cast to the waves in a cypress wood coffin.

Stealing each other's lands, wives and livestock, and then massacring each other over them, was a traditional pursuit of Irish chieftains. Their other main activity, for the last four hundred years (since 1167, to be precise, when Henry II had sent over the vanguard of colonisers) was fighting the English invader. Dublin fell in 1170. It was to remain English for 750 years. Year after year, in spite of continual wars, countless coalitions, countless revolts and massacres, countless victories, the English colonisers went on establishing themselves in town after town and in county after county. Using cold steel and a carefully organised state of permanent famine, they drove out or exterminated the native Gaelic population.

On the accession of the Tudors the English administration already had a firm hold on most of Leinster (the southwest quarter of the island) and partial control of the west. The north was still free.

Henry VIII established a Church of Ireland and put himself at the head of it, and then declared himself King of Ireland, a fictitious kingdom, legitimised by the Pope in 1555 for Henry's daughter, Mary Tudor.

The better to secure this new throne, Mary had as many title deeds as were necessary drawn up for the crown and everywhere set up English and Welsh 'planters' who coolly turned out the legal (according to Irish law) occupants. Plantation became a regular policy in 1556. It was pursued by Elizabeth (and those who came after her) who sent in large reinforcements of Protestant colonists.

To govern this kingdom, the English monarchy appointed a local Lord Deputy, responsible to the Privy Council in London, from whom he received his instructions. In 1588 the post of Lord Deputy, based at Dublin Castle, was held by Sir William Fitzwilliam, ex-Treasurer at War, ex-Lord Justice, and now a sick old man. Like everyone else in Ireland, he knew nothing at that stage of the outcome of the Enterprise of England, but he did feel threatened because Spain had always been the ultimate hope of the Irish Catholic resistance. The Irish waited for the King of Spain's armies to land much as they might have awaited the Messiah.

Spanish ships had already arrived once, bearing the papal banner, and Don Martinez de Recalde had landed his troops. But there were too few of them – 600 badly equipped men. They had been surrounded and captured at Smerwick before any of the armed Irish could reach them. The English had massacred their prisoners down to the last man.

And now rumours were rife in London and Dublin. According to some spies, one section of the Armada was going to take Ireland; according to others the whole fleet was coming to winter there before launching an assault on England in the spring.

The task of the Lord Deputy had been becoming increasingly difficult over the last twenty years. The old Gaelic chieftains were permanently in a state of revolt against English tyranny, but now there was the added problem of the 'Old English'. These were the descendants of the early British settlers who were now being threatened by a new wave of adventurers like Sir Peter Carew and Sir Walter Raleigh, Protestant speculators protected by Elizabeth. James Fitzmaurice was leading this second rebellion, which had the support of the nationals. Having crushed the uprising, the English had gone on systematically to burn or massacre the wives, children and families of the men they had killed on the battlefield. Scorched earth was all that was left of Munster. In 1583 the last remaining strongholds of resistance were destroyed in another blood bath. And now rumour had it that the young Maurice Fitzgerald, the rebel's own son, was in the Armada.

Towards the middle of September 'great ships' were sighted off the West coast of Ireland. Driving their horses for all they were worth, messengers were arriving from 'O'Dogherty Land', from the coast of Donegal, from Sligo, Galway and the mouth of the Shannon, in fact from all round the coast, with the same news. A state of panic overtook the local officials. The Lord Deputy could not sleep for worry. Was this the Armada come from the Channel? Had it not been defeated after all, not sunk, not destroyed? Or was this another invasion fleet, attacking on a second front?

Seven ships had been sighted at Carrigfoyle. In a mad panic, the Mayor of Limerick hurriedly wrote to the Council that seven squadrons had been sighted. Twenty-four men had landed at Tralee. Fitzwilliam informed London of the arrival of twenty-four galleons.

The Governor of Connaught, Sir Richard Byngham, an old soldier who had at various times fought both with and against the Spanish, sent for powder, lead and match. He also thought it 'very convenient to levy a band of footmen of this country people . . . to prevent their going away to the enemy . . . them being idle men . . .' There were grave doubts as to whether the country would be true to the English or not.

These doubts were not entirely unfounded. The Lord Deputy did not conceal from the Privy Council the fact that they had 'neither men, money, nor munitions to answer these extraordinary services' . . . nor that 'there are not 750 foot in bands in the whole realm. . . . We cannot imprest the few soldiers for the shoeing of their horses. . . . We look rather to be overrun by the Spaniards than otherwise'. The Queen immediately issued orders for 700 soldiers to be levied in England and vessels armed to send them to him.

Then little by little the authorities began to find out what sort of state these 'great ships' were in, and how dying men littered their decks. The twenty-four men who had landed at Tralee were some of Medina Sidonia's men who had survived the wreck of a small frigate. Half dead already, they begged for mercy, promised ransoms, pleaded for their lives. Sir Edward Denny had every one of them put to the sword. 'Fear and weakness could not afford to be magnanimous,' wrote the English historian, Froude, much later.

Recalde anchored by Dingle Bay, the most sacred spot of the Catholic resistance, the very spot where eight years earlier the ill-fated liberation forces had landed. All that was left on board the *almiranta* were '25 pipes of wine, and very little bread, and no water, but what they brought out of Spain, which stinketh marvellously; and their flesh meat they cannot eat, their drouth is so great'. On the 15th, the Admiral sent his launch ashore with the eight strongest men in the ship. Just to look at these fleshless sailors, at their wretched appearance, and to listen to their appalling stories, spoke volumes on the state of the King's fleet. The Catholic cause was losing ... definitely losing. The soldiers of the Crusade asked for water and the Irish threw them into prison, seized their boats, and not long afterward cut their throats. Recalde set sail again, with 100 sick men (out of 500). Four or five were dying every day of hunger and thirst.

The *Nuestra Señora de la Rosa*, in her turn, came in by Dingle in Blaskets Sound. On board, out of 700 men, 200 were still on their feet. They cast the last anchor. It dragged in the changing tide, and the galleon was thrown on to a hidden reef and split open. She went down leaving only one survivor.

The seven Spanish ships anchored in the mouth of the Shannon sent their boats in to fetch water at Kilrush, flying a white flag at the prow. There were no English troops at Kilrush, but 400 years of informing and massacres had bred fear of repression, and it prevailed there too. The authorities refused the Spanish permission to land. They pleaded for a 'barrel of water against one of wine' or as much gold as they wanted. They offered the Sheriff of Clare a great ship complete with rigging and guns, in exchange for being allowed to fill their cask. The Sheriff refused all their offers. The galleass *Zuñiga* tried to land a few tottering men by force, but they were repelled empty-handed. There was nothing for it but to set out to sea again, into the storm.

At Galway harbour, Don Luis de Cordoba put ashore a party of shivering skeletons. They were immediately taken prisoner, before his very eyes. Don Luis offered to give himself up in exchange for a promise of safety for his companions. The Mayor accepted on condition that they first hand over their arms. But while this was going on the townspeople were already throwing themselves onto the first prisoners, tearing off their gold chains, their doublets and their shirts. 'Weigh anchor,' ordered Cordoba, 'we're leaving.' The seamen collapsed at the capstan. The Mayor sent out fishermen to take the ship, and had the noblemen and mariners taken to the castle. They were so weak 'they could not swallow what food they were given, but vomited it straight away'. Don Luis was spared in the hope of a ransom. The others were shot or hanged along with some hundreds of other survivors taken in County Clare and Connemara.

Don Pedro de Mendoza, leaving his fast sinking ship, put ashore at Clare Island, carrying his treasure chests. The storm of the 20th finally put an end to his galleon and to those who were still struggling to repair the damage and pump her out. The local chieftain, Dowdarra O'Maillie, massacred all 100 of them and seized their very considerable treasure, before Don Pedro could lay hand on his curraghs (light boats of leather stretched over a wooden frame).

One galleon ran aground on the sand near Burrishole. Two hundred Spaniards were thrown onto the sand by the waves, shivering and exhausted. The local Irish rushed up and battered them to death for the sake of their shirts and their boots.

And false rumours too were rife in the country. Medina Sidonia was reported shipwrecked. The Duke of Ormond issued immediate orders that Sidonia be carefully guarded but not put in irons and that he be allowed to ride his own horse. Another rumour had it that he had died in the great ship that had set out from Torane. Elsewhere they had found the dead body of Recalde, then the body of Prince Ascoli.

The storm of 20th threw three Spanish ships onto the sand between Sligo and Ballyshannon and pounded them to pieces. 'When I was at Sligo, I numbered on one strand of less than five miles in length, 1,100 dead bodies of men which the sea had driven upon the shore. The country people told me the like as in other places, though not to the like number,' wrote Fenton to Burghley. Fitzwilliam, too, went to see the bay where some of those ships were wrecked;

and where, as I heard, lay not long before, twelve or thirteen hundred of the dead bodies. I rode along upon that strand near two miles but left behind me a long mile or more and then turned off from the shore leaving before me a mile and better; in both which places they said they had seen it, there lay as great store of the timber of wrecked ships as was in that place which myself had viewed being in my opinion more than would have built five of the greatest ships that I ever saw.

In the letters that were reaching Dublin from all around the coast, one finds the same story repeated time and again until October: Two ships lost with a 1,000 men; 140 Spaniards came ashore and were cut down with sabres; 300 Spaniards landed and were rightly put to the sword – and so on, day after day. Those were the orders. Feeding the mariners would have been expensive, and once back on their feet they would have constituted a dangerous threat.

The danger averted, Fitzwilliam countermanded the troops promised by the Queen. 'Since it hath pleased God by His hand upon the rocks to drown the greater and better sort of them [the Spaniards] I will, with his favour, be His soldier for the despatching of those ragges which yet remain. . . .'

Sir George Carew, Master of Ordnance in Ireland, estimated on 28 September that 3,000 Spaniards who came to land by swimming were slain, besides 2,000 drowned between Lough Foyle and the Dingle. Fenton was inclined to reckon 16 ships lost and 5,394 drowned, killed or captured. Richard Byngham put the figure at 4,600 drowned and claimed to have been personally responsible for hanging or cutting the throats of 1,100 survivors. On mature reflection he subsequently modified his estimate: 15 or 16 ships and 6–7,000 dead, of whom 7–800 were killed either by him or by his brother. Thus he reported to the Lord Deputy, and continued, clearly rather pleased with himself: 'having made a clean despatch of them, both in town and country, we rested Sunday all day, giving praise and thanks to Almighty God for Her Majesty's most happy success and deliverance from her dangerous enemies.'

As for the Irish peasants, they had brained or battered to death between 2,000 and 3,000 and stripped and robbed many more. A certain Nicholas Kahane, reporting to the Mayor of Limerick on the 22nd, desires him 'to content this bearer of 40 tescons for by much ado I could get him to go there, for all men be about those ships that be lost. . . . I will never have none to send Your Worship if that you do

110

not consider this boy.' And a survivor of one of the Sligo wrecks wrote:

> Whenever one of our men set foot on the shore, two hundred savages and other enemies surrounded him, stripped him naked, ill-treating him and wounding him without pity. . . . I passed many Spaniards stark naked and shivering with the cold. . . . There were more than six hundred dead bodies cast up by the sea which the crows and wolves would devour pitilessly. . . . It is the custom of these savages to live like wild beasts. . . . There is neither order nor justice in this country. . . .

Edward Whyte writes, 'They were so miserably distressed coming to land that one man, named Melaghlin M'Cabbe killed 80 with his gallowglass axe.[1] Fitzwilliam could write jubilantly: 'Don Luis de Cordoba [he was a prisoner] blames the Irish for letting the Spaniards range up and down the country after they had stripped them of their apparel and robbed them of their money and jewels.' And he concluded, on the basis of the evidence that he had, that sixteen of the fifty-nine ships sighted had been lost and that 8,000 Spaniards had met their death on the North and West coasts. This calculation did not include either the prisoners at Dingle, nor those ships that were lost at sea and whose crews had the good fortune simply to drown, nor did it include the 1,300 dead still to come on the *Girona* or those in a hospital ship that sank later on the Devon coast.

NOTES

1. The Gallowglasses were champion fighters grouped together in special units.

21

Alonzo De Leiva's First Shipwreck

Don Alonzo, in the *rata*, had anchored in Blacksod Bay and sent Giovanni Avancini ashore with fourteen men to fetch water and parley with the locals. This was MacWilliam country and the local industry

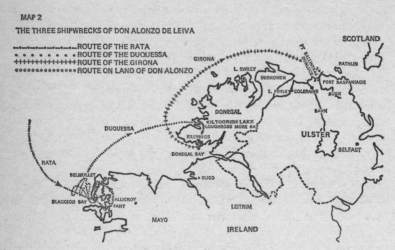

MAP 2

THE THREE SHIPWRECKS OF DON ALONZO DE LEIVA

—·—·—·—·—·—·— ROUTE OF THE RATA
· · · · · · · · ROUTE OF THE DUQUESSA
++++++++++++++ ROUTE OF THE GIRONA
◉◉◉◉◉◉◉◉◉◉◉◉◉◉ ROUTE ON LAND OF DON ALONZO

was piracy. It was not long before they encountered the leader of a small gang, Richard Burke, known as the 'Devil's Hook' or the 'Devil's Son'. He stripped them bare and kept them prisoner.

Bryan na Murtha O'Rourke of Breffni was the guiding spirit of Irish resistance in Connaught. As soon as he heard what had happened, he came to their rescue, and apologised profusely. Not long afterward Governor Byngham, who complained that he could never get

O'Rourke to pay the 'Queen's rent' reported on 10 October that '. . . Certain Spaniards, being stript were relieved by Sir Brian O'Rourke, apparelled and new furnished with weapons'. When the patrol did not return, the captain of the *rata*, Francisco Vidal, sent some seamen ashore astride empty barrels to rescue the launch. The following day a storm broke from the West.

The *rata* or carrack was a characteristic Mediterranean merchantman. A huge, pot-bellied tub, out of which rose the high, solid walls of the square fore and aftercastles. The design had not changed since the fifteenth century, when the Genoese carracks first plied the seas to and from the Hansa ports. To convert the *rata* into a warship, thirty-five gunports had been opened in her sides and the heaviest available guns placed in them. A floating fortress of that sort was impossible to take by boarding, but it was incapable of sailing into the wind and was difficult to manœuvre in battle as it was to anchor. Being without any shelter, the carrack, whose high castles presented such an area to the wind, quickly dragged her anchor, struck bottom and ran firmly aground on a gently sloping beach.

Perfected over the years, the English intelligence system was highly efficient. As early as the 22nd Edward Whyte, a member of the Council of Connaught, was writing to his brother, Stephen, an alderman in Limerick that there was a ship of 900 tons, 'cast upon the sands at Ballycrouhie; 13 of their gentlemen are taken, the rest . . . to the number of 400 are come to land and fortify at Ballycrouhie'. He meant near Ballicroy, which is inland. More precisely it was at Doona.

Once the storm died down Don Alonzo had in fact gone ashore with all his men, in good order. He fired the wreck and crossed the beach to a small fortress close to the water's edge. There he entrenched himself.

Nearly four hundred years later I followed in his footsteps along this path, a moving pilgrimage. I had seen Blacksod Bay for the first time under a sky that managed to be blue and white and grey all at once. Here was the Ireland of the picture postcards: a lake edged with golden sand, gleaming pebbles and all around lush fields cut across by dry stone walls, and everywhere sheep grazed the lush green grass. I revisited the bay in September and then another year in October, under the same stormy squalls that must have frozen Don

113

Alonzo and his noble young company, in the same torrential rain that covered the peat bogs under heavy floods. I followed his steps from the beach, where the great ship left her bones, to Doona (Fahy) Castle; only one corner of a tower and bits of a wall are left now, and a local peasant has leaned his pigsty against it. I stood dreaming for a long time as I ran my hand over the stones where he had perhaps put his.

De Leiva did not stay long at Doona. Just before the storm he had sighted another Spanish ship coming in to land. She had gone further north, to a sheltered cove of the vast bay, and anchored 'at Pollilly by Torane' (now Tirawn), in fact in Elly Cove, a very safe anchorage.

They must have had some fishermen aboard who knew the coast well (a 1572 report to the Queen mentions a Spanish fishing fleet, 600 strong around the South and West coasts of Ireland as well as several permanent establishments). De Leiva made contact. It was the *Duquessa Santa Ana,* a 900-ton hulk from the Andalusian squadron, having 23 guns and carrying 280 soldiers and 77 sailors.

The Governor of Connaught was a busy man. Byngham was virtually living in the saddle, riding up and down the coast from castle to castle on the lookout for any information, and writing letter after letter to Walsingham to keep him up to date. On 24 September, Sir Richard learned from a local official by the name of Comerford that '. . . the 600 Spaniards who were at Ballycrouhie were conveyed to the castle of Torane, a very strong place, and there joined with 800 more who came out of another great ship which lay at anchor in the road of Torane . . .' De Leiva had just joined the captain of the *Duquessa,* Don Pedro Mares, and his crew on the Mullet Peninsula. Together they were now occupying a castle in Elly Cove.

It was in the summary of the examination of a sailor of the *Duquessa,* which was later abandoned, that I found details of these events. It ran as follows:

The examination of James Machary of the Cross (within the County of Tipperary) taken before the Lord Deputy – He said he was imprest at Lisbon and put into a Flemish hulk called St Ann. . . . After the fight in the Narrow Seas, she fell upon the coast of Ireland in a Haven . . . where they found a great ship called the Rat in which was Don Alonso de Leva and . . . above 700 men. After she perished, Don Alonso and all his company were received into the hulk of St Ann with all the goods they had in the ship of any value, as

114

plate, apparel, money, jewels, weapons and armour, leaving behind them victual, ordnance and much other stuff which the hulk was not able to carry away.

It seemed quite clear to the 'Devil's Son' and his acolytes, that they had a natural right to this 'stuff which the hulk was not able to carry away'. Gerald Comerford, who was keeping an eye on the ship anchored at Pollilly, had other ideas. He had not even received any orders, but he was a good civil servant and he did not doubt that there was every good reason why the rightful place for the Spanish spoils was in Her Majesty's coffers. So he put an armed guard on the half burnt wreck of the *rata*. By 23 September he had grown somewhat weary of this and had to admit to Byngham:

The Ship that is here aground is well stored of great pieces and other munition, wine and oil and many other things under water. Here are no boats able to come by them, neither is it possible to take anything of great value out of the same as yet. . . . But James Blake, Ferriegh McTyrrell, Richard Iccoggy, MoylMory M'Ranyll, Marcus Roe M'Tyriell and Thomas Burke M'Niabbe took out of the wreck a boat full of treasure, cloth of gold, velvet etc. . . . I pray your Lordship that if they be taken they may be put safe and not bailed . . . as we wish to charge them with disloyalty for they have disobeyed commandments given them in writing and beaten and wounded our people.

Byngham was more concerned about what Don Alonzo was intending to do. What if he was planning to conquer the province himself with his 1,500 men? What if the local Irish were to join him? He certainly did not rush to attack them, but he did ask the Lord Deputy for two bands of foot soldiers to help him take Torane castle and oppose the enemy in all future enterprises. Byngham had asked the Lord Deputy for reinforcements sufficiently often to know that he ran no risk of getting them, or of having to encounter any able-bodied Spanish soldiers. His messenger set off at a gallop and had been gone barely two hours when Comerford sent him word that: 'The ship that was at Pollilly, by Torane, has sailed . . . towards the south-west . . . taking the company that was wrecked . . . with bags and baggage. . . .' Behind them the Spanish left a much relieved Governor and a tradition that is still alive today.

On 11 October the Governor wrote to the Lord Deputy:

And touching the ordnance and other munitions lost here, all diligence shall be used to save as much as may be for Her Majesty's use, but the great ship at Ballycro ... is now all broken to pieces and the ordnance and everything else utterly lost I fear me. Treasure and great wealth hath been taken no doubt, but that by such unworthy persons as it will hardly be ever any thereoff come by at all.

In Blacksod Bay, some local peasants pointed out to me the spot where the carcass of the 'great ship from Spain' had gradually buried itself in the sand. As late as 1900 people were still taking timbers from it at the low spring tides, and in 1906 the Chief Inspector of Irish Fisheries recorded that 'he had secured one of her frame timbers of Italian oak, burnt off at one end . . .'

22

De Leiva's Second Shipwreck

Leaving the bay, the *Duquessa Santa Ana* had been badly shaken in the heavy swell. Hulks such as the *Duquessa* were the direct descendants of that medieval vessel, the *nao*: transport ships of enormous capacity, high of freeboard and shallow in draught, with a rounded bow and a high, narrow poop. These ships were slow and unwieldy to manœuvre. (See plate II.) For two days and two nights the *Duquessa Santa Ana* had to tack from Inishkea to Erris Head, rolling badly and making hardly any headway. On the 27th Byngham learned from Comerford that 'one of the great ships which lay before Torane was driven back with a contrary wind, but afterwards put to sea again'.

Out in the open sea again, the *Duquessa* met repeatedly shifting winds. They had to run northwards for a whole night, and then do so again, 'in which course by a contrary wind they were driven back upon McSweeney Nc Doe's county to a place called Lougherris, where failing to anchor, there fell a great storm which broke in sunder all their cables'. So reported James Machary.

Juan De Nova and Francisco De Barja, two seamen from the *Trinidad Valencera*, later gave further details as related to them by one of the survivors. Rearranging these details in the only order that makes sense according to the map, it appears that the force of the current caused the cable of the hulk's only anchor to part. They managed to pass a mooring line ashore and make it fast to a rock. The current, however, drove the vessel aground, and seeing what condition she was in, all hands decided to go ashore, taking with them some food, some ammunition, and a piece of ordnance.

Carrying their jewel boxes under their arms, De Leiva and his young noblemen waded in to a beach on the north coast of Loughros

More Bay, near Rossbeg, with some 800 men. (Tradition thereabouts has it that until the last century, at very low tide and when the sea was particularly clear, one could still make out the timbers of the hull coming just level with the sand.) They climbed onto a sand-dune and from there they saw O'Boyle Island, rising sheer out of the middle of Kiltoorish Lake, and on the island a castle built of large flat stones. (See plate 13.) There, near the ship, they camped for the space of eight or nine days. Don Alonzo sent Father James ne Dowrough, an Irish monk, with a message for the local chieftain McSweeney Ne Doe, one of O'Neil's vassals, who welcomed them most warmly. News of this soon reached Walsingham in London.

The Lord Deputy organised a new expedition to oust them. His spies, who were acting as double agents lost no time in informing McSweeney who, in turn, informed Don Alonzo. Meanwhile the Spanish had discovered that the galleass *Girona* was at anchor further down the coast and they went to find her. De Leiva was carried in a sedan-chair. Before he landed, his leg was injured by the capstan of the ship so badly that he was able neither to walk nor ride.

A galleass! It must have been Heaven sent! The four galleasses of the Neapolitan squadron were renowned throughout the Armada. During the battle they had always been in the thick of every action, more conspicuous for the courage of their men, as it turned out, than for their success. They had not managed to repeat their earlier victorious intervention at Lepanto. With eighteen oars on each side and a rather slender hull, with two castles, and a very high freeboard, they were a cross between a galley and a galleon. They were decked vessels about 150 ft long with three fixed masts, carrying square sails on foremast and mainmast and a gaff-rigged lateen on the mizzen. 'The galleasses,' writes the historian Leti, 'were strikingly beautiful and ornate, with their cabins, towers, chapels and pulpits.' We know that there were carved figures on the castles, the prow and the sides and large ornate lanterns above the stern. The officers had their quarters in the aftercastle, where there was either a tent or a sumptuously decorated cabin, and hung inside with velvet or tapestries, and lit by stained-glass windows, with a large lantern in the ceiling. Pennants and banners fluttered at all points. In port dinner was taken on board to musical accompaniment. The table plate, candlesticks, knives and forks were gold-plated. The officers were bedecked with

118

chains and jewels; their evening dress was a velvet doublet and satin breeches. Things were different for the galley slaves, and the soldiers; they dressed at their own expense as best they could, when they happened to be paid.

There are a number of contemporary engravings of Armada galleasses. Some show fantasy ships, while others simply depict large galleys. There does however exist a set of engravings by John Pine, which give what is probably an accurate portrayal of vessels such as the *Girona* and the other galleasses. These engravings, made in 1739, are an exact copy of the famous tapestries that hung in the House of Lords until the fire of 1834. (See plate 5.) The tapestries were made by Francis Spiernig around 1589 (for a fee of £1,628) from cartoons by Cornelis de Vroom, an outstanding painter of naval subjects, who worked from the original plans and sketches that Lord Howard of Effingham had given him. It was the Lord Admiral himself who commissioned the tapestries. He later sold them to James I, and they were already hanging at Westminster in 1650. For such a client de Vroom would certainly have paid great attention to the likeness. (His fee was 100 gold crowns.)

When she left Lisbon, the *Girona* carried a crew of 121–22 officers, 2 mates, 39 gunners, 10 helmsmen, 27 able seamen, 21 sailors and ship's boys. There were 244 rowers: 161 convicts, 15 slaves and 68 volunteers (*bonevoglies*). The captains, Gonzalo Beltran and Antonio de Silva, had embarked their companies, 76 men and 110 men respectively – arquebusiers and pikemen.

The ordnance consisted of 50 bronze pieces: 6 cannon, 2 demi-cannon, 4 demi-culverins, 8 perriers, 6 sakers, 4 demi-sakers and 20 esmerils, and the ammunition of 400 50-lb. balls, 400 35-lb. balls, 400 25-lb. balls, 316 16-lb. balls, 450 15-lb. balls, 400 12-lb. balls, 1,200 6-lb balls, 800 4-lb. balls, 2,000 3-lb. balls and 1,000 1-lb. balls, plus 800 stone balls, adding up to a total of 8,166 rounds.

When the *Girona* left Naples she had 200 quintals[1] of gunpowder, 3 quintals of refined powder for use in the touch-holes, 12 quintals of match, and 30 quintals of lead for casting more cannon balls in England. At Lisbon they took on a further 208 quintals[2] of powder and 65 of match.

The provisions consisted of 750 *bizcoches*, 100 butts of wine, 62.5 quintals of bacon and the same amount of cheese, 60 barrels of tuna fish, 40 barrels of sardines, and 15 quintals of rice, as well as beans and dried vegetables, raisins, oil, vinegar, sugar, salt and semolina.

A ship as powerful as the *Girona* inspired confidence in those who sailed in her.[3]

When he set out to join the *Girona*, De Leiva left behind the piece of artillery mentioned by the two seamen, De Nova and De Boja. In 1968, I found it. Nothing remained of its wooden carriage, and it sat directly on the ground, on the very edge of the southeast slope of O'Boyle Island, forty paces from the castle ruins and still levelled on the narrow strip of land that leads to the island. It is a falcon, a small, cast iron gun, wider at the breech with the reinforcement shrunk on there, and with a long, conical cascabel button.

The gun is typical of the period. (Identical pieces have been found recently in Bermuda on a wreck of 1595.) I photographed it, measured it, and drew up an exact plan. No other cannon from the Invincible Armada was then known to exist anywhere in the world, and for 400 years this irreplaceable relic had been rusting away in the salt spray and slowly disintegrating, in the very spot where De Leiva left it. Shortly after I revealed the existence of this cannon by publishing a photograph of it in the *National Geographic Magazine*, it was bought from the local farmer and taken away. (See Appendix III for a plan of the gun.)

Carried at the head of his small army, Don Alonzo followed the coast, cutting across rivers and peat bogs. Some of McSweeney's envoys guided them from Ardara southwards along the pass leading directly through the valleys to Killybegs. Nowadays the T72/road follows the same route except that it avoids the old, stony, winding stretches where the four men carrying De Leiva in his makeshift chair must more than once have stumbled.

NOTES

1. One quintal = 100 Neapolitan pounds. One Neapolitan pound = 891 grams.
2. These were Castilian quintals each of 46 kilograms.
3. See Appendix II for further details on galleasses.

120

23

De Leiva's Third Shipwreck

This stony path followed the Stragar valley across McSweeney ne Bannagh's fief and led straight to Killybegs, a very safe harbour in McSwyne's bay, on the North side of Donegal Bay. The Spanish sailors knew the locality well; fishing smacks and merchant ships often put in there.

There were Spanish sailors over the whole area. They gave De Leiva a triumphant reception. Apart from the *Girona*, one of the four galleasses of the squadron of Naples and two other small ships had arrived at almost the same time. One ran on to the rocks just outside the harbour and as the other seemed in imminent danger of sinking, her crew had run her aground in the port.

Under its soft grey light, Killybegs still retains much of its old charm. A little way away from the modern jetty where the trawlers moor, I found the old, worn, stone quays, now lying above the high water mark. I do not know if they really were there in Don Alonzo's time, but the gulls crying plaintively as they circled over me must have circled in much the same way over his tent. Dotted around in the black sludge of the disused docks I could see the carcasses of wooden ships sinking from view. . . . Under that compost of old rope, dead seaweed and rotting fish, could one of those skeletons have been the second of the smaller Spanish vessels – perhaps the deepest of all?

Carpenters were busy taking timbers and iron fittings off the beached vessel. They would use her steering gear and rigging to repair the *Girona*, which was in poor shape and rudderless. McSweeney helped by lending them his boats and giving them a pinnace to break up the timbers. He also managed to get together some victuals of sorts for them.

It was not long before all this reached the ears of the Lord Deputy:

The Spaniards from the two ships wrecked off McSweeney Banagh's country have joined those in McSweeney Ne Doe's; McSweeney fears to hunger his country; The Spaniards are buying garrons and mares for food; The Spaniards in McSweeney Ne Doe's country have repaired one ship

And James Machary later testified that Don Alonzo and all his company encamped twelve to fourteen days, in which time the galleass was finished and made ready for the sea as well as she could be. De Leiva knew that the Lord Deputy was preparing to move against them. It was nearly a month now since Don Alonzo had moved ashore and time was short. He had been thinking. Before setting sail again there were two decisions he had to make – where to go, and who to take with him.

First, where to go? To try to get back to Spain would be mad. The head wind was still holding and showed no signs of changing. Winter was coming and the ship was not in any fit state to withstand a week of bad weather, let alone two or three. So Don Alonzo issued orders to return by Cape Clear, 'thinking that like that they might reach Scotland, where they would find help'. Cape Clear was a fantasy. The Spanish were ill-informed and had inaccurate maps, and this was a figment of their imagination. What they thought they were referring to was the westernmost point of Ireland. Actually they called virtually every single headland in the island Cape Clear, one after another. In this case 'Cape Clear' must have referred to the Bloody Foreland.

The West of Scotland was Catholic. The nobility there had close links with France and the Guises. During the whole episode of the Armada the young King James had remained irreproachably neutral. He listened impartially to his Catholic lords. The Duke of Parma had sent them 13,000 crowns in May, care of the Earl of Morton and Colonel Semple, in order that they should occupy a Scottish port and prepare to invade England when the time came. With the same grace he greeted Elizabeth's promises in August: if he stayed out of it he would get a pension of £5,000 a year, a dukedom in England, and enough to support a guard of more then 50 gentlemen and another of 100 foot and 100 cavalry. And was he not, besides, Her Majesty's sole heir, as Burghley tactfully reminded him. Her Majesty was, after all, not getting any younger. And then finally James put on a good face for the papal emissaries who arrived with welcome ducats. The bishops let it be understood that all things considered, the Vatican had no desire to see Philip reigning over too many states. The English throne, Catholic once more, would be James's. So wasn't it time he got down to opening up a second front in the North?

Once victory seemed to be in the bag, James rushed to the aid of the Queen and his undying loyalty to the Protestant cause became quite apparent. At that point, however, promises of pensions, duke-doms and guards went right out of Elizabeth's mind. When he did eventually become James I of England, although officially a Prot-estant, many felt that he behaved as a protector of Catholicism.

De Leiva well knew that even though Mary Stuart's son had been brought up in the Protestant faith, deep down he may have been Catholic. That, at least, was what was said in Spain, in France and in Rome, a theory which seemed to be confirmed by the aid which he generously provided for the Spanish survivors sent to him from Ire-land. Under his protection many hundreds of them were fed and housed before being repatriated via Flanders or France.

Who should De Leiva take with him? It was physically impossible to fit five ships' crews into one. The Lord Deputy's estimate had him take his own company 'being near 1,200, and all as may be with greatest reason thought choice men and of best account for birth and service, went aboard her, who together with the galleasses company being at the point of 700 or 800'. The Lord Deputy had got his figures wrong. Apart from a few passengers, the *Girona* must have carried 186 soldiers, 121 sailors and 244 rowers, a total of 551 men, not 700 or 800. Fitzwilliam's estimate that Don Alonzo's 'company' was of 1,200 men seems similarly exaggerated. In the official inventory of the Most Fortunate Armada, I found the exact figures for the *rata* (419 men), the *Duquessa* (357) and the *Girona* (307 plus 244) and one can reckon on another 100 for the crews of the two small ships lost at Killybegs – a total of 1,427 men to begin with. Taking off say 10 per cent for those killed in action, and another 10 per cent for those dead from disease (epidemics had not in fact taken too great a toll of any of these ships), that leaves 1,157 for crews and soldiers. Adding, say, 305 passengers for the *rata* (noblemen and gentlemen adventurers with their servants, pilots, Irish Catholics, monks, barbers, surgeons, etc.) and 30 or so passengers for each of the other large vessels (losses were negligible among this privileged group) the total comes to about 1,540 men. Of those, according to various accounts, De Leiva embarked 800, 1,100, 1,300, 1,500, more than 1,500, or 1,800. He left few, if any, Spaniards behind; but English accounts made it clear that those left ashore soon became wretched beggars.

There was one possible solution to the problem of how many shipped with Don Alonzo. Fitzwilliam learnt that De Leiva had written 'two several letters sent away by special men to Spain'. Two letters? One must have been to the King, the other to his family, perhaps. Either the letter to the King never arrived – I found no trace of it – or else it is lying, yellowed with age, having gone astray, in a dusty bundle of uncatalogued letters, lost for ever in the miles of stacks in the National Archives at Simancas or the archives of the Academie de la Historia in Madrid, or God knows where. I did not go through the family archives of the Castille Martinez De Leivas, so I do not know whether the letter to his family, if that is what it was, ever arrived, but I would give a good month of my life to lay hands on it.

Meanwhile I am inclined (and here I am in agreement with the survivors of the third shipwreck) to put at 1,300 the number of men who left Killybegs harbour in the *Girona*, just before dawn on 26 October 1588.

There is no doubt that Don Alonzo had loaded the galleass well over the safety margin, but did he really have any option? The Spaniards gave McSweeney at their departure twelve butts of sack wine and to one Murrouch Oge M'Murrough I Vayell, four butts. 'The McSweeneys and their vassals have received a substantial supply of Spanish muskets and calivers,' wrote one Henry Duke. 'McSweeney killed 40 of the best Spaniards as soon as the rest were gone a-shipboard,' reported William Taaffe to Richard Byngham. An economy measure no doubt! And this is what a neighbouring landowner, Sir John O'Dogherty, had to say about it when he wrote complaining to the Lord Deputy on 3 November: 'McSweeney having subsisted the 3,000 Spaniards till his country is consumed, directs them now for hate into this country to lie upon it and consume it.' The last days of the Spaniards sojourn cannot have been comfortable.

The days went by, a week, ten days. Where was the galleass? Not a word from Scotland, not a word in Dublin, or in London, or in Spain.

It was not until 5 November, a Saturday and late at night, that the first news began to percolate through to the Lord Deputy in Dublin Castle. He was awakened to read it. Henry Duke had learned from a spy sent up to the north that on:

> the 16th [26th][1] of this instant October, the said galley departed from the said harbour [Killybegs] with as many of the Spaniards as she could carry and sailing along the coast towards the Out Isles of Scotland whither they were then bound, struck against the rock of Bunboys where both ship and men perished, save only five who hardly got to shore: three of which five men came the next day being the 17th [27th] in company with Sorley Boy McDonnell unto O'Neil's home at Strabane where they certified of their late shipwreck. . . . This rock of Bunboys is hard by Sorley Boy's house.

This 'house' was in fact Dunluce Castle, a veritable eagle's nest, occupied by his son James. McDonnell lived at Dunanyme, near Ballycastle. (See plate vi.)

Sorley Boy McDonnell ruled over north-east Ulster. His Norwegian ancestor, who had settled in Scotland in the twelfth century, was called Sumar Lidi, the summer marauder. Just like the bear, sleeping in winter and plundering in the summer, the Vikings used to spend the winter in port and the summer looting. Having driven out of Argyll the Norwegians who had preceded him, Sumar Lidi had himself renamed Somerled, or Somhairle Duidhe, which later became Sorley Boy.

Sorley Boy was a rebel who could not be put down. Thirteen years earlier, in the course of a peacemaking expedition, the Earl of Essex had ordered the massacre of McDonnell's wife and youngest sons, along with 600 other women and children who had taken refuge on Rathlin Island, either in the castle, in the caves, or in some hideaway. Sorley Boy was powerless, because Sir Francis Drake had sunk his 'galleys' (in fact they were only smacks). He could only stand and watch the flames shooting up from the castle.

Hardly had the Lord Deputy returned to his bed when the following confirmation arrived. 'The Spanish ship which arrived in Tirconnell with the McSweeney was on Friday the 18th [28th] of this present month descried over against Dunluce and by rough weather was perished so that there were driven to the land, being drowned, the number of 260 persons, with certain butts of wine, which Sorley Boy hath taken up for his use.'

And how about De Leiva? Not a word of him. There were some survivors, but how many? Five, they said, but was it true? Don Alonzo, was he well and truly drowned? It was not confirmed. The Privy Council was concerned. With De Leiva alive the whole of Ireland was in peril. 'Further where it pleased your Lordship', wrote Fitzwilliam to the Privy Council, 'that I should make an inquiry whether Don Alonzo de Leva [sic] were drowned. . . .' The inquiry would be a perilous one. Secret agents in the pay of the English who dared to go and spy on Sorley Boy, did not always come back. His men were all 'bad types'; one could expect no good of them.

Another whole month passed bringing nothing but rumours. Captain George Thornton, of H.M.S. *Popinjay*, one of the Queen's galleons – the only one, as it happened, stationed on the west coast of Ireland – declared 'that as he passed the Rathlins and Skirrys with her Majesty's ship, it was constantly affirmed by a gunner saved out of the galleass who yet remaineth with Sorley Boy McDonnell that Alonzo de Leva was drowned'. This was not enough to reassure Secretary Walsingham.

It was, indeed nothing more than a rumour, and not the last. In January 1589, a letter from France delivered to the depths of the Escurial brought with it a new glimmer of hope. Ambassador Mendoza wrote to Philip, 'there are reports from Scotland that Don Alonzo De Leiva has landed 2,000 men in Ireland, in Mac Win land, and that the local population has risen in support of him.' The news had been not far off the truth, but it was two months out of date.

Philip knew by now just how much faith to put in Don Bernadino's 'good news' and each day that passed without any definite information prepared him a little more for the worst. Nonetheless he scratched a note to his secretary in the margin of the letter, 'Find out what province [part of Ireland] he means, and let me know.'

On the very same day Mendoza's letter was written, 27 December, the Armada's chief navigator, Marolin de Juan, who had been left behind in Calais, was writing to Mendoza from Le Havre that Don Alonzo was drowned, and all the nobles with him. He wrote:

Some Scottish ships arrived here yesterday with 32 Spanish soldiers and a few sailors from the Armada, who were shipwrecked on the coast of Ireland. . . . They were on the Venetian ship *la Valencera* . . . Don Alonzo De Leiva, with his ship's crew and the *Santa Ana*'s, embarked in the galleass *Girona*, which had sheltered in some port somewhere. No sooner had she set sail for Spain than she was overtaken by a violent storm, which broke her rudder and threw her at midnight upon the rocks. . . . Of the 1,300 men aboard, nine managed to save themselves, and it was these men who told the story to the soldiers who are come here.

(That is, to the *Valencera*'s soldiers, whom they met at Dunluce Castle, where James McDonnell was sheltering them until they could be repatriated.)

The old ambassador was overcome with grief. He was nearly blind now, racked with every sort of illness, and in such bad favour at court that every week he begged Philip to accept his resignation. He sent the letter on to Philip with no comment.

Later in a letter dated 21 January, he reported: 'A sailor passing by the spot where Don Alonzo was lost with 1,300 men recognised many of the bodies strewn along the coast. He took 300 ducats out of the belt of one of them.'

For Don Alonzo, 'who had with him all the nobles in the expedition', all Spain went into mourning. And it was said that the King minded his loss more bitterly than that of all the rest of the fleet'.

NOTES

1. The 16th according to the English Calendar (the old Julian Calendar still in use despite Gregory XIII's reforms in 1582). In 1588 it was 10 days behind the Gregorian Calendar (which we still use). All dates on English documents are therefore ten days behind those on Spanish documents. Throughout the text I have referred all dates to the new calendar.

Opposing rulers: I (*right*) Elizabeth I, from a miniature by Nicholas Hilliard; II Titian's portrait of Philip II

III (*top*) A galleass of the Armada, from a contemporary cartoon for a set of tapestries made to show the glorious English victory

IV (*above*) Having failed to make the planned rendezvous with Parma and his army, the Most Fortunate Armada sailed back to Spain via Scotland and Ireland; from a map made in 1588 by Robert Adams

v (*top*) Spaniard Rock, as seen from the top of the cliff. In the foreground are the Chimney Rocks, on the right lies Lacada Point, where the *Girona* perished

vi (*above*) Out of 1300 men, 5 survived the shipwreck. The local chieftain, James McDonnell, provided shelter for them at Dunluce Castle. He extended his rescue operation to salvaging the contents of the dead men's pockets and also collecting a considerable treasure from out of the part of the wreck left on the rocks. He used it the following year to rebuild and modernise his castle

VII (*top*) Having systematically explored the whole area, our first task was to draw up a trigonometrical plan on which was plotted the exact position of every object before moving it

VIII (*above*) With our metal detector, we were able to spot artifacts hidden under sand and pebbles

ix and x Later we went through it grain by grain, using a high pressure water jet, connected to a surface pump, to remove sterile fresh deposits

XI-XIII (*above*) It was Marc who found the anchor under a camouflage of seaweed and a crust of assorted marine life. We used a large lifting balloon to float it, and towed it to Port Ballintrae

XIV (*right*) Discovering one of the bronze cannon

XV (*overleaf*) The perrier balls and arquebus shot roll in the sand for the last time

PART II

Gold under the Seaweed

O lord, methought what pain it was to drown,
What dreadful noise of waters in mine ears,
What sights of ugly death within mine eyes!
Methought I saw a thousand fearful wrecks;
A thousand men that fishes gnawed upon,
Wedges of gold, great anchors, heaps of pearl,
Inestimable stones, unvalued jewels,
All scattered in the bottom of the sea!
Some lay in dead mens' skulls, and in the holes
Where eyes did once inhabit, there were crept,
As 'twere in scorn of eyes, reflecting gems,
That wooed the slimy bottom of the deep,
And mocked the dead bones that lay scattered by.

(William Shakespeare, *Richard III*, I. iv.)

24

A Three-Star Wreck

In 1952 I discovered Rieseberg, the American fiction writer, and his unblushing accounts of imaginary battles with giant squid, octopus and sharks, staunch protectors of those ocean treasures that he unfailingly brought back, by the chest load, from his expeditions in what he called the South Seas. His books enjoyed phenomenal success and went through many editions. I didn't believe a word of his stories, needless to say, but I had found my vocation.

I was nineteen, a student of politics in Brussels and I had recently developed two great passions, for deep sea diving and historical research. As I put Rieseberg's book down, I filled in my first index card. Today my card indexes take up a whole room.

My first wreck hunt, in 1954, took me to Vigo Bay in the Spanish province of Galicia. I was looking for the lost galleons of the 1702 Plate Fleet. *Les Épaves de l'Or* (Paris, 1958) is an account of this expedition. It is only with considerable effort that I manage to keep a straight face nowadays when I refer to it as an 'early work'. I wrote then:

> I felt sure that there were wrecks loaded with gold, that I had at my disposal the means of seeing them, touching them. I could imagine no more fascinating or enjoyable way of spending my life than looking for treasure, and maybe even finding it. Wherever else life might take me, I would always think the place I really want to be is Vigo, on my galleons.

And so I set off, giving up everything else, dropping out of university and the preordained future that it promised and that I no longer wanted. After two years of failure, in a highflown, lyrical rapture I concluded:

> But I can see gold, gold under the mud, the fabulous gold of the Americas,

lying under fifty feet of slime and fifty feet of water waiting to be found, the gold that one day will glisten under the sun in the palm of my hand.

I became a professional diver. In 1964, after a few more treasure hunts and a few more failures, I could still write, in the introduction to *Le Livre des Trésors Perdu* (Paris, 1964):

I had not the slightest wish to invent responsibilities for myself, in the way that 'they' did, only to have to spend the rest of my life coping with them ('they' were all the little cogs in the vast machine). I did not want to 'make a career' and I wanted nothing to do with their so-called 'experience' if it was going to turn me into one of them. They could keep their 'realistic view of things' which prevented them from seeing the only true reality in the world: sea and coconut palms. I wanted to look for treasure, to live under the sea, a free man, an animal capable of thinking straight, unlike all the others, someone who could live his own life, not in his little cell in the beehive but the master of his own destiny.

I read these lines again in 1967. By then I was living in London. I had had other experiences. I had been a spelunken and a cave diver and I had spent three whole years doing experimental deep sea diving. And yet as I reread them I could find little to change in them. By then, of course, I had emerged from my treasure hunter's cocoon and spread my wings as an underwater archaeologist (an amateur one and self-taught – there are hardly any others). The prospect of the *Girona*'s cargo of gold held less meaning for me now than the weight of history in her. But apart from replacing the word 'treasures' by 'historical wrecks', I wouldn't change a word. I decided to devote myself completely, for just as long as it might take, to finding the *Girona*.

Why the *Girona*? Because, in my Renaissance file, under *Spain: British territorial waters*, the *Girona*'s index card sported three stars in the top right-hand corner.

It was at Bayona in Vigo Bay that I first heard her mentioned. I had returned there in 1958 for a third expedition, which was to last six months. This time we were operating an underwater magnetometer. During the winter storm, John Potter, who was leading this expedition, was writing a master work on wrecks. I had contributed to some of the chapters. Numb with cold, for the wind was whistling through his flat, rattling the windows, he handed me the second revised and corrected draft of his manuscript. Immediately my im-

132

agination was caught by the story of the *Girona*. My blood was up! Battles, storms, five crews, the noblest, richest, bravest men in the whole fleet, jammed with all their treasures into one ship. Three wrecks in succession! At least 1,000 dead! This was what tragedy was made of, what romance was made of. This was what treasures were made of.

The *Girona* had me in her grasp. John Potter tried to put me on my guard and quoted Conrad. 'There is no way to escape from a treasure, once it fastens itself upon your mind.' The warning came too late.

I started on my research, right there in Spain. But, alas, I was pressed for time and could not do very much there. I pursued it at greater length in Brussels, in the Bibliothèque Royale, which has a wealth of old Spanish publications; then in the Archives Nationales in Paris, where they have the whole of Ambassador Mendoza's correspondence with Philip II on microfilm, and then in Holland, where there is not very much. In all this represented about 200 hours' work. But although the *Armada: general* file got fatter as I looked at it, the *Girona* file remained slim. I was finding few worthwhile references. Meanwhile my job took me for a year to Colombia, then back to Brussels, where it left me little spare time; then, for over two years, to America. Finally I went to London. I boarded the plane carrying under my arm the *Girona* file, thick with dust. Ocean Systems, Inc (affiliated with Union Carbide), an American industrial diving and underwater engineering company, had put me in charge of their London office. I had first joined them with Edwin A. Link and the 'Man in Sea' team after our record dive in the Bahamas in 1964 (two days and two nights living and working 430 ft beneath the sea).

Now if, back in 1588, someone who actually knew had happened to note down on some scrap of paper the exact spot where the *Girona* was wrecked, that piece of paper would almost certainly be in London.

Drilling was beginning on all the off-shore rigs in the North Sea gas and oil-fields and I was occupied full time by my professional commitments. Nonetheless I made it a rule for myself to set aside three evenings a week, from 6 pm to 9 pm, which I would spend under the blue and gold dome of the British Museum Reading Room, or in the rotunda of the Public Record Office Reading Room. In the space of a year and a half I must have put in about 600 hours' work. I believe that everything, still extant, ever written in England or Ireland on the Armada and its wrecks must have passed through my hands. I discovered that there was another Armada wreck, the *Nuestra Señora de la Rosa,* which went down off the Blaskets (the south-west tip of Ireland), that also deserved one or two stars. So I was conducting my research campaign on two fronts. It wasn't long before I was tempted to award the *Nuestra Señora* two stars and give the *Girona* a fourth.

But where in Heaven's name was this ship, the *Girona?* It was becoming less and less clear. The more information I collected, the more contradictions I found . . . unless, of course my own theory, which had struck me out of the blue right at the start, was the right one after all. . . .

Calling a halt to all this paper work, I decided that the time had come to go and take a look. This involved at least one team mate, a boat, a motor, a compressor, cylinders and two cars to put it all in. It was the Belgian photographer, Marc Jasinski, my companion in countless dives and caving expeditions, who would once more be my team mate.

25

The *Girona* in the Archives

'But surely,' argued Marc, 'other divers must have been there and looked before us.'

'Not many, and always in the wrong spots.'

'And they found nothing?'

'Nothing, as far as I know. But it wasn't entirely their fault. They put too much trust in the historians. Look.' And I passed him a summary I had drawn up. 'Look where these famous Armada historians made them dive.'

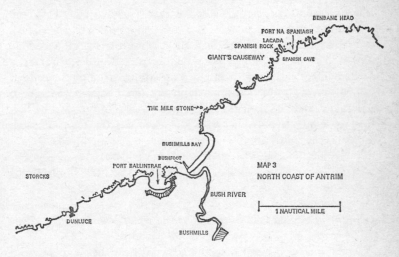

'Wait,' said Marc, 'show me the Admirality chart first.'

It was Number 2798, Rathlin Island to Lough Foyle, the north coast of Ulster, the English part of Ireland, the Six Counties. There was Portrush and the Skerries, Dunluce Castle to the East and opposite some isolated rocks, the Storks. There was a beacon on them now. Farther east we could see Port Ballintrae and then Bushmills Bay, the estuary of the Bush River. The chart showed a long stretch of beach, then the coast became rocky again, cliff, the Giant's Causeway and then . . .

'What's the Giant's Causeway? Some tourist spot?'

'Yes, apparently it's very fine, a solidified lava flow. It fissured as it cooled into a sort of honeycomb, because the lava all contracted evenly. The fissures went right through from top to bottom, and each hexagon eventually became a column. Then, still going eastwards, we have a few bays, some more cliffs, and there – see those two little points with a bay to one side? Well, pass me the other map now. No, not that one. The Ordnance Survey map, six inches to the mile. Yes, that's the one. I just got it. Sheet three of County Antrim. Right, see this little point here?'

'But it's called Spaniard Rock,' exclaimed Marc, suddenly excited, 'and Spaniard Cove and . . . Port na Spaniagh – well, well, how about that.' (See plate v.)

'Indeed, and that's not all. Look at that, Lacada Point. That's no Irish name, is it?'

I was mistaken, as it happened. Mr C. Trench has since been kind enough to point out to me that Lacada is in fact, on the contrary, a Gaelic name, Leac fhada, meaning long stone, or long promontory. But, as yet comfortably confident in my ignorance, I went on to explain, 'It could be the name of a survivor, couldn't it? Maybe that was where they found Juan or Miguel Lacada, the next morning, soaked to the skin.'

'But, Robert, if that is so, then we haven't got far to look.'

'Right, but read my summary of statements of Armada historians all the same.'

It ran as follows:

De Bavia: . . . She was so tossed by the weather that she was lost. . . . Five or six mariners managed to swim ashore.

Hadfield: Girona struck a submerged rock near the Giant's Causeway and went down in the deep sea off Dunluce. . . .

Hardy: . . . went down west of the Giant's Causeway. She was wrecked on the rock of Bunboys . . . [but elsewhere] . . . the bay is

11 With their personal belongings and their flags, Alonzo Martinez de Leiva and his men put to sea again in the hulk *Duquessa Santa Ana*: from an engraving by Breughel

12 (*top*) Driven north by the wind, they were forced to anchor in Loughross More Bay. The anchor dragged, and they tried in vain to find a mooring on the rocky promontory (to the right of the photograph). She ran aground on the sand (to the left) in a storm

3 (*far left above*) Once more DonAlonzo led his people ashore, carrying their money and jewellery, and this time, an iron cannon. They entrenched themselves in a ruined castle on an island in Kiltoorish Lake. I found the cannon where de Leiva left it a few weeks later, when he set off overland to Killybegs. There he put to sea for the third time in the *Girona* taking with him the crews of all three ships along with their valuables

4 (*far left below*) Port na Spaniagh: the local name perpetuates the memory of the tragedy

5 (*top*) In 1967, after 600 hours' research in the archives of five countries and an hour's diving, I found the remains of the *Girona*. First, a lead ingot, then two bronze cannon

6 (*left*) and 17 (*right*) After twelve years of repeated failures, I have at last found gold under the sea. Here is all the treasure that we found in 1967

18 (*top*) 1968: we were back in force with all the necessary equipment

19 (*above*) Left to right: the author, Louis Gorsse, Maurice Vidal, Francis Dumont. Behind the Asahi Pentax, Marc Jasinski

20 (*top*) We found the remains of forty-five forks, an important discovery because until now it had been thought that the fork was not in common use at that time

21 (*above*) Hilts and handles of various swords, daggers, pocket and other knives

22 (*top*) Fragments of gold plate and engraved silver

23 (*above left*) Silver candlesticks

24 (*above right*) Perhaps an inkwell lid. Could this have been Don Alonzo's?

25 (*top*) Bronze shoe and chair nails and a bronze pin

26 (*above left*) A silver chair decoration

27 (*centre right*) A silver perfume phial with its crystal dipper, with which to dab the moustache, when the wind blew from the direction of the galley slaves

28 (*bottom*) Bronze buckles

29 The ring setting: a tiny hand holding a heart and an open belt clasp. The inscription runs 'I have nothing more to give thee'

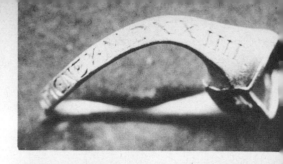

30 and 31 Madame de Champagney, 1524. I found that she was the grandmother of Jean Thomas Perrenot, who drowned in the *Girona* wearing this very ring

32 (*bottom*) A ring belonging to a Canon of the Holy Sepulchre or to a Jesuit father

smaller than Port Ballintrae where the *Girona* foundered. . . .

Kilfeather: . . . driven ashore at Dunluce . . . at a point known ever since as Port na Spaniagh.

Laughton: . . . near the Giant's Causeway, at Spaniard Rock.

Mattingly: . . . near the Giant's Causeway. . . .

MacKee: . . . struck a submerged rock . . . in sight of Dunluce Castle. . . . Under the high cliff topped by the sombre castle of Dunluce. . . .

Lewis: hit the rock of Bunboys. . . .

Froude: . . . They struck upon a rock off Dunluce. . . .

Duro: . . . They hit Dunluce rock . . . [but elsewhere] . . . the storm split her again in the canal and she sank. . . .

'What is the rock of Bunboys?'

'That bit was easy. It's spelt Bunbois or Bon Boys but on the six-teenth-century maps I've seen, the River Bush is called Boys river, and the Irish-English glossary in the Pilot Book, says that Bun means estuary, so the rock of the Boy's Bun is the rock of the Bush estuary. It's called Bushfoot now on the Ordnance Survey map.'

Marc handed me back my summary, saying we wouldn't stand much chance of finding the wreck with this lot. But these were all historians of the Armada in general. As far as they are concerned it is just one tiny detail. Weren't there any local historians or experts?

There was one in particular, the Reverend Spotswood Green, who gave a paper to the Royal Geographic Society on Armada wrecks in Ireland. He is considered the leading authority on the subject and for the most part his work is remarkable, but he above all had been responsible for sending our predecessors off on the wrong track. Just think, here was this chap, this most excellent fellow, who in 1894 knew that there was a Port na Spaniagh and a Spanish Rock and yet, God bless him, he wrote this: 'It is hard to doubt tradition that has fixed a name to a place. . . . Taking all things into account, I incline to the conclusion that the remains of the *Girona* lie off the mouth of the Bush River near Port Ballintrae. . . .'

'But what if he was right after all?' Marc argued.

'No, I don't think so. I've got another theory. I'll tell you. But there's more. Another nineteenth-century expert, Hugh Allingham of the Royal Irish Academy, achieved a really remarkable feat. By com-pletely mixing up the entire history of the shipwrecks and of De

137

Leiva he managed to cram into two and a half pages no less than eleven mistakes and major untruths. I'll spare you the details. He ended up by getting so lost in his four wrecked ships and all the other ships he added on, that in order to tie up his paper he was forced to invent still another wreck. It's in the *Ulster Journal of Archaeology*, 1897. He sinks another ship, name unknown, on Bunboys rock, to which he assigns nine survivors and three cannon salvaged, as against five survivors and some wine butts from the *Girona*.'

'Right,' said Marc, 'then we'll have to forget that. How about eye-witnesses? What do they have to say?'

Unfortunately I had to tell him that there was not a single eye-witness account. I'd thought at first that Sorley Boy McDonnell or his son, or some clerk in their household must have left some notes, somewhere, on what was after all the event of the century for them. One might have found there the exact spot of the shipwreck and details of what they managed to salvage. Nothing doing. Not even a hint of a line of even the briefest account.[1] Then I thought of Spanish sources. What the survivors had to say.

'How many were there in fact?' demanded Marc.

'I don't know. Some say none, some five, others nine, eleven, thirteen. It depends what document you read. They had incidentally no contact whatsoever with the English. No point in looking at English records except for vague, garbled accounts. The men they did tell their story to were some other survivors, from the *Trinidad Valencera*, whom they met at James McDonnell's, at Dunluce Castle. Here, listen. "Sorley Boy received them most kindly and kept them for twenty days, having masses said for them. . . . He obtained some boats . . . eighty soldiers embarked to go to an island off Scotland; the others waited there for the boats to come back. Meanwhile the Governor in Dublin had learned that this gentleman had taken in some Spaniards, and sent him word in the name of the Queen not to embark one more man, on pain of death and confiscation of all his property, and to surrender those that were still in his house. He answered that he would rather forfeit all his property and his wife's and his children's rather than sell the blood of a Christian man . . . and when the boats returned he embarked the others, etc., etc. . . ." It's rather strange, really, because just before this he had sworn an oath of allegiance to the Queen and kissed her slipper in effigy at

Dublin Castle. In short, you can see that in twenty days the survivors had ample time to go over every detail of what happened to the *Girona*. They told the story to two mariners in particular from the *Valencera*, Juan de Nova and Francisco de Borja. And when these two old salts reached Calais, via Scotland, they were questioned by Marolin de Juan, the Armada's chief navigator, who had got left behind ashore after taking a message to Parma. Marolin de Juan sent the King a summary of their story, before having an official record of their testimony drawn up. From Calais this record was sent to Ambassador Mendoza in Paris, enclosed in a letter from Marolin dated 21 January 1589. The Ambassador forwarded it to the King. And from the Escurial this document finally ended up in the Spanish National Archives in Simanca, where it is today.'

'Okay, okay. That's all very well. But where's the wreck?'

'Oh, that. Marolin de Juan just says that according to them, the *Girona* ran aground on the rocks at midnight.'

'And how about the *Girona* survivors? Did they go back to Spain?'

Some of them had returned. Some, including a gunner, were still at Dunluce a year later, but others, I discovered, got back to Corunna as early as February 1589. Marc made the point that they must have been questioned directly, and they must have had a pretty good idea what rock it was they were clinging on to till dawn, or what beach it was they tramped along. What had happened to their testimony? I couldn't find any trace of it. And I'd looked for anything that might have been written from Ireland, Scotland, Flanders or France, from anywhere along the return route, in effect, and still I found nothing. Then I gave up. When it came to the point, all there was to work on was hearsay and some guesswork based on hearsay. Marc wanted to know about the guesswork too.

The most meaningful deduction one could draw was this: if the natives managed to salvage the cannon, that must indicate that the *Girona* actually ran aground, on the coast, or else sank in shallow water, definitely not more than 30 ft deep. One could make other guesses but one could set too much store by them. Duro, for example, published an account, for which he doesn't quote a source, which says that the *Girona* was wrecked because of the current. It would seem that Don Alonzo drew the pilots' attention to the fact that the current was driving them hard towards land, but that they wouldn't listen to him and that was why they went on the rocks. One could check that one out on the spot by making a study of the currents. It would give one a probable area of study. But in fact the only major currents in the vicinity of the wreck appear to be tidal ones, parallel to the coast. The story was, I thought, spurious. That was the second hypothesis. There are more details in de Nova and de Borja's testimony which do not feature in Marolin de Juan's initial summary of their account, but only in their detailed testimony. They only confuse the issue:

> When they arrived between the Spanish sea [Atlantic] and the Scottish isle, there was a good wind blowing to get them back to Spain. The pilot said to Don Alonzo that if he gave his permission they could go about and in five days they would be in Spain. Don Alonzo replied if he was sure the good weather would hold he had his permission. But the pilot was wrong in thinking that the wind was established. It veered round, throwing them onto the Island of Hibernia [the Latin name for Ireland]. They hit a submerged rock and the galleass broke into pieces. More than 1,300 men drowned. Only nine seamen managed to save themselves, of whom one made this declaration.

'On the Island of Hibernia, that's a bit vague,' Marc commented as he finished reading the account, 'but if she did hit a submerged rock, that makes it somewhat easier to find than having to go over the whole coast. There can't be that many.'

I explained my fourth hypothesis. The rock can't have been far out to sea: 260 bodies were washed ashore with the wine butts. Only this story upset all the others, because we now had a ship going from east to west instead of west to east. It all sounded suspicious anyway, for De Leiva had almost reached his objective, and he knew it. If it had been light he would already have sighted the Western Isles. He knew too that he didn't have anything like enough provisions on board to feed 1300 men for five or possibly ten days, and that his ship was not sufficiently seaworthy. And besides, from the time he set out, say before dawn on the 26th to the time of the shipwreck at midnight, 100 nautical miles farther on, twenty hours had passed. With a good following wind, the *Girona* could do five knots and twenty hours would be about right to cover 100 miles, but it wouldn't be anything like long enough to get all the way to the Isles, bearing in mind that the wind dropped, then changed, and then, that they doubtless waited a while until the new wind seemed properly established, before working back to the west.

'But you said that James McDonnell salvaged some stuff right away. The English must have learnt of it, otherwise we wouldn't know about it ourselves, since the Irish didn't write anything down.'

'Yes, "some butts of wine". The Lord Deputy heard about them. In theory he should have claimed them for the Queen. In fact, more likely kept them for himself. He was said to be a bit of a rogue. He had declared that "the Spanish wrecks belong to the Queen as waifs ..." "Waif" is a fairly cloudy legal term, quite vague, meaning roughly a piece of abandoned property the owners of which came ashore alive. But Fitzwilliam didn't risk claiming them from Sorley Boy. And then in December he found out something else and wrote to London: "And further I hear that three fair pieces of brass, which lie within view between rocks at Bunboys where Don Alonzo was drowned, will also be recovered".'

'Aha,' said Marc in a satisfied tone of voice. 'So it was at Bunboys. And not deep.'

As usual he was one jump ahead of me, but first I wanted him to read what Captain Cuellar wrote when he too arrived at Dunluce, in 1589, from the west coast where he had been shipwrecked, 'I went into the huts of some savages that were there and learned from them of the terrible sufferings of our people who were drowned there. I was shown many jewels and valuables that had belonged to them This caused me great sorrow. . . .'

They'd robbed the 260 bodies thrown up on the beach, on the day after the wreck, of that there could be no doubt. But more than that, James must have taken the lion's share of the treasure for himself, either then or during the summer of 1589. George Hill had written 'Every Spanish ship carried aboard two exceedingly strong iron chests. . . .' This was sheer invention. Previously Hill even went so far as to specify that one was for gold and the other for silver, and that the McDonnells probably did not take any of the gold or silver (Hill was the family historian, so the picture had to be an edifying one). He also claimed that the two coffers are still preserved and in the possession of the Antrim family. Hill doesn't give his source, and there is no mention of these two chests in any other document.

141

Personally I thought he'd invented them so as to provide a pedigree for two chests that he had seen in the castle. But that was neither here nor there. What was certain was that James must have found — either in the wreck or the dead men's pockets — a very considerable fortune. I'd read in a history of Dunluce, that starting in 1590, the original square keep was rebuilt and greatly enlarged. James even decorated the entrance with a turreted Scottish baronial portal. Where else could this new fortune have come from — in 1590?

If McDonnell had left anything for us, it must be at Port na Spaniagh, and for two reasons. Firstly, everyone else had looked at Bunboys, but I was convinced that the Irish lied at the time. There they were, quietly salvaging cannon, gold and silver. They would never have talked to an Englishman or to some stranger who looked like a spy, unless it was to send him off on the wrong track. They had known the English long enough to be pretty sure that they would claim the lot. The text of the Lord Deputy's commission to his subordinates is clear enough on this point:

Whereas the distressed fleet of the Spaniards, by tempest and contrary winds, through the providence of God, have been driven upon this coast, and many of them wrecked in several places, where is to be thought hath not only been much treasure cast away, now subject to the spoil of ours, and other goods of several kinds . . . we authorise you to make inquiry by all good means . . . to take all hulls of ships, stores, treasure, etc. . . . into your hands and to apprehend and execute all Spaniards found there of what quality soever. Torture may be used in prosecuting this inquiry.

The McDonnells must have known about that order and they wouldn't have taken any chances.

'So you think that all the early reports, where they give Bunboys as the place where the shipwreck occurred, are deliberately misleading?' Marc asked.

'I'm certain of it. And that's not all. On reflection Sorley Boy must have decided he hadn't lied enough. The Bush estuary was still too near the actual spot. He probably tried to improve his story because in December 1588, Carew received further details. He informed the Queen of them on the 13th: "Don Alonzo De Leiva . . . being again driven back upon the northern coast in Ulster and from thence putting to sea again, are sithence, as I hear say, cast away about the isles going for Scotland. . . ." They lied, and quite rightly too. In the following year, the same George Carew was already looking for cannon on the west coast.'

'With any success?'

'Hardly. In 1588 the Lord Deputy wrote that only three small pieces remained of the Spanish gun. But the next summer, when the weather was calmer and warmer, he commissioned Carew to see what more was worth salvaging on the Munster coast.'

They must have used a diving bell in these salvage operations, with the whole paraphernalia of hooks and hawsers and nooses to grab the cannon from the bell. That was the method used on the Tobermory wreck and on the *Wasa*. And then they would have had lifting jacks between two boats, like the ones they used around that time in the Cadaques operation – pulley blocks and so on.

But Carew was a poor supervisor. That summer he was in the midst of his honeymoon. He wasn't the slightest bit interested in the *Girona*. All in all, he only raised some dozen cannon. Fitzwilliam was sympathetic and did not press him too hard. Soon it was autumn, and the time for a thorough search had passed. As a result none of the misleading reports were disproved.

I had another argument, too, in favour of Port na Spaniagh. The only place names that appear on sixteenth-century maps of Ireland between Portrush and Rathlin Island are Dunluce and the Bush River. Obviously these would have been the only meaningful names a spy or a civil servant could quote to his superiors. There were virtually no paths along the coast. The cliffs were inaccessible. So even if the Irish had been truthful, they couldn't have pointed to the exact spot. All they could say was that the wreck was 'near the river Boys' or else that it was 'near Dunluce'. This was where I thought the nineteenth-century historians made their mistake, and similarly the divers who believed them; they took these two names literally. They dived immediately under Dunluce and at Bushfoot, without thinking. And then, one day in 1904, the man from the Ordnance Survey, come to do his surveys, asked the locals for the names of places roundabout so as to draw up the first edition of that map we had with us. The old fishermen he asked didn't see any reason to lie any more. The tradition had been handed down among them for fifteen generations, and they told him: 'That, sir, that's Port na Spaniagh.' Like Schlieman when he was looking for Troy, I set more store by local tradition than on all the so-called experts. Everywhere I have found that the old fishermen are right, when official hydrographic charts and serious historians are way off the mark.

NOTES

1. The Earl of Antrim, Randall McDonnell, direct descendant of Sorley Boy, later confirmed that his family had never kept any proper archives. He himself has no relics of his long family history at Glenarm, apart from two iron chests of uncertain date.

xvi (*top*) Bringing up the chains of gold

xvii (*centre left*) and xviii (*centre right*) For a month we did nothing but break up and raise large chunks of the natural black magna, encrusted in the crevices of the sea bed. This was where the treasure was

xix (*above left*) and xx (*above right*) We found twelve gold rings, and four dolphins. In front, a combined tooth and ear pick, an instrument in common use at the time

XXI (*top*) Gold coins of Spain and of Naples

XXII (*above*) A Neapolitan gold ducat, bearing the effigy of Charles I of Spain and the Kingdom of the Two Sicilies, and V of the Holy Roman Empire

XXIII and XXIV (*above*) I had the good fortune to be the one to find some of the most beautiful jewels, like this delicately engraved salamander

XXV (*overleaf*) The treasures of the Armada

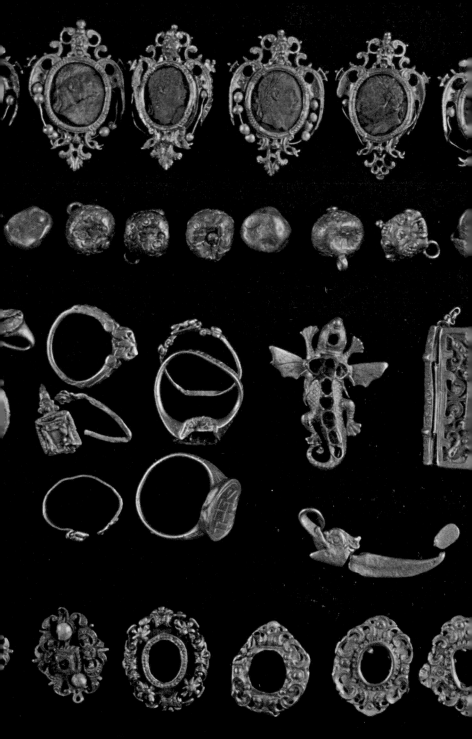

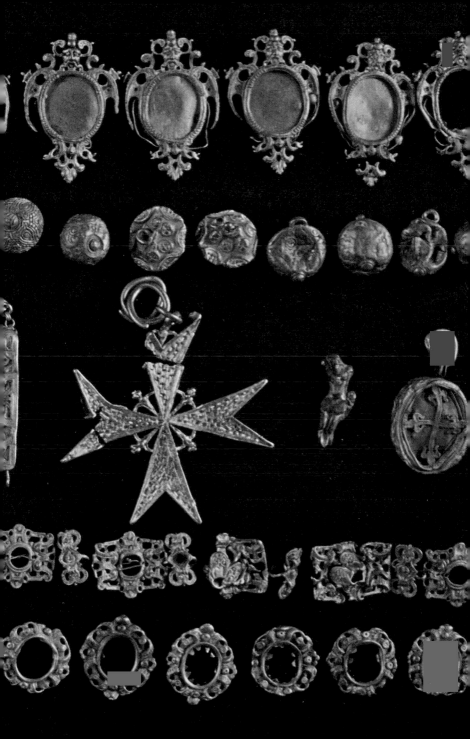

XXVI-XXVIII In this gold reliquary, which opens like a book, one of the passengers – possibly the Bishop of Killaloe – kept his Agnus Dei

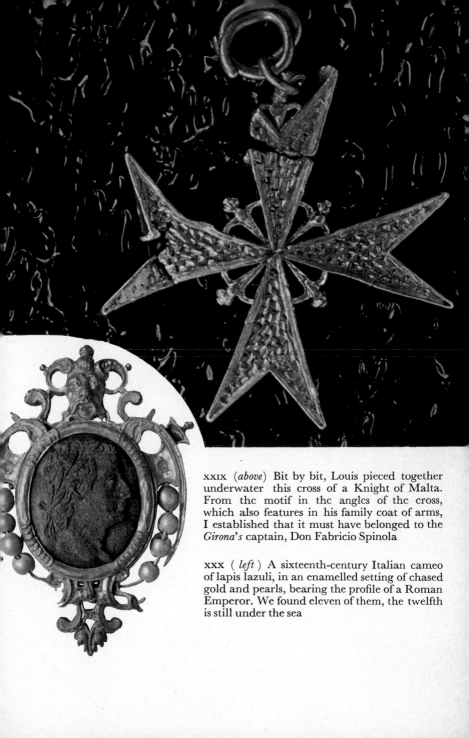

XXIX (*above*) Bit by bit, Louis pieced together underwater this cross of a Knight of Malta. From the motif in the angles of the cross, which also features in his family coat of arms, I established that it must have belonged to the *Girona's* captain, Don Fabricio Spinola

XXX (*left*) A sixteenth-century Italian cameo of lapis lazuli, in an enamelled setting of chased gold and pearls, bearing the profile of a Roman Emperor. We found eleven of them, the twelfth is still under the sea

XXXI Silver coins of Spain or the Americas, with a link of an elaborately worked gold chain, set with rubies and pearls, and a ring belonging to a Canon of the Holy Sepulchre or to a Jesuit father

26

1967: I Find the Wreck

June 1967. We left London first thing in the morning. At 12 pm the following day we were drawing up by the Atlantic. It was wild and stormy. It had been drizzling when we set out from London, in the Midlands it had been raining properly, it had poured cats and dogs in Scotland and over the Irish Sea it had come down in buckets. Now that we were in Ireland it seemed that the heavens had opened.

Marc unfolded an oilskin. He opened his door. A gust of wind slammed it shut again. There was no question of going out to sea today. Bent double under the squalls, we floundered across to the Giant's Causeway. Judging by the number of souvenir stalls it seemed that tourists must come in their droves on days when it wasn't pouring with rain. Farther along was a sheep track swept by a stream.

We walked some distance. Port na Spaniagh is out of this world. An amphitheatre of 400 ft high cliffs, sheer and terrifying. The wind howled round our ears. Beside the cliffs sea birds hovered, circling ceaselessly in one spot and their raucous cries, endlessly modulated, echoed into infinity. The rock was black — the cliffs were black, with gashes of red where men have cut out paths. Occasional patches of green pasture were specked with nimble white sheep. Mounds of fallen debris were piled up at the bottom to form a chaotic mass of boulders where the beach ought to have been. All the floating wrecks from miles around end up here.

Below us, the green ocean showed its power. The breakers' rippling backs heaved as they approached the shore, and broke on Lacada Point, sending fountains of milky spray rocketing up to the sky. In front of Spaniards' Cave flakes of foam flew up, spinning in the air like flights of yellow butterflies.

Neither of us spoke. The wildness of the spot made a deep im-

145

pression on me. It's a place that calls for death, cries out for tragedy. It's too much. A film set. Nature has overdone it. I could see the great ship being pounded to pieces down there by the waves that never stop. Her sides crack, and men are thrown out on to the black rocks, snatched up by the breakers, hurled down again, smashed, broken up like old puppets.

Marc turned to me after a long silence. 'What can be left of the wreck after 400 years of this?'

When we got back, Marc went into a tourist shop and bought a one and threepenny guide book to the Giant's Causeway. He flicked through it. Suddenly he roared with laughter.

'How much of your precious youth have you spent poring over Armada archives? How many hours altogether? Six hundred? More like eight, probably? There was an easier way, old man. Here. Try this next time.'

And this was what I read: 'In 1588 ... the galleass *Girona* was wrecked at a little cove, near the Giant's Causeway, still called Port na Spaniagh.'

It was easy enough to laugh then, but if I'd just read it there in that one and threepenny guide like everyone else, I'd have done exactly what everyone else has done before. I'd have shrugged my shoulders and gone about finding some more serious source.

The next day there were gale force winds.

Apart from Portrush there is not another proper port on the whole coast, only small coves with little or no shelter from the open sea. To get into them you have to know how to wind your way between the reefs. The fishermen use these coves whenever the weather begins to look a bit threatening, winching their boats up the beach on rollers. We had reconnoitred all of them on foot, with a map, before deciding on Port Ballintrae for our base. We managed to assemble the boat between two storms.

For this first exploratory expedition we had with us only the very lightest of equipment: a small inflatable dinghy with an eighteen horse-power Johnson, four double-cylinder aqualungs and a small high-pressure air-compressor. With our wet suits, photographic equipment and our bits and pieces, it all fitted into two cars.

We inflated the dinghy, and as it was still very rough, went to have a look at Dunluce. Sir John Perrot, Lord Deputy in 1584, gave a good description of it in a letter that he wrote to the Privy Council while he was besieging it.

I set up camp with the whole company in front of Dunluce, the best fortified spot in the kingdom. It is built on an overhanging rock and cut off from the mainland by a natural trench; the only access to it is by a narrow rocky bridge, which also has a deep cleft in it. . . .

It was exactly as he had described it. A fairy-tale castle, perched like an eagle's nest on a sea-swept rock promontory. There are caves there, which we looked at, that were once lived in by early troglodyte Christians.

Around the thirteenth century a square fort was built, which later fell into the hands of the clan McQuillan. A rival clan, the McDonnells, wanted it for themselves. They tried to appropriate it first by a peaceful alliance and later by more forceful means. At the battle of Bun na Mairge they virtually exterminated the McQuillans. But a few survived, including some of the more powerful members of the clan. The McDonnells invited them to a picnic at Minehill, to celebrate their reconciliation. To create a more friendly atmosphere and foster better relations between the two families, they placed them alternately in the seating. Beside each McQuillan sat a McDonnell. At the end of their feast, when they had all eaten and drunk their fill, the bards in their long, coloured robes began to sing, accompanying themselves on the harp. At a given signal every McDonnell turned swiftly to his left, plunging his dagger deep into the heart of the McQuillan beside him. The castle was theirs.

Sir John Perrot captured it in 1584. He left a garrison and a high constable there to guard it in the name of the Queen. He had hardly turned his back when Sorley Boy McDonnell retook the castle by force, hanging the English constable by the neck from the highest wall. Sorley Boy installed his son in it, and it was he who was living there in 1588.

From the castle windows, one can see the Western Isles; James McDonnell was well placed to organise the evacuation of Spanish survivors.

The atmosphere in these ruins is heavy with history, fascinating for those who are as steeped in it as I am. I have often been back to look at the Scottish baronial door and the new additions that James McDonnell built after 1588, with what I cannot help thinking of as 'my' money, taken from 'my' wreck, in 'my' coffers.

About 200 yards from the castle is the old church of Dunluce, where the *Girona* survivors went to pray and offer their thanksgivings to God. James McDonnell had a special weekday Mass said for them there. Now all that is left of it are four walls overgrown with ivy and honeysuckle. All around and inside the tombs have collapsed. Some have quite disappeared in the long grass. One after another we scrutinised the tombstones. Tradition has it that the bodies that were thrown up on to the beach from the galleass were buried here. But there must have been hundreds of bodies. How could they have been carried so far? Loading them on to a boat and then on to carts would have involved more than thirty journeys, considerable expense, and at least a week's work. In any case how could so many bodies have been laid to rest in such a small area? We found no sign of any Spanish graves. The earliest date on any stone was 1630. There were some older ones, even more worn and pocked by sea spray and salt air, on which the dates were no longer visible. But the names on those were Irish. Don Alonzo and his companions must, I think, have been buried in Port na Spaniagh itself, straight in the earth under the boulders.

On 27 June the sun managed to break through between showers, and in this new light the watery landscape seemed suddenly to become vaster, bursting into colour as it broke out of its cocoon of rain. As the countryside awoke so something in us awoke with it.

The fishermen shook their heads as they watched our absurd little boat heading out towards the open sea, riding wave after wave of the incoming swell from Iceland. Immediately we left the port we were right out in the open. Marc steered towards the one-mile stone at the other end of Bushmills Bay. From there to Spaniard Rock are jagged cliffs, marked out by the Chimney Rocks, hexagonal columns of solidified lava, which rise dizzily on the edge of the abyss.

Seen from the sea Port na Spaniagh looks even more sinister. What if the engine broke down? There one would be, utterly defenceless against the raging sea, infinitesimal at the bottom of those soaring cliffs; 1,300 men were drowned there! A myriad of clichés come to mind. Dante, Villehardouin, Shakespeare. . . .

'Abandon hope, all ye who anchor here,' Marc called into the wind as he dropped the dinghy's grappling anchor next to the reefs, those two bared teeth in the middle of Port na Spaniagh. 'How reckless is he,' I said, 'who places between himself and death the thickness of a diving suit.' I put on flippers, face mask, gloves and lead belt and worked out what bearing to follow under water. I toppled backwards and Marc went on declaiming for the benefit of the seagulls:

> 'O Lord, methought what pain it was to drown,
> What dreadful noise of waters in mine ears,
> What sights of ugly death within mine eyes!'

I dived and silence was all around me. I felt the biting cold on my face, cutting right through my sinuses. I went down slowly, following

the anchor line. Everywhere, greys, greens, browns. Moving at one knot, the tide was pulling westwards. The grappling anchor had caught on a sea tangle, a long glistening stem, fixed to the rock by a large tendril and ending above my head in a huge brown frond. I wedged the grapple between two rocks and waited for a while to get used to the cold.

If Port na Spaniagh had been the first to get its Spanish name, and the rocks and the neighbouring cave had been named after it, that would mean that the *Girona* was in the bay. If, on the other hand, the rock had been named first, we should have to look there. I decided to start in Port na Spaniagh, exploring the two reefs, which are covered at high tide and could so easily foul an incoming ship.

149

Guided by my compass, I reached the base of the twin reefs. The sediment stirred up by the stormy weather had not yet settled. Swimming in this pea soup it was impossible to see farther than four yards in front of me at the most. I swam round and round one reef and then the other, but found nothing. The sea bed here is rocky and chaotic, but following my bearings I worked along parallel lines from north to south – still nothing. Then I moved in a hard southwesterly direction towards Lacade Point, moving very slowly, trying to see the sea bed through the algae, which sway ceaselessly in the swell, rather as one watches the road through moving windscreen wipers.

When you are looking for 400-year-old wrecks, it doesn't do to take Shakespeare too literally. Intent on finding gems reflecting in '. . . dead men's skulls, and in the holes. Where eyes did once inhabit . . .', it's all too easy to swim on without noticing some faint reddish protuberance which would betray the whereabouts of the caked remains of a cannon ball, not quite buried by the sea.

I stopped in a cleft in the rock and moved three stones to stir up the sand – still nothing. My depth gauge needle had moved up from 30 to 20 ft. Suddenly a cliff barred my way. Where was I? It must be the east face of Lacada Point. The cliff ran along the edge of a vast platform leading to an enormous rock. A white shape caught my eye. Ah! I went closer. A lead ingot.

In a flash I remembered something I read, sitting under the blue and gold dome of the British Museum Reading Room, avidly devouring the story of a man called Boyle, who discovered another Armada wreck in Donegal at the end of the eighteenth century. 'With several good swimmers and expert divers . . .' he found apart from a few gold pieces and some bronze cannon, 'a piece of lead which he supposed to be ballast, a yard long, triangular, the sides being pointed towards the ends, getting thick in the middle'. My ingot fitted the description perfectly. Arching my back, I heaved it over, and there stamped on the upper face were five Jerusalem crosses.

I had found the wreck. I closed my eyes, and felt my mouth, frozen with cold, turn up into a smile. The elation I felt was calm, a slow but very deep joy, a feeling of relief almost.

So, we had won the first round. Now for the second. I swam on, ferreting about in a long corridor which led me straight to a large verdigris-coloured cylinder. A bronze cannon. It lay crossways, protruding between stones, about two feet longer than my armspan, its calibre – four fingers, a little over three inches. A demi-saker. There was nothing else around. An underwater shelf inclines sharply down to Lacada Point. If the ship ran on to this, everything would have rolled down to the bottom of it. I followed the tortuous slope all the way down. There, lying in an oblong crevice, I found another bronze cannon. But what a strange shape it was. Box-like with a barrel coming out of it. Of course, a breechloading piece! The breech blocks[1] must be somewhere near. I couldn't take my eyes off this unique object. A Spanish Armada gun. There wasn't a museum in the world that had one, not even a cannon ball, not even a nail.

Lying just beside it were the powder chambers – two, three, four, *five* of them. A chalky crust, impregnated with copper oxide, had soldered some of them to the rock. Others were loose, and two were of a large calibre. Perhaps they belong to one of the guns Sorley Boy fished up? There were lead ingots everywhere, twelve at least, and some thick rectangular plates. It all tallied with the inventory drawn up before the departure from Lisbon. There were holes and marks on the plates that must have been left by the round-headed, square nails that were used to fix them. The nails must have been made of iron, for nothing was left of them. Shapeless lumps had fused to the rock and filled up the fissures. Cannon balls were everywhere, and traces of rust on the sea bed, round stains, where shot had succumbed to the combined effects of corrosion and erosion. From between two stones, I picked up a copper coin. Enough, it was time to make my way back.

I was smiling so broadly when I caught hold of the dinghy that I dropped my mouthpiece from between my teeth. 'I've found it, Marc,' I said. But he had guessed as much already from my face.

NOTES

1. That is to say the powder chamber (*recamaras* or *servidores*) loaded in advance, then half screwed into place and secured by hammering in a wooden wedge. When a shot had been fired, one man changed the chamber, while another cleaned the barrel and a third put in the shot. By this method it was possible to fire up to three shots a minute

27

380 Years After

The following day the wind was up before us, blowing from the south while we ate our porridge. It changed, as we dressed, to south-west, and by the time we left the port a strong west-sou-wester was blowing. After ten minutes of switchbacking over the waves, the wind had swept in so much spray that we had taken six inches of water. We had to turn back, baling all the way.

It was the beginning of three days of really bad weather. A stiff west wind blew without a break.

To allay our impatience we went back to Port na Spaniagh by the coastal path. Rabbits were out playing all over the slope. Using clods of fallen earth for stepping stones, we climbed down to the spot where the Spanish bodies were thrown up by the sea. Today buoys, cork floats and tons of driftwood are still tossed ashore just like those drowned men. The whole bay is white and thick, cakes of foam form between the stones. We found bones everywhere. The remains of the shipwreck victims? No. Dead sheep, probably.

By 1 July the sea was calm and we were able to dive again. When I first saw the cannon it had been quite clear. After three days of storms it was half buried under huge stones. I took Marc to photograph it, and showed him the ingot. While he was focusing his camera, I picked up a flat, round, grey pebble. 'What a laugh,' I thought, 'I'll make him think it's a piece of eight.' I examined it. Just an ordinary pebble. I turned it over. It *was* a piece of eight. A silver piece of eight. No doubt about it. There was the cross, the Jerusalem cross, almost worn away, but it was there all right. I waved my arms about with excitement and pushed the piece of eight under Marc's nose. I watched his expression, sure that he was saying to himself, 'Ha, ha. What a joke. He's trying to make me think it's a piece of eight.' I showed him the cross. He took my hand and shook it, ceremoniously, mumbling congratulations into his mouthpiece. There in the same place, by the entrance to a large cave, was another, lying flat on the pebbles, just waiting for me to come along and find it.

We went back up to change cylinders. The silver coins were Spanish and, like the cannons, they were of the right period. The amount of lead and the number of cannon balls proved that the wreck was that of a warship. Was it an Armada wreck? According to the documents the only one on the north coast of Ulster was the *Girona*. It remained to be proved.

That the cannon had got half buried like that in three days, shows how thoroughly the seabed here is stirred up in bad weather. Storms, real ones, must send small stones flying, roll large ones around and generally turn the whole seafloor upside down. Heavy wreck débris, anything made of metal, for example must have collected on the solid rock bed under a layer of light sediment.

I spent the whole of this dive digging around the first ingot, in front of a huge boulder. I shifted three stones. There was a cannon ball, encrusted with that brown magma of iron oxide and chalky deposits, typical of the gangue that all cannon balls acquire under water over the centuries. I dug down farther, to find more cannon balls and then just like that, a piece of eight, firmly wedged. It had not rolled around at all. The silver was very well preserved. The arms of Spain were clearly visible, a capital T with a small o underneath: it was minted at Toledo. I slipped it into my glove and then, oh . . . gold . . . it's gold. My pulse raced. Yes, a little gold ring, there between two stones, all shining. I had to take off my glove to get at it, not noticing the cold. At last, after twelve years of laughable attempts, after twelve years of monotonous failure, I have found gold under the sea. There, shining in the palm of my hand. Enough. Into my glove with it and on with the job. Here were some lead plates from the lining of the hull, a green marble egg with a hole through it. What on earth could that be? And then, more. A little fragment of gold chain, six gold links shaped like flattened figures of eight, entwined together, of the most exquisite delicacy. Where could the rest of it be? I would have to look further, to dig right down to the bottom. But how? I didn't have the right tools. And besides, I'd run out of air.

Meanwhile, Marc was reconnoitring Spaniard Rock and the little cove in front of Spaniard Cave. Nothing there. As he described it, the sea bed there was quite smooth, flayed by underwater erosion: giants' kettles, devils' cauldrons – a real lesson in geology. Then farther out, some way away from Lacada Point, he found an anchor. A big one, 'one Jasinski armspan plus one foot from fluke to fluke'. It was heavily eroded, missing its shank and one fluke, hidden under a mesh of fine algae. 'A less experienced eye,' he added, 'less acute, less sharp than mine, might easily have missed it.'

And now what were we to do? That evening, sitting by the fire, we made a plan. What could we possibly do, just the two of us, without any proper equipment, and with a find like that on our hands? We had seen two cannon. There must have been fifty. If we had found pieces of eight as easily as that lying on the surface, there must have been ten or a hundred times as many buried farther down. And if there were silver coins, it followed that there must be gold ones. In the 1580s the Americas were producing ten pounds of silver for every one of gold, and the proportion of coins in circulation was roughly the same. So for every ten pieces of eight, we should find one gold escudo. Only there was no getting away from the fact that there were 3,000 or 4,000 cubic feet of chalk, sand, gravel and rocks to be meticulously sorted through. To get at them we would have to move mountains or break them up. We would have to shift the boulders on top of the sediment. And there were boulders of every shape and size, some as small as a pumpkin others as big as carriages. It would mean at least two years' work, and two years' work by a large professional team of experts, at that.

This was the first Armada wreck found since Boyle found his. What Boyle did with his 'pretty made and pretty shaped bronze guns' was to bring them to white heat over a peat fire and then break them up (a wandering tinker had suggested this method to him). He sold 'three cartloads of brass at 4½d a pound'. The gold coins that Boyle found have disappeared, made into rings, perhaps, for they do say roundabout that there isn't anywhere else that the family fortune could have come from. My plans were quite different. I wanted this to be the first Armada wreck to be properly excavated and scientifically studied.

What we wanted to do was not the sort of thing one can do just like that. And in any case it was 1 July. We both had our professional

154

commitments. It would be autumn by the time we had the thing set up. There was only one answer. Wait.

We decided to come back fully prepared the following year. From now until then we must keep the secret to ourselves, for there is in England no legal provision by which my rights as finder could be protected in my absence. We must offer prayers to Poseidon, night and morning, that no other divers would find our wreck. *Dura lex, sed lex*. Before leaving, we must replace all our odds and ends of treasure, piece by piece, at the back of the cave.

28

A Two-Star Wreck

Back in London, I began, on reflection to have certain reservations. The *Girona* deserves three stars. There's no doubt about that. But the *Nuestra Señora* has two, and so have many other Armada ships that left their bones along the coast of Ireland. Before rushing into this perhaps we should, after all, go and have a look at the other wrecks. I went through my notes once more, and picked out two other tempting wrecks and some groups of wrecks.

In September Marc and I were on our way to Eire. Besides our light equipment, I took along a magnetometer this time. It's a detecting instrument that reacts to any disturbance in the magnetic field caused by a foreign magnetic mass, twenty or thirty iron cannon, for example, or an anchor, or a few tons of iron shot. We spent five days at the first site. Very promising. . . . But definitely less so than the *Girona*. That wreck would have to be left for another expedition. The next group of wrecks proved to present trickier problems than had appeared on paper. To be reconsidered.

Without any feelings of regret we now made for the *Nuestra Señora de la Rosa*. She was the one that sank like a stone between the Blaskets and the Kerry coast, on the very south-west point of Ireland. To get there we had to drive right down the west coast of this beautiful country. Its very poverty has made it one of the few parts of Western Europe to have maintained a real identity.

23 September. Our cylinders were full of air and we, likewise, were full of ourselves. The sun shone. The sea was like a mill pond. Marc was driving, and between the 'oohs' and 'aahs' and the 'did you see thats' at the fantastic landscape, he asked why I had given the wreck two stars. I said, 'She's the *Rosa* isn't she, and an *almiranta*. She was the Guipuzcoan flagship.' I argued that the King's gold was divided

among all the squadrons on the *capitanas* and *almirantes*. They were the only ships that had *contadores* and *pagadores* on board, officers entitled to sign cargo on and off, and therefore, to hand out the King's money, on orders from the squadron commander or from the admiral. I didn't know exactly how much royal gold there was on board. In theory Medina Sidonia was supposed to be taking 200,000 ducats. There was a lot of money talk in his letters to the King. I had been over his expenditure letter by letter; in the end he did take most of it with him. What wasn't at all clear, was why the Pagador General of the Armada, one Juan de la Huerta, swore on oath that he left Lisbon with 430,690,091 maravedis. It was possible that this represented the total funds, for fleet and army together, but I didn't know where it came from.

Marc asked, 'How much does that number of maravedis equal?'

'About 1,148,240 ducats. But there were expenses at Corunna. All that was left would have been on the *almirantes* and the *capitanas*.'

'But Robert, the *Girona* was neither a *capitana* nor an *almiranta*.'

I explained that of course she wasn't. There wasn't any treasure on the *Girona*, not official chests, anyway. All we could hope to find there was the money that noblemen and gentlemen adventurers would have had on them, as well as their jewels, no doubt, and then whatever the five crews might have had in their pockets. Just before sailing they had received two months pay. The Duke received 3,500 escudos a month, plus expenses; his 'Ayuda de Costa', a Maestro de Campo, got 500; a cavalry general, like Alonzo de Leiva, 300; a captain in the Guards, 100 escudos; a ship's captain got 100 too; a doctor, 30; an alguacil, 24; soldiers and seamen must have got between 4 and 10, depending on their length of service and seniority.

On the other hand the treasure of the *Santa Maria de la Rosa* was down in black and white. The sole survivor swore to the English: 'In silver there are in her 50,000 ducats; in gold as much more: more rich apparel and plate, and cups of gold.' That's what he is quoted as saying in *Certain advertisements* . . . , a contemporary propaganda pamphlet, in which a translation of his evidence was published. Only his evidence is taken up again in other pamphlets and in them it becomes 15,000 silver ducats and 15,000 gold, and then in his second

157

examination, he mentions only 'three chests full of money'.

'Do these sort of amounts seem at all realistic to you?' asked Marc.

The answer was yes. Killjoy historians have pointed out that this sole survivor, a Genoese, called Giovanni de Manona, was in no position to know what he was talking about, because he was only the pilot's son, and that in any case his evidence is full of errors. But all the same, the *Rosa* was an *almiranta*, and all the *almirantes* and *capitanas* I knew about, whether they were lost, captured or got back to Spain, were carrying a sizeable treasure. And then, quite apart from the treasure, this was a fascinating wreck, because she went down in deep water, at least 100 ft, which meant that she could have remained fairly intact.

'Yes, okay. But to get back to this treasure. How much do you reckon?'

I had made a note of all that was on the other flagships, and had the figures with me. The treasure on the *Rosa* must have been roughly the same:

Santa Ana, capitana of the Biscayans, ran aground at le Havre, 50,000 crowns of ten reals, deposited in safe hands in France.

San Lorenzo, capitana of the galleasses, looted by the English – nothing, according to them, but according to the historians, 50,000 or 22,000 escudos.

Nuestra Señora del Rosario, capitana of the Andalusians, 52,000 escudos, or 25,300 or 22,000 according to whose evidence you take, a Spaniard's or an Englishman's – not counting Pedro de Valdez's own money, say 4000 reals – or his silver. This was all Drake's loot.

San Salvador, vice *almiranta* of the Guipuzcoans, captured in the Channel, said to have then contained a chest, but it disappeared.

Oquendo's *capitana*, another *Santa Ana*, the Guipuzcoan flagship, as it happens: 55,000 escudos, brought back to Spain.

Apart from the fact that somewhere Juan de la Huerta mentions the sum of 4,000,000 maravedis on one ship, possibly the *San Salvador* – this was all that was known.

'But, Robert, this is really something. I mean to say, it's a fortune.'

Marc was right, it was a fortune on paper, at any rate. The ship went down in the presence of an eyewitness, Marcos de Aramburu, who was just a few cables away on the *San Juan Bautista*. He gave all the details. All one had to do was to dive along the dotted line, still on paper, of course. Then Spotswood Green, the good Reverend, who we mentioned before, constructed a theory that seems to stand up. He thought that the ship struck Stromboli reef and went down at the foot of it, to the southeast in view of the tide, and according to the map, about 90–100 ft down.

'The wreck must have held together then?'

'Yes, apart from the wood, it should all be there. And as well as the treasure, you know, there were 50 field cannon on board, and bronze ones at that, if the pilot's son knew what he was talking about.'

'But it's a dream come true!'

'Isn't it? For independent archaeologists, not living off handouts from some committee or commission or ministry, it really is a dream come true. A dig that pays for itself. I always have thought that profitability wasn't necessarily synonymous with badly carried out excavations, and that a loss doesn't necessarily imply scientific accuracy.'

'Quite, poverty is no virtue. But how about some lunch?'

We had just arrived in Limerick. Before sitting down to lunch I bought a local newspaper, the *Evening Press*. Splashed across the front page was an enormous headline:

GOLD MINE OFF KERRY. DIVERS FIND £1 MILLION ARMADA WRECK
'After a four-year search amateur divers claim they have discovered the wreck of a flagship from the Spanish Armada off the County Kerry coast; the discovery could be worth at least a million pounds. Mr Sidney Wignall, 44, has declared. . . .'

Somehow we weren't hungry any more. I had already experienced that sensation, like the time that some other divers found the wreck of the *De Liefde* in the Shetlands, and the wreck of the *St Gerans* off Mauritius, the *Chameau* off Nova Scotia and any amount of other treasure ships – wrecks I had spent hours diligently studying and carefully indexing when I should have been out looking for them. This time, too, it was not the lucky divers I felt sore about. I felt like hitting myself.

Sidney Wignall, leader of the expedition, that found the *Nuestra Señora*, deserved to have us take our hats off to him. He had been searching for six years. First he had looked for the *Girona* and failed.

This time he deserved to succeed. We drank his health in large dry sherries in a pub in the main street in Limerick and wished him all the luck in the world.

For us, then, it would have to be the *Girona*. On the way back we made a long list of all the equipment we would need to take. On reading through it I realised we had left something out: a lorry to load it all on.

On the equipment side, our friend from Marseilles, Henri Delauze, founder and president of COMEX, and pioneer of experimental and industrial diving, was to be our patron. He was going to lend us the lorry, ready filled. On the diving side we needed more men, real professionals. On the money side the question was how best to spend the few cents I had managed to bleed out of my publishers during the last ten years. The National Geographic Society in Washington D.C. to which I had contributed for some time, had promised a small extra sum. And then above all we would need time. My Managing Director was willing to release me from professional commitments in my London office for the summer. Finally we would need an Armada expert. I undertook to become one.

But for the whole of that winter I knew I wouldn't be able to open *The Times* in the morning without getting into a cold sweat.

29

1968: Topography of a Shipwreck

On 27 April 1968, three overloaded vehicles drew up in front of the Manor Guest House, Port Ballintrae.

In the Peugeot van were 2 Zodiac inflatable dinghies (Mark 5 and Mark 3), 2 outboard motors (50 and 35 hp), 2 compressors (8 and 10 cubic metres/hr), a powerful force-pump, 12 double air tanks, 6 sets of diving equipment, 9 crates and 11 sacks filled with accessories and tools; and 2 French divers.

In the Opel station wagon were cases filled with photographic equipment, cameras, underwater camera housings, sacks of lenses, underwater lights, flashbulbs, a small compressor, a metal detector, cylinders, carboys of acid and chemicals, drawing and topographical material, and two Belgian divers.

In the Alpine and its trailer, two sets of diving equipment, a low pressure compressor for two hookahs, rolls of Admiralty charts, crates of documents and photocopies, cases of reference books (histories of ordnance and navigation, books on naval construction, numismatics, preservation and treatment of artifacts, and so on) files, and the leader of the expedition.

But expeditions, like wars, are won by men first, equipment second.

Marc Jasinski was to be with us for two months. Marc is one of the best underwater (and underground for that matter) photographers in Europe. He is a chemistry graduate, so as well as his cameras he was going to take charge of the preservation of underwater finds.

He had brought with him Francis Dumont, known as Jules, designer and architectural student, veteran speleologist and novice

161

diver. He was to take charge of all charts, plans and sketches.

Henri Delauze, our friend from Marseilles, patron of the expedition, had picked the two other members of the team from among the top French professional divers.

Maurice Vidal, 33, with fifteen years in the French Navy; comes from Cannes and could talk the hind legs off a donkey. To shut him up you'd have to knock him out, which wouldn't be easy. He is an instructor in unarmed combat, a frogman-trooper, commando, instructor in demolition-sabotage, and a combat diver. He developed these skills mostly in Algeria and in Indochina, and returned the mildest, most peaceloving man imaginable. From the Navy he went into professional diving.

Louis Gorsse, native of Auvergne, but now living in Toulon, is as taciturn as Maurice is verbose. He spent three and a half years in the Navy doing what must be the nastiest of all jobs, underwater explosive disposal. It didn't put him off, though, and immediately afterwards he became a professional diver, specialising first of all in public works, and later in the most arduous branch of the profession, offshore oil rigs. His qualifications, like Maurice's, are many and varied.

Come the evening the boats are already inflated, the cylinders were filled and we were ready to go.

On 28 April, we set out. The sea was calm but swept by hail and sleet. We were shivering by the time we got to Port na Spaniagh and the sight of those rocks, blacker even than usual, chilled us to the marrow.

First of all I wanted to draw up a precise plan of all the wreck remains. Underwater archaeologists excavating Roman and Greek wrecks in the Mediterranean, on an even mud bed, in deep water, use the classic methods of land archaeology. A grid of metal squares placed on the sea bed serves as the basis for all measurements and general reference. Colour stereophotographs are taken systematically at every stage of the excavation, followed by careful layering in each square which enables them to locate every object precisely in three dimensions. Later they can plot on their chart the exact layout of the cargo and of the ship herself. But here there isn't a ship any more, nor any cargo. All there is here is an irregular chaos of cliffs and crevices with shallow basins here and there filled with

162

pebbles, coarse sand and enormous boulders all over the place; between these we could get as lost as ants in a pile of gravel. Laying out a metal grid here would be about as easy as it would be on the top of Milan Cathedral. And besides it would be utterly useless. The first square we put down wouldn't last three days, and even if the square itself stayed put, even before the ink had dried on our chart, everything in it would have been tossed about and scattered into the next square and the next. Every movement of the ocean upsets the seabed, fills up holes, covering and uncovering cannon at random.

Of the actual ship which must have split on the rock, nothing will have survived. Of that we can be certain. Only the whereabouts of heavy objects will be able to tell us anything of how the *Girona* met her end. Her anchor, cannon, ingots and cannon balls have not moved far. They have just rolled down as far as the first ledge. Everything else has been swept along like dead leaves in a tornado, resting one day here, another somewhere else.

So to draw up our chart we must use the simpler method of bearings and measurements taken from set control points.

I started by stretching a red rope between the first and second cannon. The rope was marked out in metres and zigzags to link the two pieces to the most obvious points. Another rope ran from the cave to the first ingot. These formed the backbone of our plan. Meanwhile they provided guidelines for Louis and Maurice, who were doing an exploratory dive to get to know the area and the local diving conditions.

Back in the cave I reclaimed our embryo treasure. It had stayed put. Then just casually in passing, I turned over a stone and there was a handful of silver fragments, a gold link, a silver half escudo and two more pieces of eight for the evening's inventory.

The thing that really worried me was the weather. Already by the next day it was beginning to deteriorate. Visibility was down to arm's length. No question of being able to make a start on the systematic circular exploration that I had planned. It was impossible even to find one's way around, and there wasn't a hope of being able to work on Lacada Point, where Marc had meant to finish setting out the buoys. I made one attempt to go and take a look, but the surf enveloped me and somersaulted me into a vertical cleft. I made my way back to the dinghy only to have Louis point out Maurice to me. He had strayed out to sea and was heading eastwards; already he was no more than a tiny speck, swept swiftly along the surface by the irresistible tidal current.

Having recovered Vidal, we returned to the harbour.

And there we were to stay for three days. My room faced the sea. At night the wind from Greenland would rush in through the badly fitting window, streak under my frozen nose and then dart out under the door on its way to the Azores.

In the morning, I could tell just by listening what the weather was like. If I heard the thunder of waves breaking on the beach, there was nothing for it but to resign myself to going back to sleep.

On 2 May it was the silence that woke me. The sea had calmed. We could go on with setting out the buoys. Taking advantage of the crevices, Marc and Francis laid out white ropes marked off in metres, to north and south, perpendicular to the red rope. They numbered the intersections. These would serve as a general grid for the chart of the area. Louis and I worked as a team, plotting every object and control point with distance and bearings. For a simple triangulation I took bearings using a fixed wheel with degrees marked on its rim, while he stretched a tape to the selected control points. To fill in the details Marc would systematically photograph it all from top to bottom.

We had worked hard. We deserved a little treat as a reward. We would go on a treasure hunt. Immediate success: some gold coins.

Louis and Maurice brought back the first ones, two pieces of four escudos, bearing the shield of arms, and above, the crown of Aragon, and therein lies the whole history of Spain. There wasn't a mark on them, not a sign of wear. 'Extremely fine', certainly 'very fine'. As well as these they had found two dozen or so pieces of eight reals, some badly worn pieces of four, some exquisitely engraved gold buttons, a heap of broken silver forks, and assorted artifacts and tiny fragments. The pace was set for such finds. It would not slacken and it wouldn't be long before the 'treasure site' chart was covered with symbols and arrows.

We decided to split up like that every day, one team plotting charts, another surveying, and the third out hunting for treasure.

But barely were our measuring lines in place when the sea got up again. By the time we were able to go back, the red rope, a half-inch nylon climbing rope, had snapped right through and tangled itself up into a cat's cradle, and the white ropes were snaking about in the seaweed like overcooked spaghetti.

We had to start again. And it was not always possible to work in the shallows of Lacada Point where we began before. Louis tried once or twice at the beginning, but in the swell it took both hands just to stay in one place and one couldn't work with one's teeth: they were already taken up with the mouthpiece. There was nothing for it but to give up.

There was nothing we could do about it, so on bad days we all concentrated on the treasure in front of the cave, where it's deeper and somewhat more sheltered. I had already found several engraved gold medallions there, or rather empty settings, all missing their central cameo miniature or cabochon. Doggedly, I searched everywhere, but never did I find a single one. They were lighter than the gold and would have been swept away like dead leaves. One finds these same jewels in portraits of the period, sewn on to a hat, or a doublet, or occasionally worn on a bracelet.

I found a gold coin. I kissed it. My first gold coin, my very first.

Fifteen years I had been looking for that coin, fifteen years I had waited to bestow that kiss and it was not the dry kiss of a miser. It was not the metal I was kissing, nor what it could buy. What I was kissing was the symbol, the dream come true.

For a long while I just looked at it. Then I found a second one. In less than an hour I had filled my jam jar with gold and silver, not only that but a mustard pot, a pickle jar and a band-aid tin as well. Finally I was stuffing things into my left glove.

How we needed that glimmer of gold between the pebbles to keep us warm! After a few hours on the sea bed the cold started to drill its way into one's sinuses. One's neck went rigid; it paralysed one's muscles. The pain was excrutiating. We were used to letting our feet get paralysed, to letting our calves go rigid. When it got to the point when one's knees wouldn't bend then it was time to get back while one still could.

We tried everything. Francis wore three neoprene suits one on top of the other. Maurice wore three layers of woollen underwear under a dry suit and Louis a dry suit over neoprene. I myself had to give up dry suits, because the sleeves cut into my wrists so badly that they drew blood. I finally found the best thing to be a new Piel wet suit, which is cellular and designed to maintain a constant thickness. A little bottle of compressed air with a reducing valve reinflates it at depth.

In the evenings we took the cold with us in our bones from the sea back to the shore. We took it into dinner with us, and then to bed. It lingered in the marrow of our bones until the next morning, and finally left us just as we began to dress for a new dive.

30

Treasure Cave

We lived by the rhythm of the sea. Our daily life was utterly dictated by the whims of her temper, her anger and her moments of tranquillity. Her anger confined us to the harbour, her periods of tranquillity sent us to work. There were days when we dived blind, when the water was so dense that one could not see one's hand at the end of one's arm. We would get lost in the places that we knew the best. Huge black masses would hurl towards us, veering off only at the last minute, or else the darkness around us would quite suddenly intensify. We did not know it but we were nothing more than the playthings of the swell which was throwing us at a rock or sweeping us into a cave.

On days like that we would come ashore in the evening, pitching and rolling like drunks, and later, even lying in bed, we would still feel the sea rocking us.

Diving keeps one's hands busy but it leaves the mind free. As I humped my stones around I let my mind wander happily. At last there was nowhere else I would rather be, nothing I would rather be doing. After all these years I was living out my dream. When I got up that morning I felt shattered already. I would go to bed more dead beat still. Hardly time to eat or sleep. That's how I like it. What I really enjoy is the discomfort, the exhaustion, the biting cold, the wretchedness of sea-sickness and the agonising need for a pee.

Under my hand something yellow moved and cut short my soliloquy. A gold coin? No, a shell. It's so easy to be fooled. Let's have a good look. It'll teach me a lesson. I won't get caught like that again. *Santiago y a ellos!* I am away on a crusade. *Santiago y Cierra España!* It's not a shell. It's a gold medallion, with the cross of St

James on it. It's the insignia of an order of knighthood, could it be the Order of Santiago? Then it must be Don Alonzo's. I wave my arms about in excitement, talk to myself. But no. On the other side there is a saint beautifully engraved, but he has neither a shell nor a staff. It can't be St James. Keep calm, now. Let's examine this cross. Well, yes . . . no, it's not the military order of St James of the Sword. There's no blade and there's no pommel. The ends of the arms are shaped like fleurs-de-lis. On the reverse, the saint's side, a tree. What saint can that be the symbol of, a tree? A new bit of research for the winter.

The floor of the cave was covered in a dense amalgam of round stones, shot and conglomerated remains – so was the floor in front of it, with a thick layer of pebbles on top.

'Have you seen this?' I said very learnedly to the others when I came up. 'Highly significant. Typical Spanish ballast. I found exactly the same sort of thing in Vigo, in some 1702 wrecks.'

'Really,' said Maurice sarcastically. 'How interesting. I wonder why they put a whetstone in their ballast and a pair of dividers?' And he pulled both these things out of his jam jar.

Louis was not much more impressed than Maurice. He turned out his little green bag. 'But what are all these gold coins doing then, in the middle of this "significant ballast"?'

My theory was getting a bit shaky. It finally collapsed the next day when I lifted up one end of a splendid gold chain and found that it went right down into the black magma and came out again on the other side. My 'significant ballast' was in fact natural concretion. Rust from the cannon balls, gunpowder, chalky deposits, empty shells and sand had petrified with time and now covered most of the remains of the wreck.

Should we try to remove this husk underwater? Dangerous. There was always the risk of breakage. It would in any case have been a lengthy business. So for the first month our work consisted of shifting great chunks of the sea bed out of their honeycomb of solid rock, raising them and loading them aboard, heaving and sweating and straining our backs. Once ashore, and taking every possible precaution, we spent every evening breaking up the concretion, pebble by pebble. From out of this vile magma came escudos and reals, maravedis and ducats, copper buckles, little gold chains, broken pots, lead bullets, leather straps, fragments of cartridges, knives, spoons and forks.

It was there in the cave that the swell had collected the bulk of the débris. Every morning at breakfast, in between the porridge and the eggs and bacon, I would say: 'Francis, Maurice, Louis, Marc, listen! No more risks in the cave. Better to leave a few coins behind than one of us.'

The cave, so-called, was in fact two enormous slabs held up by a few pillars in the middle and some large round stones in front.

The left-hand side was a regular gold mine, the right a silver mine. We shovelled out tons of stones and gravel by the bucket load before painstakingly raking over the bottom. Our efforts created a sort of funnel effect in the cave. In rough weather the water would surge in through the enlarged opening and spray out of the little holes at the back, like a turbine. Gravel flew everywhere and stones rolled around. The ground swell would knock one over if one let it, so one had to work clinging on, with the hoses of one's regulator flapping and bubbles of air escaping in horizontal dotted lines.

We had already jacked out one supporting stone, to clear the way for a large chunk of magma. Now we were setting to work on the pillars, Maurice on one side and me on the other. The pillars were built up of stones tightly packed and 'cemented' together. The natural concretion supported the stones, the stones supported the pillars and the pillars the roof, all two hundred tons of it. We were working right there underneath it at the very back. If the roof had given way we would have been squashed flat as two pancakes. But in among the stones that held up the 200 tons of the 'Rock of Damocles' was a silver candlestick in perfect condition. I could touch it, but it was jammed – only by the little stone that rested on the stone that held the one that supported the other . . . and so on. The trouble was that only the day before I had broken down two other pillars that happened to be on top of some silver phials – could they have been for the apothecaries' potions? – and uncovered a regular vein of pieces of eight. At arms' length, with one eye on the way out and the other on the ceiling, I slipped my crowbar under the stone. Should I push it? I did. The rock moved. Suddenly I was out in the open. What on earth had happened? What was I doing outside? Reflex action? What had that noise been? There had been a sound of stones rolling. Something

169

must have collapsed in the other part of the cave. But Maurice was outside too. He must have set the stone rolling, the idiot. 'Look here, Maurice, come off it.' I made angry signs and snarled into my mouthpiece. 'You're crazy.' I pointed at the massive roof, and mimed – collapse – pancake. After all, I had said it again that very morning! He didn't look impressed. 'How about you, then? I saw you.' He pointed at his eye, at me than at my crowbar. Maurice's sign language is remarkably eloquent. I quickly grasped what he was trying to say. If one of us was a stupid ass, a blundering oaf, an elephant in a china shop, it certainly wasn't him. He had been watching me. He had seen it all. I was a public menace. *He* had been very methodically removing a few tiny pebbles, here and there, of no structural significance whatever. On his side there were still three pillars. Three. He held up three fingers. There was no denying it. But wait a minute. How come he got out in such a hurry too?

Next day I had my candlestick, but the stones I had removed had revealed, in a gaping hole at the base of the pillar, the dull sheen of another. The other half of the pair. I had to have the pair. The following day I had it, but then I spotted a real gem, a brilliant gold object, the biggest yet. A piece of table plate, it must be. A plate? A meat dish? A fruit bowl? A bath? Perhaps we could try shoring up the whole cave somehow. A long job though. Let me see. If this stone moves, then it means it is not holding anything up. That one is a bit trickier. But see how it shines. I am blinded by the reflection of my torch light. An hour later I have the great jewel in my hands. It's a large saucepan handle. Copper. But behind it . . . behind it I can see a long section of the little figure of eight chain, so fine and delicate, disappearing under the base of the last pillar. . . .

The cave is still there, scraped down to the last wrinkle of the last crevice of the last cranny. And no one left any bones behind. The slab is hanging there suspended, defying gravity, a monument to our temerity.

31

'Is the Minister of Defence Aware?'

The people of Port Ballintrae are the nicest in the world. Week after week, our two compressors, lined up like guns in the harbour, back-fired for four hours a day, battering their eardrums, spoiling their quayside walks, ruining week-ends for the whole village, upsetting their holidays and disturbing their convalescences. Anywhere else than in Ireland we would have had stones thrown at us, insults heaped upon us. We would have been asked to go and do our com-pressing elsewhere. Petitions would have been got up and we'd have been accused of disturbing the peace.

But here, the local people used to just put their heads to one side, smile good morning to us and raise their voices slightly to say in our ears: 'Pretty awful weather again today, eh?'

The people of Port Ballintrae are also exceedingly discreet. There we were, diving every single day at the same spot, which just hap-pened to be called Port na Spaniagh, and where – though, of course no one believed it – according to local tradition, there lay the wreck of a large Spanish ship. It must be a coincidence . . . but all the same . . . every evening we used to bring back huge sacks, dripping wet, and immediately stuff them into the lorry and every day a large metal trunk used to go from the lorry to the boat and back again. More coincidences. The fishermen and anyone else who happened to be standing around would discuss yesterday's weather with us, today's inclemency, tomorrow's probable meteorological conditions, and then they might ask one or two general questions, just to be polite and friendly. Louis would reply, with a gentle smile: 'I wonder, could you say it in Auvergnat?' And Maurice would answer: 'Sorri mi not

171

spik ingliche.' I would try to be a bit more precise myself. 'Ah, yes. Didn't I tell you? We're doing a general geological survey of the sea bed, of the volcanic system around Giant's Causeway. Fascinating examples of eruptive crystallography, you know, resistance of lava to marine erosion. All that sort of thing . . . we're making a film about it.' And our Irish friends would keep a straight face and comment nonchalantly. 'Yes indeed, how very interesting. Of course that's what it is.' They looked forward to seeing our eruptive, volcanic underwater film one day; in fact they could hardly wait . . . and they would change the subject. 'And what about lobsters? Do you see many lobsters down there?'

Every day we used to ask our perfectly delightful hostess, Mrs McConaghie, for more empty jam jars, more pickle jars. (Some of us, you see, were rather clumsy and kept breaking them.) Right from the start she must have found it the most natural thing in the world for geological film makers to want. She remained quite unsurprised by it. Not once did Mrs McConaghie even begin to inquire or seem in the least bit puzzled.

With the help of a Belfast solicitor, I had taken certain precautions to ensure the full rights of the expedition in case of any incidents. I had spent days on end in London examining the minutiae of British law concerning the recovery of wreck and sunken ships. A very well informed lawyer had pointed out to me that English law establishes, by a clear and indisputable precedent, that any salvor who is working uninterruptedly on a wreck that he has discovered and buoyed becomes the sole 'salvor in possession'. In the case of the *Girona*, the 'salvor in possession' was me, which meant that I was allowed to fend off any potential rival who might be tempted along by the rumours of the whiff of gold.

So that everything should be in order we had anchored a large red plastic buoy near the cave (not too near, one couldn't be too careful) by a steel rope. It read:

NOTICE TO ALL DIVERS

ALL SUNKEN OBJECTS WITHIN A RADIUS OF 400 YARDS OF THIS BUOY ARE UNDER AN ARCHAEOLOGICAL SURVEY BEING CARRIED OUT BY MR. ROBERT STÉNUIT AS EXCLUSIVE SALVOR. IT IS STRICTLY FORBIDDEN TO TAMPER WITH ANY SUNKEN OBJECTS IN ANY WAY WHATSOEVER. IMMEDIATE ACTION WILL BE TAKEN IN COURT AGAINST TRESPASSERS.

I had also informed the Coleraine Receiver of Wreck of what we were doing and had promised to let him have a complete inventory of finds every two weeks. The Receiver of Wreck is a civil servant in the Department of Customs and Excise, part of the Board of Trade. It is his job to see that 'wreck', properly so called, is placed in the Queen's bond to be sold by the Crown, with a fee to the salvor if no claimant comes forward within one year. Legally, what we were bringing up from the cave was not 'wreck', however.

Our legal position was watertight, but we still felt that with a little discretion and a few white lies we might improve our chances of being spared angry set-tos with other divers, and that would be in everybody's best interest.

The day came, however, when we had to abandon our policy of discretion. We had finished marking out the first section with buoys, and our next job was to raise the gun to uncover what lay underneath, so as to complete our chart. Louis fastened a lifting bag to the small breech-loading piece. Maurice opened a cylinder under it. The rubber filled out, expanding like a frightened blow-fish. The gun quivered, bucked and then, very slowly, moved up to the surface under the fat black bag which was spitting out silvery bubbles. And there waiting for us in the hollow imprint left by the cannon, was a sounding lead.

I made a chain with Louis to shift the blocks in the fissure where it had been lying. Lying among the stones and shapeless cakes of rust and remains of cannon balls were two very simple bronze pestles. Were they apothecaries' pestles, or were they powder pestles? Gunpowder used to be carried in barrels ready made up in large quantities (five parts saltpetre to one of good willow or alder wood charcoal, and one of refined sulphur). But the so-called fine-corned powder was not always fine enough. It contained more saltpetre and was used as a fuse (a trail of 'fine-corn' worked quicker than cotton match steeped in saltpetre) as well as for small arms, muskets, arquebuses and pistols. Perfectionists used to make their own powder according to their personal recipes.

We had previously found, not far from there, two flat mortars, plain bronze slabs, hollowed out on top, where the various ingredients would have been carefully ground up – bronze on bronze so as to avoid any risk of sparks. Musketeers used to steep the mixture in brandy to make it blend better, and then sieve it when it was dry.

I think, in fact, that these are powder pestles and not for medicines.

Elsewhere, at the bottom of a round hole full of silver and cannon balls, I found a superbly decorated apothecary's pestle, a much nobler instrument altogether, in quite another class. Scattered next to it lay fragments of an old crucible mortar, such as one still sees in the shop fronts of old-fashioned chemists.

But back to the cannon. All that was left to do was to secure it properly and tug the whole lot — balloon and all, very slowly — back to Port Ballintrae, now that the tide was pulling with us. Everything went without a hitch, but inevitably our manœuvres were conspicuous. The secret was out. As four of us carried the small cannon to the van, the whole population seemed to converge on the harbour, on foot, on bicycles or in cars. They all wanted to get a look, to touch it, to know all about it. One inquisitive local nearly got his nose caught as the van doors closed behind the gun. From the harbour, the news flew from pub to pub and then, mysteriously, from newspaper office to broadcasting studio. The following day we were beseiged by the press.

But these journalists didn't speak French ... my English was a little imprecise ... and of course an old diver's hearing is not as sharp as it might be. A wreck? What wreck? Had they heard something about a wreck? But tell me where. Oh, I see. We were supposed to have found one? Oh, you know what wrecks are like. Big place, the sea. The Armada? Just a moment, now. Just remind me, who was this fellow Yarmada? A cannon? You know what they are like round here, they'd say anything. Why are we still diving at Port na Spaniagh for the second year? Seems a bit odd? Does it? Well, yes, thank you, our survey is going very well. But the wreck? The gold? Chained skeletons of galley slaves? A film, yes a kind of underwater film. As for the rest, I'm afraid we have an exclusive contract with the *National Geographic Magazine*, very strict. ... I can't tell you any more about the geology. I am so sorry ... thank you again for your interest.

The following day, back at their typewriters, these journalists were tapping out their stories. 'Mystery hangs on cannon barrel found off Antrim coast ... a team of mystery divers are believed to have located the wreck of one of the ill-fated Spanish Armada warships . . . they are reluctant to comment on the matter,' and so on.

Then the television crews put to sea in a hired boat, cameras levelled. How had they found out about it? Once more I had to explain that yes, indeed, there was that cannon; but no, it was not possible to film it. A question of contracts, that was all. Treasure? You mean historical treasure? Why, indeed, yes, some cannon balls of the greatest archaeological interest, stone and iron ones. Gold? But my dear chaps, that's the kind of things you see in the movies. A man doesn't take his safe with him when he goes to war. The *Girona* was, after all, a warship, not one of those galleons from the Americas, packed with jewels and pearls, or with gold and silver ingots. No, no. Only the *capitanas* and the *almirantes* were carrying any of the King's treasure. (That at least was true.)

The programme was broadcast on 24 May, but was fortunately interrupted by a wildcat strike of company technicians. Ha, they said, another cunning move by the mystery divers to tighten the web of silence they have spun round themselves.

One thing did rather worry me. In a recent press conference the public relations officer of the Belfast branch of a big English diving club had made a public announcement of the club's future plans. I read the hand-out in a Coleraine newspaper (*The Northern Constitution*, 18 May), which I picked up quite by chance:

Members of the . . . club are searching for the remains of a Spanish galleon, the *Girona*. . . . We will be diving in three different spots . . . where we have been told the galleon went down. The hunt could take years. Until now we have been hiring local fishing boats with echo sounding equipment. . . . Diviners have been helpful in finding wrecks in other parts of the world and we were wondering if any local diviner would give us suggestions as to the possible location of the *Girona*.

If they were intending to use echo sounding equipment and a diviner to look for a 400-year-old wreck under a chaotic bed of rock, I could well believe that their search might take them years. I did feel, however, that I ought to inform the club of our discovery and invite their members to come and look at what we were doing. So I got my solicitor to send a letter to the chairman saying that I was the finder and 'salvor in possession' of the *Girona* and ready to stand up for my rights. I ended by expressing my warm desire that the club committee would accept our invitation to come and make an observatory dive around the remains of the wreck. The following Sunday the pirates attacked.

On 26 May, twelve of them arrived, twelve divers from Belfast, armed with jemmies and ice axes, housebreakers' sacks and lifting balloons.

There they were, in the harbour dressing beside their cars. They did not announce themselves. They did not introduce themselves. They ignored us. I inquired whether they had received my letter. No answer.

'Careful,' I warned them. 'Don't touch anything. We are in the middle of plotting a chart of the wreck, and besides I am "salvor in possession", and have sole rights over it. You will see our marker buoy; it makes it quite clear.' They look at each other, then at me, but say nothing. I warn the boat-keeper who is taking them out. 'Take care, a boat used for illegal purposes can be seized. If anything happens in the vicinity of the wreck, in the eyes of the law you are an accomplice.'

'Come along now,' he said, 'what will you be thinking of. These gentlemen are going out to look for an outboard motor that was lost last year, and a few lobster pots of mine that have got caught on the bottom. ...' And off he went, making straight for Port na Spaniagh.

A man from Port Ballintrae who went with them, and has since become a good friend of ours, told me in detail what happened. They had taken with them an extra specially clear sighted diviner-sooth-sayer-clairvoyant. He was standing on the prow, eyes fixed on the horizon, using both hands to hold his copper wire dowsing stick. He turned to the boatman. 'Think of something.' 'Gold,' said the mariner. The dowsing stick writhed and twisted. from the way he carried on you would have thought the poor soothsayer could hardly keep a grip on it. It went on like that the whole journey. It could only be a gold mine.

We left after them, but soon overtook them and were the first to anchor above the cave. We had all agreed, whatever happened, they would not take anything away.

Team after team, they came, weighed down with all their appar-

33 We found eight gold chains. The longest measured 2.56 metres and weighed 1,800 kg.
It was absolutely intact

34 Spanish gold coins: one, two and four escudos from the reign of
Philip II. 35 Rare Neapolitan gold escudo from the reign of Charles V,
and his mother, Joan the Mad. 36 A very rare Neapolitan gold ducat
from the reign of Charles V. 37 Father, Charles V, on a Neapolitan gold
ducat. 38 Son, Philip II, on a Neapolitan gold escudo. 39 Portuguese gold
coin: a St Vincent from the reign of John III

40 (*top left*) and 41 (*top right*) Medallion of an unidentified Knight of Alcantara. The cross was originally covered with green enamel. The pear tree and the fountain identify the saint, Julian del Pereiro. The Knights of Alcantara were once known as the Knights of St Julian of the Pear Tree

42 (*above*) I identified three of the Caesars. They are almost certainly Byzantine emperors. Left: Stauracius (unless, of course, it is Julius Caesar). Centre: Michael I Rhangabe (no possible doubt). Right: The younger Constantine (Constantine II) or possibly Vespasian

43 As a child, I often used to dream of the frontispiece of the *Mariner's Mirror*

ORIZONTE

44 (*top left*) An astrolabe being used to measure the height of the sun and to calculate the latitude

45 (*top right*) I was thrilled when I found those very same instruments on the sea bed: the sounding lead, nautical dividers and astrolabes

46 (*left*) A sixteenth-century astrolabe, possibly Spanish, in the National Maritime Museum, Greenwich. It is similar to ours, although ours are unfortunately in very bad condition

47 Maurice raising the esmeril

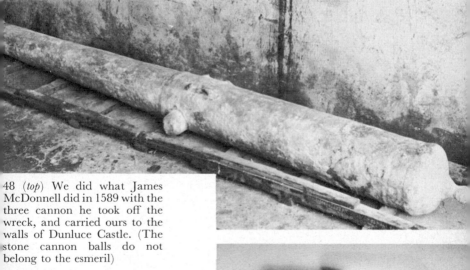

48 (*top*) We did what James McDonnell did in 1589 with the three cannon he took off the wreck, and carried ours to the walls of Dunluce Castle. (The stone cannon balls do not belong to the esmeril)

49 (*centre*) A demi-saker, possibly one of the guns that Medina Sidonia provided for the galleasses from his own arsenal

50 (*right*) The 'servidores' or breech blocks still had inside their cartridges of powder, poplar wood stopper and cotton match

51 The treasure mounting up

atus and searched for hours, all over the place, but nowhere near the wreck. Then one group found the end of one of our lines and followed it to the cave, only to come face to face with our guard. One look at Louis was enough. Bolt upright, motionless, arms crossed, chin set for battle and with an icy glint in his eye, he was about as welcoming as a prison door. Four marauders turned sharply to starboard and made themselves scarce, farther out to sea.

Meanwhile their hired boat had gone back to Port Ballintrae to pick up the next batch. They climbed up on to a small rock to wait for it. On this very same rock where they saw nothing, immediately under where their feet had been, we later found forty gold coins and a little heap of jewels. I really must tell them one day.

And now the next team arrived. They too found one of our lines and followed it to the breech blocks. 'Tankards, apparently,' was how they described them afterwards to the press. This time I swam above them, watching them, without being noticed. Then at the very tip of Lacada point I saw the last one stop. He picked up a small square lead plate, and stuffed it swiftly into his bag. Not only was this stealing, but that piece wasn't even plotted on our chart yet. What really shocked me was having our excavation programme upset like this. We had put too much hard work into it to stand for some irresponsible gang coming along like this and messing up our results.

The souvenir hunter moves on again. I dive down and swim up to him, tapping him lightly on the shoulder. He turns, as though he's just had his foot bitten by a shark. I point to his sack and shake my head. I turn it upside down. The lead falls out. Suddenly I am surrounded. Someone is shaking me from behind. They are all waving their arms about. One of them is trying to pull off my flippers. I kick but he hangs on. I get free and go up to the surface. Four heads bob up. I protest. 'I warned you that you had no right to take anything at all off this wreck.' They threatened me, they remind me in no uncertain terms that we are 'only foreigners' and that we 'better be careful'. And now the abuse starts. What right have I got to take the law into my own hands? And what about that cannon? I had no right to take that either.

Our Zodiac comes up. Louis leaps out to the rescue. Francis is ready to join him. Six divers jump out of the enemy boat and advance like skirmishers. Only the invaders can't forget the fact that they are members of a club. A committee meeting is clearly called for. So in the middle of the ocean motions are proposed, amendments suggested. They vote, and decide, by the required majority, on a retreat. The minutes are taken and they leave, empty-handed. We can get back to work.

A police car was waiting for us when we returned to the harbour. Apparently one of the divers from the city had complained about our 'violence' (not that he had anything to show for it). An extremely polite and rather embarrassed policeman asked us whether we could spare him a few minutes, once we were dressed and warmed up, unless, of course it would be more convenient another day. The club secretary was overcome with confusion and utterly charming. She apologised profusely. No, my letter hadn't arrived (which was true. My solicitor in Belfast hadn't posted it yet). 'What an unfortunate misunderstanding. And when I think,' she added, 'that we dived there only seven or eight weeks ago and didn't see a thing. . . .'

Of course it had all been nothing more than a misunderstanding. The club's Belfast Chairman told the press that the divers in question were a group of members acting quite independently. The official club dive for that Sunday had been held somewhere completely different (which was true). Summoning an extraordinary meeting of the committee, the club called upon its members not to dive at Port na Spaniagh any more, while the legal situation remained unclear. When I started legal proceedings before the Supreme Court of Northern Ireland to insure the protection of our expedition, four of the divers made it their business to assure me, either by telephone, in writing or in person, that they hadn't touched a thing. It was the others. Personally they found the whole affair deeply shocking.

The incident upset me all the more in that the club, at national level, has an outstanding record in the diving world for courtesy and responsibility. For many years I have had some very good friends among its founder members.

But such epic battles are rare in the quiet little village of Port Ballintrae and the next day the BBC broadcast an account of it. It was both detailed and objective. But according to Radio Belfast: 'Belfast divers were rammed when they attempted to take some things off the wreck.' (The prow of an inflatable dinghy is about as lethal a weapon as a beach ball.) For the big London dailies it was a godsend. Better than the Loch Ness monster! Front page headlines: 'Storm on the Sea Bed as Rival Divers Clash' (*Daily Mail*); 'Deep Sea Fight Over Wreck' (*Daily Express*); 'Spanish Treasure Ship Divers in Under Sea Clash' (*Daily Mirror*).

The incident took place on 26 May and I spent the whole of the following week in Belfast in the marble passages of the Law Courts. This time I was diving into the mysteries of British legal procedure. By the following week-end a bewigged judge had clearly reaffirmed our rights.

> There is good evidence that Mr Sténuit is indeed the exclusive salvor in possession. . . . Any person who has taken any object from the wreck, has not acted legally. . . . All underwater swimmers and archaeologists should abstain from taking any object on the bottom of the sea in the vicinity of the wreck of the galleass *Girona*. (Mr Justice Lowry, Supreme Court of Judicature of Northern Ireland, May 31.)

But on 30 May, in the House of Commons in London, the Hon. Member for North Antrim was asking the Minister of Defence the following questions:

> Is the Minister of Defence aware that a wreck at Port na Spaniagh, County of Antrim, ownership of which is vested in his Department, is being damaged and looted by foreign frogmen, and what steps is he taking to deal with this situation?

The M.P. had clearly got his information from Belfast. The Minister replied.

> Ownership of this wreck is not vested in the Ministry of Defence and the prevention of looting of such wrecks is not a Ministry of Defence responsibility . . . It is the responsibility of the Board of Trade.

But meanwhile, some of the good folk of Port Ballintrae, who knew us well and had been shocked by the incident, had taken it upon themselves to telephone their Member of Parliament in London in the middle of the night to explain to him exactly what had happened. The question had already been tabled and it was too late to change the text, but the following day in his comments to the press after the House had risen, the Honourable Member, who now, at last, knew

179

what he was talking about, put the record straight, showing a truly
British sense of justice and fair play.

As far as I know, there is no one who claims ownership of the galleon and as
the Belgian team of frogmen have kept in close touch with the Receiver
of Wreck at Coleraine, they are completely within the law. The Belgians, I
understand, are highly skilled underwater archaeologists and we are very
fortunate that men like these should have come to North Antrim to investi-
gate the possible galleon. . . . I have had to word my question in a particular
way to get it on the Order Paper in the House, but I am casting no reflection
whatever on the divers.

That was the last of the stormy visits.

32

Gold under the Seaweed

It was getting on for the middle of May. The sun was shining and in the space of a week the algae had blossomed into life.

They were everywhere, always moving, dense as a field of sugar cane. They engulfed us, drove us mad. One couldn't talk of a sea bed any more, just thousands of these fluid rubbery tentacles. Paralysed, trapped, swallowed up, enraged, you cut through twenty, forty, a hundred. They didn't move. You pushed them out of the way, in a moment they were back. You could carry them right away and by tomorrow the current would have brought them back and filled up the hole you had just dug.

June. Living at the bottom of the ocean, we didn't see the sun even when it shone. But we had our own barometer: the turned-up nose of our most loyal supporter, four-year-old Wee John McConaghie. Red and peeling already, it told us all we needed to know about the weather. Wee John, the youngest son of our hosts at Port Ballintrae, came down to the harbour every morning to cast off for us, and every evening he was at his post to supervise unloading.

There was often a land breeze now, which brought with it a strong smell of cows. The sea was calmer. We could actually stand up in the Zodiacs to put on our equipment. The fishermen said 'You're lucky. It's the best spring we've had for twenty years.' The water was warmer too, and now we could dive comfortably for five or six hours a day. Our chart was beginning to take shape. For weeks we had been working on it and now we had put a name to each section of the site: the canyon, the corridor, the mound, the basin and so on. The 'esplanade', for example, was actually a basin 100 ft by 50 ft opening out in front of the cave. On the solid rock bed lay a layer of pebbles, stones and rocks of every size, ranging in depth from 1 ft to 10 ft. At first we screened those pebbles with great care, moving them systematically from one section to the next, exposing the solid rock underneath. In this shifting gravel, we found nothing but perfectly round white perrier balls, of beautiful chalky stone. All the metal objects had collected, like nuggets in a riverbed, in the fissures of the rock. Pounded by 400 years of storms, any jewels here had been shattered to smithereens. The sea had bent gold rings, torn stones from their settings and miniatures from their frames; unlinked precious chains; smashed goblets and tankards, leaving only the handles and knobs of the covers (the thickest parts) intact; and crumpled the silver plate. Lead musket balls lay flattened between stones. Small, heavy things, on the other hand, like gold coins, soon sorted themselves out from all the rest and found a sheltered spot at the bottom of a crevice. They remained there undamaged and were still perfectly intact when we found them.

The upper strata here proved to be sterile, so we could shift them without further ado. In the inflatable dinghy a self-powered water pump roared, much to the annoyance of the seagulls, which had to strain to make themselves heard above it in the wind. Attached to it was a 100-ft-long hose, which plunged down into the sea ending in a nozzle, like a fire extinguisher. Using both hands, wedging himself in position with feet and knees, the diver had to try to hang on to it, helped by a lead weight holding down the nozzle. In spite of that, because of the powerful backthrust, it threatened at any moment to turn the hose into an epileptic sea serpent. We had a Galeazzi non-recoil nozzle, an ingenious system which drives some of the jet of water backwards to counteract the backthrust of the main jet. But the wastage of power is considerable and with the small pump which was all we had room for in our tiny boat, we could ill afford it. So the only answer was to hang on for all we were worth.

The high-pressure water jet itself is invisible, but it stirs the sand up in huge dark swirls; pebbles are sent flying, stones jump and roll around, scaling the slopes. One diver can move mountains. The feeling of power is tremendous. But as soon as one reaches solid rock one has to stop and begin sifting through very carefully, by hand, every tiny wrinkle on the sea bed. Here the pieces of eight were worn and smooth, the forks prongless, the ewers and meat dishes were in pieces. Only the gold had remained intact. Because of its weight it fell straight down away from the danger of erosion, and it is not susceptible to chemical corrosion. The escudos that lay waiting for us to find them were shining and bright. Three-quarters hidden in a crevice, they had that same cheeky look about them that a collar stud has when one finds it in its proper place in a drawer after looking for it under every bit of furniture.

It stayed light now until 11 pm. The glistening sea tangles were full of sap, thick as one's arm and taller than a fully-grown man. Their brown thalluses, their fronds and their long velvety strap leaves were themselves covered with the purplish red algae that spread everywhere, all over the red rock and over the grey and black boulders. The interplay of colours on the sea-bed dancing in the sunlight never ceased to be a delight.

The holiday makers had arrived, and in the evening they crowded round the boat-filled harbour to count the gold ingots and the silver. 'I do wonder,' said Maurice 'what on earth they find to do in other years, when there aren't any frogmen.' One might ask what they find to talk about too, those years. Already the most fantastic rumours were going around concerning what we are doing.

According to them, we have, very discreetly, exported to the United States enough gold to replenish Fort Knox. An American photographer is supposed to be slipping the 'little stuff' over. A local telephone call warned the customs of this, but, alas, too late. Another story is that a customs officer, an accomplice of the divers, that is, was stopped at the border with Eire and found to have jewels and gold coins in the back of his car.[1]

The teacher in the village school set her little class 'The Frogmen' as a composition subject. She showed us the results. There was no doubt in the minds of the local children. We had found 200 tons of gold ingots, as well as several gold cannon. For their parents even that was not enough. We had also, it seems, found some silver pistols, in perfect condition.

Nonetheless it is true that with our joke boats, our navvies' tools and a few rubber bags, those of us who followed behind the photographic team, were everyday bringing up the sort of treasure one reads about in story books. I had found in the cave a marvellous chased gold salamander, winged, with every scale engraved and encrusted with rubies. A few feet away Louis found a strange gold fragment, a point, apparently off some star shaped jewel, with a fleur-de-lis shaped link to hang it from, and a double gold ring to thread a ribbon through. Two days later, a bit farther along, he had spotted, with his practised eye, a straight edge on the side of a little black ball, about the size of an apple and made of that magma that clogged everything up. Carefully he scratched the edge. Under the black, it was gold.

That evening I plunged the ball into a dilute solution of acetic acid. The next morning there was some black liquid in the jar and a slightly pocked gold Malta cross. With the star-shaped fragment the jewel was complete, except for the end of one of its eight points. I knew I could count on Louis, and by the end of the week he had the last piece. This fragment still had traces of the white enamel on it that originally covered both faces of the cross.

By that stage, we had twelve gold coins on the inventory (one, two and four Spanish escudos, and scudi from the Two Sicilies). In my wildest dreams I had visions of the day when I would find another twelve all by myself. The time I found fifteen all in one day I enjoyed a minor triumph. I paid for it the next day, when Maurice found twenty and I found only a bronze bootnail. And to tell the whole truth I must admit that modesty was not the only reason why my triumph that day was so minor, or why afterwards I took care never to mention the fifteen-coin day again.

The moment I surfaced, I rushed to have Louis photograph me, first in black and white and then in colour, hands full of gold. And then to make it look more natural, I tried spilling the coins like manna from one hand to the other. One of the fifteen coins, a four escudo piece from Seville, spilled so realistically it jumped out of my right hand on to the back of the dinghy and then – splash – into the water.

Rarely in my life have I felt so abashed. I broke off the photographic session there and then. I gave Louis the coins (or maybe he snatched them out of my hands immediately, to put them away somewhere safe – that's the sort of detail I prefer not to remember), and I dived down again. I never did recover that fifteenth coin.

As the weeks went by we widened our area of research. I now realised that the sea must have scattered the wreck débris over an enormous area, for wherever we looked, our luck seemed to follow us. Ten or twelve gold-coin days were standard now. On 12 July we celebrated our hundredth gold coin, and by then we already had 500 silver ones on the inventory.

And that was not all. As a child I had pinned up on my wall a reproduction of the frontispiece of *The Mariner's Mirror*, published in 1583. It showed a pilot in a greatcoat holding a sounding lead, and on either side of him an astrolabe and a pair of dividers. This picture of my childhood was recreated for me again, in colour this time, the day I found an astrolabe lying slightly askew on the sea-bed, and again when Maurice brought up the identical bronze dividers, scarcely bent, and Francis found the sounding lead. (See plate 44.)

One day, at the far end of the site, on Lacada Point, sticking out from under a protective coating of black magma, harder than stone, made of rusted cannon balls, kitchen débris (animal bones, charcoal, broken pots) and cartridges, and cemented again by the gunpowder, I spotted a small piece of wood. 'Part of an oar,' I motioned to Maurice. He came and looked. 'No,' he waved, putting an imaginary gun to his shoulder. The next day, after three hours work with a hammer and a chisel, I had uncovered 6 in. of a musket stock. On the third day, having worked my fingers sore to get through that dense mass, I could see the chamber. All that was left of the barrel was a grey paste sticking to the wood and to the rock. It was disintegrating before my very eyes with every movement of the swell. The firing piece had gone down loaded. I found the round lead ball still in the breech. Working at the rate I was, it took me the rest of the week to finish digging it out. Then, firing piece in hand, I swam up and in pantomime fired a victory salvo into the air.

At the same spot, I found a scrap of black velvet in the magma, a bit of doublet perhaps, and some leather thongs. And then one day I came across the most fragile object of all, the most unexpected: a delicate hexagonal point, made of rock crystal, about two inches long, set in a little silver top. And suddenly everything fell into place. The countless rounded silver phials that we had been finding bits of everywhere, had not as I thought originally contained apothecaries' remedies, but scent. (See plate 27.) Every nobleman, every hidalgo must have had one. When the wind brought to their nostrils the suffocating stench of 244 rowers, living in a shirt and chained night and day to their places, they would pass the crystal dippers, loaded with scent, under their curled moustaches. (Another explanation has been suggested to me by an English expert: because of its strange optical qualities, rock crystal was thought to have certain magical powers. It might have been some sort of charm to hang on a chain.)

And finally, amid the kitchen remains, I found an absolutely unique relic, unhoped for, incredible, perfectly preserved, in the dense gangue that must have encrusted it from the very first, protecting it from erosion and from all contact with oxygen. In a mass of magma, made of broken crockery, charcoal and one bird's feather and in mint condition, I found the only Armada plumstone in the world.

NOTES

1. In fact everything we found on the expedition was noted down the very same day on the official inventory for the Receiver of Wreck, and then deposited in a safe in a Belfast bank, or, where necessary, given immediate preservation treatment. This was carried out either in the house where we were staying or in the preservation laboratory in Belfast, founded jointly by Queens University and the Ulster Museum. Our experience has shown that honesty in activity like ours elicits one of two responses in conversation: incredulity or piteous contempt. The most common response is of the wink, nudge and conspiratorial smile type, accompanied by asides like: 'Why, naturally, but you pocketed some for yourself on the quiet, I hope' – a remark which gives an interesting hint as to what the behaviour of the interlocutor would have been in our place.

33

The Summer of the Century

The summer was drawing to a close. The tourists were leaving, and there were six divers who were beginning to feel a little lonely.

Only Wee John McConaghie stuck loyally to his post. 'The best summer of the century,' they said. Even the hotel keepers agreed. There never was a summer like it in Ireland, not in living memory. The barometer needle never moved from set fair. The sea was limpid. Never did we feel the least bit cold. Once more the scene under water had quite changed. A new layer of white algae had started to grow on top of the red ones that were already covering the brown algae.

We raised the anchor under a huge black balloon, and the second cannon. While Francis was measuring it before drawing up his plan of it (see Appendix III), I remembered what Carew wrote to the Lord Deputy in 1589. 'Yet those pieces that be under the water I presume are there still. . . .' Well, yes, Sir George, you were quite right. (See plates XI–XIII.)

Like other objects that sank to the bottom, the lead too escaped the notice of the Scottish captain hired by Sorley Boy to harvest the crop of shipwreck. We raised a ton and a half of lead in the form of ingots or plates. It was not ballast, as Boyle had thought. At that time Spanish ships were ballasted with round stones, taken from river banks. The lead was raw material for casting musket shot and arquebus balls. Most of the ingots had Roman numerals stamped on them, or crosses potent. These markings did not relate to the weight, for ingots of equal weight were stamped differently. Perhaps they indicated for which ships' companies the ingots were earmarked.[1] One of them had on it the monogram of St Peter, a P inside an E, forming a key. Could that one have been cast for a Vatican galley?

Every evening, after work, I made a tour of the site to check on the others' progress for the daily report.

Francis's flippers could be seen from way off, flapping about at the end of his long legs among the fronds. He was working head down on Lacada Point. He must have been waist deep in a narrow pot hole, feeling his way around. From the knees down he was hidden in a fine sand cloud. I spotted two sword pommels in his jam jar, finely decorated with plaited copper wire. The pommels were wooden ones, typical of the sixteenth century. All the rest, blade, hilt guard, and hand shield would have been made of iron. Nothing was left of them. He emerged for a moment from his sand cloud to drop three gold links into his jar. We found one or more of these links virtually every day throughout our three excavation seasons. The heavy chain that they made up had been scattered by the sea over some 1,000 sq. ft. And yet elsewhere Maurice found far more fragile chains still intact.

Maurice had said to me: 'If you come over to my corner today, you won't know where you are. You won't recognise it. I've practically built a motorway.' It was true. Five- and six-ton boulders had been bound with three steel bands and raised under bunches of lifting balloons, leaving behind a wide avenue. Maurice was nowhere to be seen. His air cylinder was lying on the bottom, with a long rubber hose running out of it. I followed it, looking for the other end of the demand valve and for the man who had it in his teeth. A bit farther on I saw bubbles percolating up from under a large flat stone. Maurice was probably crawling about busily under there, torch in hand, in pursuit of the missing rubies from the fragile, intricate baroque pendant, of which as yet he had found only fragments, mixed up with various rings and Neapolitan gold ducats bearing Philip's profile.

It was Maurice's first dive for a fortnight. He had been out of action with a dislocated finger and a crushed left hand. This was the story as he told it to me.

'I had just rolled back my stone, you know, the big four-ton one. Underneath there was another five or six hundred-pound one. It moved. Great! I thought I could roll it out of the way. I was just pushing it upwards, to get it over a ridge, when – crash! My support slipped. Down it came. Right on my hand. It hurt. Everything was spinning. I'm going to faint, I thought. I'm going to drown. Drown. Was I scared! When I came to, I found myself pinned to the bottom, caught by my left hand. What was I to do? The first thing you think of is your air. How much longer did I have? Then I remembered that I could still reach the crow bar with my right hand. I managed to stretch out my arm, grab hold of it and slip it under the boulder. I pushed as hard as I could and managed to release my hand. But when I took my glove off later in the boat it was not a pretty sight.'

Louis was currently working east of the red line rock, in a vast expanse of stones and sand. He moved with calm and precision, but he moved with great power. With his parachutes, his bucket and shovel, and his tireless left hand sweeping the sand up like a windmill sail, he sifted through 30 cubic feet each day. In the green bag where he put all his finds, there was a diamond ring – there must originally have been ten stones in it, but only two were left – a little solitaire ruby in a gold setting, two two-escudo pieces, some silver goblet handles, a few shapeless bits of copper and some fragments of gilded table plate.

Marc had laid aside his cameras and was now on the lookout for lead. Gold and precious stones had little attraction for Marc. His thing was lead bullets. That was all he ever found. But he found them everywhere. One could not risk leaving an empty container lying around. The next thing one knew it was full of lead. Little bullets, big bullets, round ones, flat ones, musket balls, arquebus shot, pistol bullets and case shot – he did not miss one. He stopped only to feed large fat pink worms that he found under stones to our familiar fish. The fish had found himself a girl friend; quite a bit smaller, pink with brown marbly streaks, pretty though. Now there were two of them, following us wherever we went, gulping down the assorted prey – larvae, worms, and other creatures – that we disturbed as we went. Marc was going over everything again, checking our work with a specially designed metal detector. He would reprimand us for every little forgotten fragment. 'For the archaeologist,' he would say, quite rightly, 'a piece of a lead bullet is just as important as a chest full of doubloons.'

For all of us the remains of the wreck were strangely evocative. The gold summoned up figures of long dead hidalgos as clearly as if we had stolen the ducats from their half open purses. The silver crucifix that Francis found, all eroded and covered with a black patina, astonishingly simple and modern in style, carried with it a strong whiff of the mendicant friar who wore it. We could see it hanging from the girdle of his rough robe, beating against his legs as he strode up and down the deck of the galleass. The copper, pewter and lead medallions, mass-produced, bearing images of the Virgin Mary, Christ or the Holy Family, medallions bought on some pilgrimage, told us of the death of the galley slave who must have clutched them in the palm of his hand, as he murmured a silent prayer and his irons and chains dragged him down to the bottom, with only his ragged shirt for a shroud.

Since the day I first met them in Florida, I have been in love with dolphins, man's cousins returned to the sea. Like all divers I am deeply envious of their perfect adaptation to this world where I can never be more than a tolerated intruder. I have studied them, fascinated, and it was with much pleasure that I once wrote a book to their greater glory.[2] The day Francis brought up with great ceremony a gold-plated dolphin that he had just found, I felt a real pang of temptation. My collection, after all . . . I have porcelain dolphins, ceramic dolphins, copper ones, stone ones and any number of others. But a sixteenth-century Armada dolphin . . . a dolphin with an upturned tail, on a base of waves, with two big round eyes, a dolphin that must have formed part of the decoration of the base of a table clock, like the one I had once admired in the Jewellery Room in the Victoria and Albert Museum in London – that would be the jewel of my humble collection.

And how about the other one? The little silver one that looked like a tadpole or an inverted comma, and which must have been a cup handle or the knob of a lid? And the gold dolphin? The gold dolphin whose nose was a tooth pick and whose tail was an ear pick – an instrument in common use at the time. (The American treasure hunter, Kip Wagner, found among the remains of the *capitana* of the 1715 *Flota* in Florida, a gold oriental jewel on a gold chain made of 2,176 flower-shaped links, which combined the functions of whistle, insignia of office, tooth pick and ear pick.)

And the dragon dolphin, wrapped around a silver naval pea-whistle, forming a ring to hang it from? That whistle must have been the insignia of office of one of the five ships' captains drowned on the *Girona*. Whistles of this type had been in use in all fleets since the thirteenth century; originally for giving orders, they subsequently became the actual insignia of office.

It was at night particularly that temptation really needled me. I visualised the little showcase that would house my enriched collection, the right plinths, the angle of lighting, and then, finally, with a heavy heart, I put the complete fortnightly inventory in the post for the Receiver of Wreck, with no omissions.

One day Maurice and I went to take a sounding quite some way from Lacada Point, in a little cove where I reckoned any drifting bodies would have been piled up by the swell.

The sea was like oil. The sun – all things being relative – positively tropical. Not a ripple on the water, not a breath of wind. The rocky shore is almost vertical here. There would be no chance of finding a foothold here in bad weather, especially at the end of October, when there aren't even any algae to hang on to. Farther along the shore is nothing but a mass of rocks. Any survivors who came anywhere near would have had their heads cracked open on them by the waves. The thick layer of foam that lies on the water when it's rough would have suffocated anyone who tried to swim away. At the foot of the vertical rock stretches a long stone-paved corridor. Recently, when I was doing an exploratory dive there, I found one of those veined marble eggs, pierced through from end to end (what they were for remains a mystery). It was clearly visible among the stones. I had found one like it earlier in front of the cave, where we later found hundreds of coins and dozens of jewels.

It was not very deep, only about 14 ft of water. It was possible to work there only when it was absolutely calm – the Zodiac bobbing about overhead. Yet another advantage of these extremely seaworthy and stable dinghies is that one can take them anywhere. Where a wooden boat would be smashed into a hundred pieces and a steel frame would bend and burst its rivets, this sort bounces off the rocks unharmed, like a football. The pump was on board and Francis was on duty, keeping an eye on it.

Maurice wedged himself in between two rocks and set to work clearing the corridor. Almost immediately he found a gold ring. Excitedly, he swam over to show it to me. It is bent and the setting is empty but one can still read the inscription: MADAME DE CHAMPAGNEY MDXXIIII. Our first dated find! What an excitement! But wait – 1524 . . . 88 minus 24 equals 64. Whoever the beauty was who gave this ring, she gave it 64 years before the Armada sailed. So it can't have been her lover who was wearing it, unless he was well into his eighties and most exceptionally faithful to his first love. (See plates 30 and 31.)

Already the name fascinated me. I swore to search until I knew every detail of the family history. I must know who it was that wore the ring at Port na Spaniagh on 26 October 1588. And why. And whether Madame de Champagney was dark or fair, pretty or ugly.

I left my hole to go and work with Maurice. He held the hose and looked in the direction of the jet, watching the fan of flying stones. I looked from on top. It was a worthwhile precaution: he spotted a four escudo piece that I missed as it flew up, and stopped to pick it up. An hour later, it was I who saw a gold ring rolling among the pebbles, which he hadn't seen from where he was standing. It was intact. The setting was an exquisite little salamander, gracefully coiled into an S shape. Another salamander! Could it have any connection with the first one? Did one of the noble lords on board have a salamander in his coat of arms?

For three hours we watched the water jet carve its way through the stones. We moved the whole floor of the corridor in one direction, and the next day we went over it all over again in the opposite direction, just to make quite sure. But there was nothing more.

The following day it was still like a mill pond. Francis and Maurice took advantage of it to empty out all the potholes and crevices at the top of Lacada Point. You had to be a diviner even to spot them because they were all full to the brim and cemented over by rock-coloured stones camouflaged by algae. They found some earthenware pots, a fragment of window glass, a few scattered links, a gold chain, some spherical buttons, and then, under a protective layer of bullets, a complete pewter plate.

I had found myself in a vast basin some way off from Lacada Point, full of pebbles, dead algae and vegetable debris. It was only logical to assume that in a basin such as this fifty bodies at least must have piled up, along with all their money and their jewels. We were going to pick their pockets.

As soon as Louis turned the hose on the pebbles he stirred up an inky black mushroom cloud of mud. Suspended vegetable compost made the water so dense we could hardly see farther than 6 in. ahead. With my nose to the jet, I kept my eyes skinned for the glint of gold, at the same time pricking up my ears for the dull clunk of a gold coin. We worked in strips and progress was slow. As soon as we had passed, the ever shifting stones filled the basin again. Nothing. Nothing at all. If there were fifty bodies here, then they must have been paupers' bodies.

The most beautiful jewels of all came to light during the last few days. Our finds were beginning to be more and more spaced out. We didn't talk about it but we were beginning to feel that the end was in sight. Still I wondered whether we had actually exhausted the lode, or whether we had done no more than skim the top of the cream. And thinking forward to the next season, I made some rapid soundings everywhere we hadn't already covered.

In the spring Louis had found two oval, baroque medallions in finely worked gold, topped by a triton with a long seaweed moustache, and enamelled emerald green and purplish red. One had been in front of the cave, the other nearly 50 yds away. From both of them the central stone was missing.

Then, just as I was coming to the end of a series of soundings in a virgin area, on the sand and gravel that I was scooping from under an unsteady rock – there, new and shining, was a lapis lazuli cameo of a Roman emperor in profile, wearing a crown of laurels, set in one of Louis's gold medallions and framed by eight perfect pearls.

Under the same stone, after an hour's feverish work, breathing out as hard as I could so as to squeeze further under, I caught hold of another one. I felt sure that there must be more. I was using my hand to sweep little heaps of gravel towards me. Then, like a poker player who fans his cards open as slowly as possible, I spread out the little pile, grain by grain, storing up the suspense for as long as possible. To get to the back, I had to go right inside, twisting like an eel. The edge of the face plate of my mask jammed when I pushed my head forward. It filled with water. I had to screw up my face to unstick the bottom edge and blow into it through my nose to empty it as it filled. But I had gained 6 in. and, stretching my arm out of joint to scrape the last corner, I felt the pearls of a third jewel under my finger tips.

For some time I stayed quite still, looking at them lying there on a pink rock. Each profile was different. The likenesses must have been copied from classical models. Could they be the twelve Caesars of

193

Suetonius's history? It really is true: the sea-bed is without doubt the richest museum in the world.

Louis and I spent the next few days eagerly turning over every stone around there. I found a sixth jewel, intact and with not a scratch on it. Louis, meanwhile, followed my example and had edged himself in to work in a narrow crevice, between two large boulders leaning one against the other. When he found his air was getting low and decided to go up, he had to come out backwards. His cylinder jammed. Trapped, he couldn't get out, couldn't move. His knife was strapped to his left calf. He stretched to reach it but failed – he tried again. By twisting both his wrist and knee he managed to inch them closer together. He gripped the handle of his knife with his fingertips, and feeling his way, tried to find the cylinder straps behind his back. He hacked away at everything he could reach. Snap! He released the cylinder. It swung round. He was free. He backed out and swam calmly up, carrying the air tank.

He went back there the next day and raised the rock under one of our bunches of balloons. The seventh Caesar was waiting underneath for him. And then, quite by chance, a few days later, some way away from there, he came across an eighth medallion, without its central cameo. My question was answered. The next year we should have four more Caesars still to find.

It was the end of September. The harbour was completely deserted. Even Wee John had abandoned us. For two days we saw him walking smartly up and down practising carrying his satchel. Now he had gone to school.

It was back to school for us, too. We let the air out of the dinghies. I counted the cannon balls again, photographed the jewels, the chains and the buttons, cleaned the black crust off the last of our 140 gold coins, our 600 silver coins and 60 copper ones. We said our good-byes and were on the road again.

It was libraries that led me to the treasure and now the treasure was sending me back to them. That winter, in Brussels, I must clear up all the mysteries.

Who was she, this Madame de Champagney, who must have already been a great-grandmother in 1588? What was the significance of these two salamanders, and the order of knighthood, if it is one? Which order, whose, and who was the Knight of Malta,

On the cameos, who's who? I thought I had recognised Julius Caesar, and the one who looked like Mussolini might be Vespasian. But how about the others? Who made them, in what workshop? I knew nothing about glyptics. I would have to start from scratch. Which Renaissance goldsmith engraved the medallions and our marvellous jewels, and where, in what town, what country? For what patron and what fee? And the saint's profile – or is it a Pope – on a large lead plaque? And the church on the other side, what church is that?

And the young mistress, who with one hand gave her ring and her heart, while with the other she unclasped her belt, was she fair or dark? Who did she mourn? And after the tears, was she quickly consoled or did she die of a broken heart?

And these thousands of fragments of silver? How on earth could one fit the puzzle together? And what were the two guns called, exactly? Those lead things of all sizes, shaped like truncated pyramids, with a round hole through them, that we found everywhere, what could they have been for? And the pierced marble eggs? And what other vital questions were there that I hadn't even thought of asking yet?

NOTES

1. In a letter to the King from Lisbon, the Duke wrote: 'The lead ingots have been distributed ... 30 quintals to each of the five regiments.
2. *Dolphin, Cousin to Man.* (New York and London 1968)

34
Madame de Champagney

'Madame de Champagney 1524.' Engraved in fine capitals in gold, that name more than any other was going round and round in my head. I thought about it all the way back. It was a large man's ring, much too big for my finger, obviously made to be worn, clearly visible, over a glove. But who wore it and for whose fair eyes? I could hardly wait to get back and race off to the Bibliothèque Royale.

From the archives to the sea and back again, I had to complete the circuit. I was determined to, because it is this fundamental interaction between the library and the ocean, between the intellectual effort of research and the physical exertions of diving, that has always given me the total physical and mental satisfaction that comes only with total exhaustion.

The first thing I found out was that there were three villages in Franche Comté called Champagney. One was in Haute Saône: in the fifteenth and sixteenth centuries the lordship of the manor belonged to the Abbots of Lure. To the Abbots? No Madame, then. What about the others? The second was in the Jura (in the Dôle region) and the third in the Doubs region, near Besançon.

In 1588, the lordship of this Champagney belonged to the diplomat Frédéric Perrenot – well, there's an old friend, who was Chancellor to Charles v, King's major domo under Philip ii, Governor of Antwerp, then Head of the Finance Committee in Flanders. But he sided with the people against Philip ii and was exiled by him to Franche Comté, where he ended his days in deepest gloom. Born 1536, died 1602. He was Count of Champagney and Baron of Renaix.

So he didn't die in the Armada. In any case he was no fighting man, and can have had nothing to do with it, since he was the man who in

1588 was leading the Spanish delegation at the Bourbourg Peace Conference. His Madame de Champagney was a very rich widow, Constance de Berchem. He had married her thanks to the good offices of the Duke of Alba. Constance was not born in 1524, so the ring must have been a family heirloom.

From incomplete family trees in various general or universal (but invariably contradictory) biographies, I set myself to work tracing back through this whole complex family history. Finding this was a step in the right direction: 'His brother Jérome died in 1554, from a gunshot wound received at Montreuil and left him the estate of Champagney in Franche Comté, of which he took the name.' This brother Jérome, the heir to the title, was indeed born in 1524. The ring, then? Was it not a present from the happy mother to her husband on the occasion of the birth of this son, who was to inherit the maternal land? And so if our Madame de Champagney was the proud mother, what was *her* name?

A few more hours spent leafing through fat, worn, leather-bound volumes, and I had my answer. Jérome was the son of Nicolas Perrenot (1486–1550) and Nicolasa or Nicole Bonvalot, daughter of Jacques Bonvalot, citizen of Besançon, and Lord of the Manor of Champagney. She was renowned for her beauty from Burgundy to the Netherlands. It was she who brought the title as her dowry to her husband, Nicolas Perrenot, Chancellor, Guard of the Seals, Minister of Charles v and already Lord of the Manors of Granvelle, Chantennay, Cantecroix and other places.

On the death of his Chancellor, Charles v wrote to Philip: 'My son, I am deeply grieved at the death of Granvelle, for we have lost, you and I, a loyal and trusted friend.' Nicole had borne him eleven children: six daughters and five sons. The eldest was Antoine, the famous Cardinal de Granvelle (1517–1586), patron of the arts and a highly cultured man. He was successively Bishop of Arras, Councillor to Margaret of Parma, Inquisitor in Flanders, Cardinal, Archbishop of Malines, Viceroy in Naples, and Philip ii's Prime Minister in Spain. Jérome, born in 1524, was their third son and sixth child. After Antoine came Thomas and Jérome, then Charles and Frédéric. As for the daughters, they are not considered worthy to be included in the biographies.

I now knew who my 'Madame de Champagney' was and I knew the

possible reason for her gift to her husband of a ring engraved with her name and set with a fine, large stone. If it wasn't for the birth of their third son, it might have been to mark their tenth wedding anniversary. Although the date of Nicole and Nicholas's marriage is not known, we do know that their second child, Antoine, was born in 1517. If he was conceived in 1516, the first Marguerite was probably conceived in 1515, so the marriage could well have taken place in 1514.

Now I wanted to know on whose hand the ring reached Port na Spaniagh. I waded about for a bit and then the answer came to me in a flash. It was in Antonio de Herrera. In fact, it was in the third part of his *General History of the World*, published in Madrid in 1612. He devotes six pages to a complete list of important participants, taken from Zuñita: 'It is only right to name the men of quality who accompanied [the Armada], following in this the detailed account of the chronicler, Geronymo de Zuñita. . . .'

de Antonio de Herrera.

de Orgaz, don Tomas Perrenoto, ſobrino del Cardenal Granuela; don Diego Odorio, ſobrino del Marques de Aſtorga, don Ramon La-

nando de Queſada, de Vb Fernando de Ricalde Nevi Iladolid, Ruy gomez de H Cuellar, don Melchior Pi

Reading through his endless list, I found, at the top of page 97 (lib. IIII, capitulo IIII), this name: Don Tomas Perrenoto Sobrino del Cardenal Granvela. . . . The Cardinal's nephew! Nicole Bonvalot's grandson. Finding this name in the Reading Room of the Bibliothèque Royale, I found at the same time a fresh pleasure, an echo of that which I had already experienced under the Atlantic when I first found the ring. The mystery was solved.

All the same, I still had to make quite sure, to cross-check. The young Don Tomas had sailed, I knew that, but on which ship? I soon unearthed another list (published by Duro) which gave his name among the passengers on the *rata*. Perfect. He had left on the right ship. But he might have disembarked on the way, or changed ships as so many others did – Prince Ascoli, for example, Marolin de Juan, Recalde. . . .

Did he ever get to Blacksod Bay? Yes. James Machary, the Irish sailor who was left behind at Killybegs, mentions him in his account to the English of the *rata*'s passengers arriving on his ship (the *Duquessa Santa Ana*).

> A great ship called the *Rat* of 1000 tons or more in which was Don Alonzo de Leva and an Earl called Count de Paris [de Paredes] ... also a gentleman named Don Tomaso de Gran Bello [de Granvelle,] a man much favoured with the King, of great revenue and a natural Spaniard born; with divers good Captains and other gallant gentlemen. ...

Perfect, all was well as far as Lough Ross More Bay. Don Tomas had indeed re-embarked on the *Duquessa*. But what if he had been left ashore at Killybegs? This time it was a letter from a survivor of another wreck (de Cuellar) written from Antwerp in 1589 (and already quoted) that held the answer. In describing his arrival at Dunluce, whence he intended to reach Scotland, he goes into some detail:

> I travelled across the mountains and uninhabited regions and suffered much hardship, as God knows, then after twenty days' journey I reached the place where Don Alonzo de Leiva, the Conde de Paredes and Don Tomas de Granvela had perished, with many other gentlemen whose names would fill a score of pages. ...

I too felt that I had arrived.

I wrote to the Library at Besançon for a portrait of Tomas and one of our Madame de Champagney. With great courtesy, the librarian, Madame Paris, sent me a copy of the complete family tree drawn up by General Jean Tiburce de Mesmay. She went into even greater detail:

> Your discovery is most interesting. The records do in fact contain mention of Cardinal de Granvelle's nephew, who met his death in this disaster at the age of 22. It was Jean Thomas Perrenot, Lord of the Manor of Maîche, son of Thomas Perrenot, not Jérome, Lord of the Manor of Chantonnay and other places. Curiously enough, he does not feature in the most complete of the printed family trees, but in one or two manuscript documents. ... His grandmother was indeed Nicole Bonvalot. ... Unfortunately, although there are quite a few portraits of the Cardinal and of his father, here in the library we have neither of the two people in whom you are especially interested. According to one scholar: 'the portraits of all Chancellor Perrenot's descendants, have perished, in their dozens; leaving both history and art the poorer.'

There is, however, a famous portrait of Nicole Bonvalot by Titian, painted in 1584, now apparently in the United States.

I never did find this painting, in spite of lengthy researches. But what I did find at Besançon was a portrait (painted at the same time also by Titian) of her husband the Chancellor. Alas, although he is wearing a ring, it is not ours.

Jean Thomas, born in 1566, cannot have had a very clear memory of his grandmother, who died when he was only four years old, but there is no doubt that it was her ring that he was wearing when the suffocating yellow foam of Port na Spaniagh flooded his lungs, when the stormy waves beat him unconscious and drowned him at the foot of those black rocks.

We had also found two gold salamanders, one a ring setting, the other a pendant (43 mm. long, 33 mm. wide, 5–6 mm. thick, weight 19 grams). Who did they belong to, and why salamanders?

It did cross my mind that it might be a charge from the coat of arms of one of the dead men. We had found the salamander ring right beside young Thomas's. It might have belonged to him as well, and the three gold and three silver coins that we found nearby might have been the small change from his pockets. Champagney, Granvelle, Chantonnay – in none of their coats of arms does one find anything but gules lions, spread eagles issuant and boars' heads. As for the Lords of the Manor of Maîche, they did not bear arms.

Working from Zuñita and all other lists and mentions of passengers on the three ill-fated vessels, I drew up a complete list of all those who might have been in the *Girona*. To make doubly sure, I added all those who took more than one servant with them. But, however hard I looked at their shields in the illustrated armorials, I could not find so much as the smallest salamander twisting anywhere among them. I tried working backwards from a classification by heraldic charges, but not one of the families with a salamander was represented in the Armada. One of the salamanders had wings, so I thought I would look under dragon. Still no luck.

So? An English expert has pointed out that salamanders were frequently carried as a charm against fire. Legend has it that salamanders can extinguish flames and live in fire. The salamander is the

Cabalistic spirit of fire, and in coats of arms it is almost always shown surrounded by flames. (Francis I had it on his shield to symbolise his ardour in love.)

Ours may well have been mere charms, or perhaps I was looking for something that just was not there to be found. Salamanders were also a fashionable Renaissance motif, and ours may simply have been decorative, like the scrolls and flowers on some of the other jewels, like the dolphins or the grimacing old men on some of the forks.

35

'Fabricio Spinola, Captn.'

Now for the Malta Cross. Who had that belonged to, but first, was it actually a Malta Cross? An English Knight of Malta, who, like all his friends in the Order, was fascinated by our find, had his doubts.

I applied myself to the study of military orders of knighthood and learned that in the sixteenth century there were sixteen active orders. Only three, apart from the Order of Malta, had as insignia the eight-pointed cross of St Stephen. The eight points symbolise the eight beatitudes mentioned in the Gospels (Matthew, v, 1–12) and, by extension, perfect happiness. The four arms stand for the four virtues: prudence, temperance, fortitude and justice.

There was the French Order of the Holy Ghost, set up by Henry III in 1578 to replace the declining Order of St Michael, but their white enamelled cross was pommelly. It had little apples or balls at its points and was cantoned (i.e. decorated between the arms of the cross) with lilies; in the centre it had a dove. All one hundred members of the Order had to be French.

Then there was the Tuscan Order of St Stephen, founded in 1562 by Cosimo de Medici to combat pirates and defend the Catholic faith, but that cross was enamelled in red, edged in gold (while ours still had traces of white enamelling) and was cantoned with crowns and lilies.

And thirdly, there was the cross of the military Order of St Lazarus of Jerusalem, founded by the Crusaders in the twelfth century, originally to help lepers. It became a military order a century later. Their cross was an eight-pointed one, with lilies between the arms, but the Order had hardly developed outside France, England and Austria, and was in any case declining fast by the sixteenth century.

There could be no doubt, then: our cross (diameter 62mm., width from point to point 20 mm., weight 37 grams) must have belonged to a Knight of Malta. But which one? (See plate XXXIX.)

The only Knight of Malta mentioned in the countless documents on the Armada is Hugo de Moncada, the Captain General of the Squadron of the Galleasses of Naples, killed at Calais on the *capitana San Lorenzo*. An engraving reproduced in a number of books actually shows a Hugo de Moncada with the white, eight-pointed cross on his breastplate. I think this engraving is in fact of a different Hugo de Moncada, the one who was first Captain General of the Ocean Sea and who was killed at Genoa in 1528. Not that our Moncada was not also a Knight of Malta; this much is clearly borne out by documents of the period.

But his cross could never have been on the *Girona*, because after Calais there was absolutely no contact between the survivors of the *San Lorenzo* and the rest of the Armada. Don Hugo's cross must have disappeared in the pillaging after the ship had run aground, probably finding its way into the pocket of one of Lord Howard of Effingham's officers, unless one of his servants managed to take it to France with him when he fled.

I went back over the list of noblemen who sailed in the *rata*, the *Duquessa* and the *Girona*, delving into their lives, going through their genealogies. I set off on many a long journey through families, over the centuries and across continents. The conquistadores took me to Chile, to Peru, to Colombia and Florida – a paleologue to Byzantium. Admirals took me across the seven seas. But while many of them must have been knights of one military order or another, I found no definite mention of the fact.

I then followed up each of the references. I re-read all the other lists and in particular the most complete, Geronymo de Zuñita's list of all the nobility and gentry.

This time I found six knights of St John.

Besides Hugo de Moncada, there were Gomez Perez de las Marinas and Francisco del Corral, both passengers in the galleon *San Martin*, who in all probability returned with her to port; there was Don Christobal de Torres Osorio, of whom no more is said than that 'he died on the voyage'; there was Lope de Vega, twenty-six and as yet neither a playwright nor famous; and there was Diego, Marquez de

Medina. None of them, alas, as far as is known, ended their voyage on the *Girona*.

What was I to do now? Should I perhaps make a closer study of the Order itself? And its connections with Philip II? Yes. Maybe I would find a lead there.

Like the Knights Templar and the Order of Teutonic Knights, the Sovereign Order of St John Hospitaller of Jerusalem was born out of the Crusades. It retained its original character until the Renaissance.

The Order started as a Benedictine hospital, established around 1070 in Jerusalem, initially for travellers from Amalfi, and later for all pilgrims. The Brotherhood was established in a hospital adjoining a church dedicated to St John the Baptist, from which the Order derived its name.

In 1113, His Holiness Pope Paschal III took the Order and their possessions under his protection in exchange for services rendered to the Crusaders. Unlike the Knights Templar, a military order, the Order of Knights Hospitaller devoted themselves primarily to medical research, to the training of surgeons and doctors, and to the building and equipping of hospitals in Jerusalem and at other stopping points along the pilgrimage routes. It was because they were frequently called upon to defend the pilgrims against the Saracens that their order became, perforce, a military one.

In 1291, Palestine fell and the Order moved to Cyprus, and from there, in 1310, to Rhodes, where the Knights became Christianity's foremost sailors and its most redoubtable corsairs. The Order then became known as the Knights of Rhodes. It was an international order. The Knights had to prove noble birth for at least four generations. The Order was ruled over by an elected Grand Master who presided over the Sagro Consiglio, the Supreme Council.

The Knights were 'of the nine Tongues', the Venerable Tongues of Auvergne, Provence, France, Aragon, Castile, Portugal, England, Germany and Italy. The Order also included Chaplains of Obediance, ecclesiastics, who were the real hospitallers, and serving brothers who were soldiers and were required merely to be 'respectable'. The titles of Magistral Knight and Knight of Grace, given by the Grand Master, were only honorary ones. All knights and serving brothers took vows of chastity and obedience and, in theory, the Order paid direct allegiance to the Pope, but only in theory. The Knights were allowed to fight only against Moslems and not against Christian princes.

The sea power of the Knights of St John and their great fighting strength was a source of some concern to the Barbary Turks and the Ottomans. Suleiman the Magnificent began his reign by besieging Rhodes, and in 1522, after a lengthy siege, the Knights were expelled from the island. They left with the honours of war. In 1530 Charles v, who saw in them the most solid rampart of his kingdoms of Naples and Sicily, gave them Malta, where they established themselves. The Order was renamed the Sovereign Order of Malta, and was known as the 'Maritime Marshalsea of Europe' because of its persistent privateering, and the fact that in all encounters between Christians and Moslems, the Knight's galleys were always in the front line.

The Order had maintained close links with Spain, to whom it owed its territory. But when it came to the ultimate ordeal, the great siege of 1565, during which they were besieged for several months by Suleiman's 30,000 Janissaries and soldiers, commanded by Dragut and Mustapha, it seemed to the Grand Master, Jean Parisot de la Valette, that the calculated delay on the part of the Viceroy of Naples, Don Garcia of Toledo, in sending help, was tantamount to betrayal. Perhaps what Philip ii had really wanted was to leave the Turks and the Christians to wipe each other out so that he should be able to reclaim the island for himself? From then on the Order turned towards France. Nonetheless at Lepanto (1571), the greatest victory of Philip ii's reign, the Order's galleys were up with the Spanish and the Venetians in the heat of the battle.

In 1588, the Grand Master was Hugues de Loubens de Verdalle, of the Venerable Langue of Languedoc. The Order as such took no part in the Enterprise of England. The English might be heretics, and their Queen excommunicated, but they were not Moslems. The Order had lost its Langue of England after Henry viii's Reformation and his anti-papist activities. In 1533 Henry had sent the Grand Master, Jean d'Omedes, an unacceptable ultimatum. Two years later he had dictated an Act of Parliament whereby all the confiscated possessions of the Order and all its property reverted to the Crown. Mary Tudor had quickly restored the Order in 1553, and Elizabeth, once crowned, had suppressed it again, equally quickly. But the Knights of the Venerable Langues of Castile, Aragon, Portugal and Italy, having once fulfilled their duties to the Order (one year of the 'Convent', which meant service at sea, followed by three years in the galleys and, finally, two years residence ashore), could choose to go into the reserve and return to their families. They would be summoned only if the Order was in peril, as it was, for example, in 1565. While 'under pain of losing their habit' they were forbidden to bear arms against a Christian prince, they could not as individuals refuse to fight wherever they were summoned to do so by their King.

I must have gone through ten or a dozen histories of the Order of Malta, and I found countless knights, but not a single one more who had definitely sailed in the Armada. The exercise had been a pleasant one, but futile.

For a long time I had been wondering whether contemporary portraits might not have something to offer, those sixteenth-century paintings in which the grandees of the period never failed to don any and every medallion they were entitled to wear. If, by some stroke of luck, I were to find a cross identical to ours, perhaps then I would have my answer. My task was made easier from the very beginning by the fact that a great many sixteenth-century knights are shown wearing a simple cross with no decoration in the angles between the arms (those, for example, painted by Giorgione, Bassano, Carravaggio), so ours would be that much easier to spot. The rule was that knights were forbidden to decorate their crosses with any motif or personal symbol, but by this time no one took much notice of such rules. Several Grand Masters inveighed against 'the knights who decorated their crosses with diamonds', wrote Mlle Claire Eliane Engel, the eminent historian of the Order in a personal letter to me, 'clear proof that it must have been general practice'.

A portrait by Paolo Farinatti in the Louvre (sometimes attributed to Titian) shows a 'Knight of Italy', red haired and bearded, whose cross is cantoned with long petals. A sixteenth-century cross in the Musée de la Légion d'Honneur in Paris has fleurs-de-lis between the arms. A portrait of Lope de Vega shows him wearing a similar one. Later crosses are almost always personalised.

It was by ferreting about in museum catalogues that I found, or rather, thought I found, our cross. It was on a ribbon, entwined in a gold chain, around the neck of Don Fernando de Toledo, natural son of the Duke of Alba and Military Commander in Flanders (portrait by Antonio Moro, in the Imperial Gallery in Vienna). I examined the cross under a magnifying glass. It looked very like ours, but painting is not photography. The angle decorations could equally well have been rather loosely painted fleurs-de-lis, whereas on our cross they were thorns, shaped like cloves, with a tiny, finely engraved grenade at the end, clearly separated from the point. Struts in right-angled segments, reinforcing the arms of the cross to form a circle, join the thorns and give them from a distance the appearance of four fleurs-de-lis.

In any case, Fernando de Toledo, who was also a Knight of Alcantara, was not in the Armada. There was one Don Francisco De Toledo among the passengers, but he disembarked from the *San Felipe* at Nieuport when she ran aground, and four de Toledos of minor importance, a Don Garcia, Don Juan, Don Pedro and a Don Alonzo. Another false trail – Fernando's brothers were called Federico and Fadrique.

I had almost given up hope, when another letter from Mlle Engel finally put me on the right track. 'It is very difficult,' she wrote, 'to get any documentation on the sixteenth century. Del Pozzo ... gives an incomplete list ... of Knights of the Langue of Italy. Among Italian Knights Vertot mentions only some Spinolas from Genoa.' Spinolas ... wait a minute! Hadn't I seen the name Spinola somewhere before?

In 1967, I had looked at a copy of Pedro de Paz Salas's General Inventory of the Felicissima Armada (Lisbon, 9 May 1588) in the British Museum. It is a particularly interesting copy in that it belonged to Lord Burghley. Burghley, whose information was always good, and quick, had been among the first in England to get hold of a copy of the inventory. In his *Annals*, Stow records that he noticed on it several notes in Burghley's own hand, made shortly after the defeat, giving details of which captains had been captured or killed and which ships had been sunk. Fortunately I had had these pages photocopied at the Museum. I looked them up. On the left of the page next to the name *Girona* Burghley had written: 'perished on the coast of Ireland', and on the right he had written: 'Fabricio Spinola Captn.'

The command of a galleass was, traditionally, the preserve of officers of noble birth (eligible therefore for the Order of Malta) who swore on their lives 'not to flee before 25 enemy galleys and not to refuse battle with them'. If Fabricio Spinola was a Knight of Malta, I was doing more than just getting warm, I was burning.

The Spinolas (originally Spinula) were one of the biggest families in Genoa. They had made their fortune in trade with the Levant, and then turned to public life, as early as the twelfth century. The first politician was Guido Spinola, Consul of Genoa. After him came several captains and generals. Once the wealth and influence of the family were well established, they gave thirteen cardinals to the Church and to the Republic countless ambassadors, consuls, doges and magistrates, as well as 127 senators. By the fifteenth century one

¶ Las quatro Galeaças de Napoles que eſtan a cargo de Don Hugo de Moncada.

	Toneladas.	Nauios.	Gête d' guerra.	Gête de mar.	Numero de todos ſeㄇㄛ.	ſiete de Pieças de Pelote-ria.	artillería.	Poluora,	Plomo.	Cuerds.
Lagaleaça capitana nombra la S.Loreço.										
Lugs hiſpana. capitan	544									
Juã Perez. la Loayſa	118	262.	224.	386.	300.	50.	2500.	232.	16.	22½
	262									
Galeaça Patrona.										
Hernãdo de queſada	116									
Andres Verdugo.	62	178.	112	290.	370.	50.	2500.	228.	16.	22½
	178									
Galeaça Girona.										
Gonçalo Beltran.	75	269.	220.	289.	300.	50.	2500.	230.	25.	22½
De Antonio de Sylua	9t									
galeaça Napolitana	161									

finds the family's increasingly illustrious name linked with every important event. During Philip's reign the most famous members of the family were without doubt Fredericu and Ambrogio, two brothers who distinguished themselves in the service of Spain by raising, at their own expense, a galley fleet and an army 'more powerful than any that a king could have provided for himself'.

Aubert de la Mire, the famous polymath, has written, among many others, two works of particular interest here: *Origine des Chevaliers et Ordres Militaires* and *Gentis Spinulae Illustrium Elogia*. As I set out on this new track, I told myself that if I didn't find Fabricio there,

there would be nothing for it but to give up. Fabricio wasn't there. There were sixty-seven Spinolas and any number of Fernandus, Fredericus, and Franciscus, Knights of Santiago, Alcantara and Calatrava, but not a word about our man. But the list was very incomplete, giving only the principal heads of families; Fabricio might have

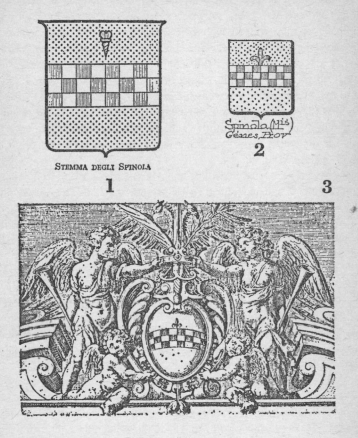

STEMMA DEGLI SPINOLA

1

Spinola (Mis)
Gênes, Prov

2

3

died in his prime, before holding any important public office or earning any entitlement to immortality.

Following Mademoiselle Engel's advice, I made it my job to plough once more through both volumes of del Pozzo *Historia della Sacra Religione Militare di San Giovanni . . . 1571–1688*. It is a remarkable work, extremely detailed. Alas, it disposes of the 'ill-fated attempt at invasion' in only three lines and mentions a grand total of two knights of the name of Spinola in the seventeenth century.

The Abbé de Vertot in *The History of the Knights of Malta*, written in 1776, lists thirty Spinolas under the Venerable Langue of Italy, between 1416 and 1702. Ah, at last! This time, amongst all those, I must find my man. Alas, among the Italians, only ten, going by the dates when they were received (from 1562 to 1583) could have been of the right age to be in the Armada and not one of them was called Fabricio. As for the Venerable Langue of Castile, only one knight, received in 1588, would not have been anachronistic and he had the bad taste to be called Francisco Spinola de Covaccio.

Still there was no cause for despair. Vertot's list is notoriously incomplete, he admits it himself. I had to steel myself once more to setting off on the heraldry track. Maybe the Spinolas had a salamander in their coat of arms.

Very early on the Spinolas had shown signs of pretensions to nobility and had acquired titles on the basis of a genealogical table. According to Joseph Lefèvre in *Spinola et la Belgique* it was 'drawn up possibly at their instigation and expense, which claimed to show their ascendance and alliance back as far as the eleventh century. One might be forgiven for being a little sceptical at the prospect of these trees, growing just a bit too high into the air'.

Once more I opened the illustrated books of heraldry and there, on the arms of the Spinolas of Genoa, I found straight away the motif that was between the arms of our cross. There could be no doubt about it. This time it was the real thing. It was a fesse chequy silver and gules, a thorn gules in pale in the middle of the fesse. On the Spinola's original coat of arms the thorn (*spina* in Italian) is shown on its own. It is quite clearly a thorn, with its separate grenade shaped head. On later coats of arms, it became half thorn, half fleur-de-lis. On the arms of Philip Charles Francis Spinola, carved in marble at the top of his mausoleum in the Eglise de la Chapelle in Brussels, where I went to look at them, the hybrid thorn has given way to a full blown fleur-de-lis. Our cross shows it at the intermediate stage.

Captain Fabricio Spinola, forgotten by Vertot, unless Burghley or his spies simply got his Christian name wrong, must indeed have been a Knight of Malta. It was he, without doubt, who lost his cross, personalised with a charge from his own arms, in the wreck of his ship.

36

The Unknown Knight

The medallion[1] that I had foolishly assumed to belong to a Knight of Santiago (De Leiva's!) – wishful thinking – turned out on closer inspection to be nothing short of a tiny marvel. On the obverse each arm of the cross ended in a fleur-de-lis. The decorated frame had been a little twisted in the course of time, and the enamel that must have covered the surface was missing (for the cross is cloisonné, meaning that round the outline is a raised frame, which would have contained the enamel). Under the cross is a simple gold plaque backed by another, with a fine engraving on the obverse of a bearded, long-haired saint with a halo and dressed in rags. He is walking through a ravine. On his right are a tree and a waterfall. On his left is what looks like a small basket, perhaps, or a boat that he is pointing at, or carrying, and in it is the stylised head of an animal. The rest of the basket is hidden by the crushed frame. It must have been hung on a ribbon by a tiny soldered ring that we found a few weeks later, not far away. (See plates 40 and 41.)

At that time there were three military orders of knighthood in Spain: the Orders of Santiago, Alcantara and Calatrava, all dating back to the twelfth century.

The Marquis de Casa Valdez, who is the present Secretary of the Real Consejo de las Ordenes Militares de Santiago, Calatrava, Alcantara y Montesa (and whose help in my research was as generous as it was valuable) wondered whether our medallion was not simply a decorative jewel, imitating the cross of an order of knighthood, quite a common occurrence:

The Knight's habit . . . was a very large cape with the cross of the Order either embroidered or sewn on and a tunic with a cross on the breast, worn short in battle with a helmet, mail coat, knight's sword and belt, a costume probably very similar to the one worn at the time of the Crusades. . . . These orders, being religious and military, the equipment of a knight did not include jewels, either for war or for the church.

This was true in the early days, when the knights, poor and chaste, virtuously devoted every day of their lives to serving the order according to their vows. But, by the sixteenth century knighthood had become mainly honorary, and because of the rich commands that could be obtained it was, above all, a good financial proposition. 'The Grandees preferred to be received in it [the Order of Santiago] than in the Order of the Golden Fleece, because they hoped thereby to obtain for themselves commands and other not inconsiderable privileges.' The rule, which required that no jewels be worn in view of the vows of poverty that had been taken, had fallen into disuse and the knights had as little respect for it as they had for the rule of chastity (abrogated long before in any case for those married by the Pope).

One only needs to look at the portraits of the period: Juan Martinez de Recalde in a well known painting is shown wearing the insignia of a Knight of Santiago, very similar to ours; so is Pedro de Valdez; Miguel de Oquendo wears a slightly different one; so do the Marquis de Santa Cruz and the Governor of the Netherlands; Luis de Requesens wears his on a gold chain, Gonzalo Chacon is wearing the Cross of Alcantara without a medallion. I have also seen a jewel of a Knight of the Order of Calatrava very like ours but studded with stones, and also several Orders of Santiago set with rubies, amethysts and white topazes in the Jewellery Room at the Victoria and Albert Museum.

So at the time of the Armada, it was not unusual for knights to wear such jewels. (I was to learn later that it was Pope Benedict XIII, in 1411, who gave the knights permission to lay aside the hood and scapular of the Cistercians for the cross with fleurs-de-lis of either vert or gules.) Two questions remained: which order, and which knight?

Most of the literature on the history of military orders of knighthood is in Latin. I was going to have to brush mine up a bit if I was going to identify ours. The task was all the more agreeable in that the subject is fascinating in itself. It is not by chance that knights feature so prominently in folklore, like princes in fairy stories.

It was clear from the start that Santiago must be ruled out. The knights of this Order wore the cross of Santiago el Mayor, Santiago Apostol, or St James of the Sword. The cross was a flory fitchy, the ends of the upper arms having the shape of a stylised lily, the lower arm forming a sword point, the pommel ending in an inverted heart. The flory cross that featured on the sacred banner of Santiago in the thirteenth century had long ago fallen into disuse.

That left Calatrava and Alcantara. The crosses of these two Orders are flory crosses identical to ours. The only difference between them is the colour: green for Alcantara, red for Calatrava.[2] The enamel on ours had disappeared without trace.

Fortunately there was still the saint engraved on the reverse, with what must have been his characteristic attributes, the tree, the waterfall and the dog basket. The obvious answer was of course to call him Saint John the Baptist and to further decide he was just coming out of the wilderness, as symbolised by the tree and the ravine. The beard and the rags would have fitted and his right index would then point towards a lamb to indicate, as it is the job of that particular saint to do: ECCE AGNUS DEI.

However, one major attribute of Saint John the Baptist is lacking, his ribboned crook (unless it is hidden by the crushed frame), very seldom in the rich iconography of the saint is the wilderness symbolised by one single tree and the theory would leave the fleur-de-lised cross on the reverse completely out of context.

So, I felt that an alternative explanation was needed, if only to allow everyone to make his own choice.

Perhaps the two possible orders had a protective saint, a patron? Then it would be him.

That was the direction in which I was going to have to look. What else could I do but make another detailed study of the lives of the saints on one front, and on the other, of the history of two Orders.

In all the research I had done on Calatrava, I had come up with only one knight who sailed in the Armada: Don Gonzalo de Eraso, a passenger on the galleon *San Martín*. I was sure there must have been others.

The Order of Calatrava dates back to the wars against the Almohades, who, in the twelfth century, still held the southern part of Spain. A certain Raymond Serrat, from Saint Gaudens, a Cistercian,

Abbot of Fitero (an abbey that he had established in Navarre), founded the Order to defend a town against the Moors. The town had previously been abandoned by the Templars as indefensible. It was called Kalaat Rawah. King Alfonso VII gave the Abbot the town but only on condition that he defend it. With his friend Fray Diego Velazquez, the Abbot set about populating it. By distributing land to anyone who swore to defend it, he managed to attract some 20,000 people within its walls and in the surrounding countryside. In this way he built up a semi-military, semi-religious militia of 'Knights of Calatrava'. Alexander III gave the Order official recognition in 1164. They wore a white mantle with a crimson cross (the red cross of war) having fleurs-de-lis (for purity) at the ends of the arms. The Abbot was canonised after his death (in Toledo in 1163) and made San Raimundo de Fitero. Ah! I had found a saint. But was he the right one?

I set out to find all the portraits, statues and medallions of St Raymond that I could dig out of the very best hagiographies. Heaven is full of St Raymonds, but there are three important ones, including Serrat. Nowhere, however, was this holy man depicted in rags, nor with a tree, nor with any animal.

I then followed up the fact of Serrat being a Cistercian: the original rule of the Order of Calatrava was that of the Abbey of Cîteaux, founded by *Saint* Benedict and made famous by *Saint* Bernard. Another dead end! Neither of these two saints had any connection with a tree.

As for the arms of the Order, they, for some unfathomable reason, are two hobbles, two lengths of rope with a buckle at each end. So, how about the arms of Alcantara?

On the shield of Alcantara was . . . a pear tree. In 1156, the town of Alcantara (El Kantarah) was also threatened by the Moors. In order to defend it two gentlemen of Salamanca, Don Suero Fernandez Barrientes and his brother, Don Gomez, founded a military order, also under the rule of St Benedict. On the advice of a hermit named Arnaud, held in high esteem locally by reason of his piety, they built the Order's first home, a fortified priory on the edge of Rio Coa (in the diocese of Ciudad Rodrigo, on the Portuguese border) immediately next to the hermitage. The hermitage was dedicated to St Julian, Bishop of Le Mans, and because his little chapel was set in a grove of pear trees, it was known as the Hermitage of St Julian of the Pear Tree. Because it was there that the Order was started, the knights were also known as 'Caballeros de San Julian del Pereiro' (*pereiro* being Portuguese for pear-tree). In his *diario*, Medina Sidonia refers to the Knight, Don Diego Tellez Henriquez, son of the Grand Commander of Alcantara, as 'El del Peral', or knight of the pear orchard, to distinguish him from the other five Henriquezes (including two Diegos) in the Armada.

The Maestre-General of the Order remained there until 1252, when the Order was temporarily amalgamated with the Order of Calatrava. In 1411 Benedict XIII granted permission for the knights to wear the green silk flory cross on their breasts. Later their medallion was a gold cross enamelled in green on a green ribbon. By the time of the Armada, the Order had thirty-seven commands and fifty-three bourgs, either taken from the Moors, acquired in some other way, or given to them. Their power and their wealth, in fact the power and wealth of all three orders, made for unending conflicts between the grand masters, the Church and the King. Finally the King of Spain took over the three orders, making himself Grand Master.

According to the most detailed histories, 'they took for their arms a pear tree, with exposed roots and bare branches on a gold field'. The pear tree on our medallion is in full leaf and its trunk disappears deep into the earth.

But, in fact, although one does frequently find such a tree on the arms of the Order (for example in the frontispiece of *Diffinitiones de la Orde y Cavalleria de Alcantara*, Madrid (1569), one also often finds a perfectly ordinary tree (in the frontispiece of the *Cronica de las Tres Ordenes*, by Francisco de Rades, printed in Toledo in 1572, for example, or in the frontispiece of the *Historia de las Ordenes Militares*, by Francisco Carro de Torres, published in Madrid in 1629).

Clearly the tree pointed to the saint being St Julian of the Pear Tree. But how about the animal? And the fountain?

Heaven be praised! Heaven had forty-five St Julians! Forty-five unless any had been left out of the *Biblioteca Sanctorum*, forty-five among whom reigns the most indescribable confusion. The one worshipped by the hermit, Arnaud, was St Julian, first Bishop of Le Mans in the fourth century. There are thousands of details recorded about his life, all edifying, all invented long after the event by his falsifying biographer, whose one aim was to bring fame and fortune to the diocese of Le Mans, for his own personal advancement. But the best known characteristics attributed to him, which I discovered from a more reliable source, are that he preached the Gospel to the Gauls (along with sixty-nine other disciples of the Apostles), that he went to Rome to find some relics that caused several miracles to happen (could the animal in the basket have something to do with

the things he brought back from Rome?), and above all, that, one day, he miraculously caused a fountain to spring out of the earth. It is said that the springing forth of this fountain brought about the conversion of a very large number of princes indeed, along with their subjects.

It converted me, anyway, that fountain playing on the left of the saint on the medallion. And I have decided for the time being that the holy man is San Julian del Pereiro, Bishop of Le Mans, that he looks like Saint John the Baptist because he was himself a very little known and not very often painted (or engraved) saint and the engraver, not

217

knowing where to look for a model, took one of the saint of all saints, the Baptist. So the jewel must have been indeed the insignia of a Knight of Alcantara.

With positively pious devotion I worked until I could hardly see, trying to pin a name on the medallion. Whom had it belonged to? I did not succeed. I discovered only two Knights of Alcantara in the whole Armada. Neither one of them perished with the *Girona*. The first was Don Diego Tellez Henriques, son of the Grand Commander of the Order, whom the Duke referred to as 'El del Peral.' Captain Francisco de Cuellar says that he buried him, with his own hands, on the beach at Stredegagh (near Sligo) after 'the Irish savages' had slaughtered him for his ducats and his clothes. The second was Don Henrique de Guzman, Marquis of Pobar, but Carro de Torres says that he served in the Enterprise of England and 'having returned' continued his career.

One Diego De Leiva, who sailed with Don Alonzo in the *rata* with a company of 145 soldiers, might have been a brother of his. They were drowned together, but nowhere, alas, is there any mention of his being a knight of any Order whatsoever. Another brother, Don Pedro De Leiva, Knight of Alcantara, and General of the Galleys of Sicily and of Spain, served from childhood with his father, Don Sancho, and with his elder brother, Don Alonzo, as lieutenant of his galley squadrons. He was involved in several actions in Barbary and was a great sailor, recognised as such by his contemporaries. But Carro de Torres, who always (or almost always) says which knights were involved in the Enterprise of England, does not say whether or not Don Pedro was, or, if he was, how he died. As a final blow, although the chronicler Zuñita mentions in his list of *caballeros aventureros* in the Armada, apart from Don Diego, a Juan De Leiva, and, in his list of captains, an Antonio De Leiva, nowhere does he mention anyone by the name of Pedro De Leiva.

So, was Don Pedro there, unnoticed? It would take too great a stretch of the imagination to believe that.

If one stretches a point, and translates *caballero* as knight (caballero means noble in general, and knight is only one special meaning of the word), and if one stretches another point and receives this knight into the Order of Alcantara, and if one stretches a third point and decides that this Juan was also Don Alonzo's brother, then one could conclude that he was sailing at his side and the problem is solved. But that's a bit too much stretching for my taste.

I spent the whole winter searching, buried deep in my papers, and then in the spring I gave it up. The Knight of Alcantara, drowned at Port na Spaniagh, must forever remain 'the unknown knight'.

NOTES

1. Size of medallion: oval 27.5 $\times$ 23 mm., 4.5 mm. thick, weight 14 grams.
2. In the Jewellery Room at the Victoria and Albert Museum in London, I also saw two seventeenth- and eighteenth-century jewels with crosses similar to ours, marked 'Insignia of a Familiar of the Inquisition' and 'Insignia of the Inquisition'. The Familiars of the Inquisition were lay auxiliaries recruited for their energetic devotion to the cause. According to the experts they wore 'antique crosses bordered with gold thread'. 'Antique crosses' in this context means nothing in particular. If one chooses to take it as meaning 'flory cross', the fact still remains that the arms of the London crosses are enamelled lengthways half white, half black. Our cross lacked the central vertical cloison that would have been necessary for the jeweller to lay two different enamels. The second cross, mounted in gold on an aquamarine the size of a pigeon's egg, seems more like an ornamental jewel.

37

1969: We Return to Port na Spaniagh

We returned to Port na Spaniagh in April, with the sand-martins.

The gulls and seamews, ever spiralling up and down by the black cliffs, greeted us once more with their raucous cries. We were very curious at the first dive. What would we find this time? Would the winter storms have churned over the sea bed, demolished the cave and destroyed all our efforts by mixing excavated sediments with virgin deposits? Or would they have revealed some golden pavements or lines of cannon – or Shakespearian skulls, their eye sockets stuffed with diamonds?

I was bubbling over with impatience. The temperature of the water brought me rudely to my senses. Hell, it was even icier than last year, 6°C according to the thermometer. Other than that, nothing had changed. All our holes had been filled up again, but with stuff that we had already excavated. I need not have feared for my eyes. There was no dazzling display of newly uncovered jewels.

We wanted to take advantage of the early part of the season, while the algae were still small and thinly scattered, to make a systematic exploration in the bay of Port na Spaniagh itself. As Louis had pointed out to me in 1968, we had after all found only signs of a ship having gone down, not the remains of a complete vessel.

'There were fifty guns on the *Girona*, weren't there?' he demanded. 'Well, we've found two. Where are the rest?'

Sorley Boy fished out three in 1589, or, to be more precise, that Scottish captain fished them out for him. Maybe the captain made a deal with him, half and half: three cannon for the noble lord and three for himself, in exchange for services rendered. But even allowing for that, it still left forty-two or forty-five cannon unaccounted for. The English never came to get them, so where were they? Perhaps the galleass broke in two on Lacada Point. One half might have drifted off with the rest of the cannon and the bulk of the treasure, somewhere in Port na Spaniagh.

So Louis thought, but I doubted it, because all the lead stores from the ship were on Lacada Point. In fact there was actually more than there should be if we were to believe the inventories, and then there were so many cannon balls.

'But what about the rest of the stuff?' Louis argued. 'On a ship that size there must have been millions of things. Where are they?'

'Disintegrated!' I told him. 'Look, here are the inventories. Supplies, for example. What the sailors didn't eat will have been eaten by the sea. Biscuits, bacon, tuna fish, sardines, semolina, sugar, salt . . . you can't imagine any of that being left. Look at the small arms: arquebuses, muskets, halberds, pikes, half-pikes, partisans. De Leiva left a lot behind at Killybegs and the rest wouldn't have lasted two years on the sea bed. What else? Corslets – same thing. What else? Gunpowder, water and wine butts? Sorley Boy drank his way through some of them, the rest are long gone. Other than that, there would have been wooden mugs and bowls for the sailors, jugs and dishes for handing out rations in, leather water bottles, lamps, lanterns, candles, match, oil for the lamps, cow hides and tow for repairing shot holes and damaged caulking, cuir bouilli buckets for the gunners' powder, steelyards. . . .'

'But we did find one steelyard. Remember? The lead weight backed with a bronze plaque?'

I admitted there might be some left. But as I turned over page after page of the inventory – sacks and sacks of canvas, rope, siege equipment, carpenters', sailmakers' and caulkers' tools, galley slaves' irons and chains – I was sure there couldn't be much left of any of that.

Louis persisted. 'How about the musket? That was still there, wasn't it?'

He was right, we must go and look to make quite certain.

In order to go and look, we had to mark out the area. First we laid a line from east to west, fixed at intervals, right across the bay and then, day by day, we worked our way along equi-distant lines to north and south. Much to our surprise we found the algae already tall

221

and dense, at the height of the previous summer, and already covered with little pink algae. That slowed down our search somewhat, but in fact, apart from some bits of modern rubbish, we found nothing. So what was not on the sea bed must have been thrown ashore. Back in 1588, the MacDonnell clan must only have needed to bend down to reap the harvest of the wreck, and the following year the Scottish captain must have just dabbled his toes in the water.

Louis was still shaking his head. 'But where have those forty-five cannon got to, then?'

I thought I knew where they were. There were 6 cannon on board, 2 demi-cannon, 4 demi-culverins, 8 perriers, 6 sakers, 4 demi-sakers, 20 esmerils and then another 40 mascolos (they were more like arquebuses than cannon). The 40 mascolos De Leiva gave to McSweeney before leaving Killybegs. There is a letter in my files from a certain Henry Duke informing the English of this. We found two small guns, and Sorley Boy raised at least three. In 1597 Sir John Chichester, who was then Governor, wrote:

> The McDonnells have planted three pieces of ordnance, half cannon and culverin which were had out of one of the Spanish ships coming upon that coast after our fight with them at sea in 1588. I have demanded the said pieces . . . but they have utterly refused to deliver them. . . .

The names he gives to the pieces are almost certainly inaccurate. Firstly there were no culverins on board, and secondly it doesn't tally with the breech loading cannon that we found the blocks for on Lacada Point.

It's always possible the Scottish captain kept that one for himself. But in any case that was the only description of cannon recovered that I'd found, apart from a rather vague letter from someone called Lady Agnes Campbell, who wrote asking Sorley Boy for 'a large piece of Spanish artillery', in December, 1589.

But where were these cannon now? A mystery! Hill, who wrote the history of the McDonnell family says: 'The cannon subsequently appear to have been sent to Scotland, perhaps as early as August, 1589, and perhaps mounted on the McDonnell stronghold of Dunstaffnage Castle. . . .' He's wrong, about the date anyway, since Lady Campbell was asking for one of them in December and Governor Chichester was still after them in 1597. These cannon were

222

a source of bad luck to everyone – to De Leiva, to James McDonnell and finally to Chichester as well. There was trouble in November 1597 between the Earl of Carrickfergus and James over some stolen livestock – one might almost say that the whole of Irish history then was made out of small battles over a couple of stolen cows. To cut a long story short, Chichester got mixed up in it and accused James McDonnell of treason in having fortified Dunluce with cannon from the galleass. He attacked. And won. James counterattacked, reinforced by some of the Scottish McDonnells. He imprisoned Chichester and cut off his head. The Lord Deputy appointed Chichester's brother in his place, in spite of James's protests, and in 1601, the brother, Sir Arthur, had James poisoned in his castle. At least everyone suspected him, although it could have been Burghley himself, who was trying to get O'Neill poisoned at the same time.

'Yes, yes,' Louis went on, 'but have you actually been to look at Dunstaffnage?'

We hadn't because our friend John McLennan lent me a book, published in 1860, called *Castellated Architecture of Scotland*, which contains the following statement:

Three beautiful Spanish pieces, relics of the Armada, were seen on the ruined walls of Dunstaffnage as recently as twenty years ago.... There are also openings in the walls for said guns....

But the castle was currently undergoing restoration. It had been going on for years. I had written to the local schoolmaster, who answered that the cannon were not on show at the moment. They had been put away for safe keeping until the restoration work was completed. According to him the most serious book on Dunstaffnage is the one by W. Douglas Simpson, which said nothing about *three* cannon. He had enclosed a copy of a passage from the book mentioning two old cannon, one very rusty iron one, said to have been dredged up from the sea-bed not far from the castle; the other, a bronze one, 6 ft 6 in. long, $3\frac{3}{4}$ in. calibre, with the usual dolphin decorations, and engraved round the breech ASVERVUS ROSTER ME FECIT AMSTELREDAM. That one is supposed to have come off the Tobermoray wreck. A false trail, in short.

'It's absolutely classic!' said Louis. 'There can't be a single iron chest or cannon in the whole country that's not called "Armada

223

chest" or something to that effect. But there isn't a clue as to where those forty-five missing cannon are.'

'No,' I said, 'but don't forget that De Leiva embarked 1300 men at Killybegs, 700 more than the normal crew of 600, and in a patched up ship at that. Reckoning say 140 lb. a head, 700 men equals about 49 tons of human flesh. Forty-five cannon, taking an average weight, come to about the same — 49 tons. So, in order to embark 49 tons of Spaniards, he must have had to throw overboard 49 tons of bronze. Quite simple. . . .'

'Well, then if they are at Killybegs, what are we waiting for?'

'It's big, you know, Killybegs roads. They could be anywhere, and wherever they are they would be in deep mud. Each time I've been there, I've asked the local fishermen about them, but no one knows anything. There have, in fact, recently been some big dredging operations there; it seems that they found nothing at all.'

38

Archimedes, or How We Resort to Extreme Measures

This year Louis and Maurice had brought along with them a young French diver, Patrick Couture, to reinforce the team. It was not long before he began to make out very well. Francis was still with us and the Belgian speleologist, Bob Destreille, the bravest cave diver I know, was to join us shortly. Marc was coming a little later, just long enough to make a short underwater colour film for television, using an underwater camera of his own design, with special corrective lenses. His assistant, young André Fassotte, was going to stay with the team until the end of the season. Altogether there would be eight of us.

We were also better equipped to move the hundreds of tons of rock under which we were once more going to dig. I did not want to use explosives for fear of destroying the very things that we were looking for. We had a hydraulic jack capable of lifting the twenty-ton monsters a few inches at a time. If the jack gave way, the sea bed shook with the impact. Fortunately these monsters were few and far between. I didn't like to see divers edging under huge boulders, precariously propped up by our makeshift scaffoldings of small rocks, in place of pillars.

Apart from the monsters, there were any number of six to eight-ton rocks. Last year we could not have touched these 'big guns', but this time I had had special air bags made to lift two and four tons each.

We had drawn up a list. For those of us who had hovered greedily around, sniffing and scratching as far as our arms would stretch, each boulder still remaining in a fertile excavated area obviously promised great riches.

We each had our own boulders, ours as it were, by right. Considering their position and the wealth of artifacts that had been found around them, they ought to have been covering rivers of diamonds and bucket loads of pearls or, at the very least, Alonzo De Leiva's gold plate. To avoid fighting over the largest bags we had to work according to a rota. Under the first rock, in the middle of the canyon, Louis found a sizeable piece of a musket ball, under the second a whole lead bullet, under the third nothing, under the fourth another rock, and under the fifth a perrier ball. Under the sixth he found a lead ingot, two whole arquebus balls, and a large piece of the weighted underside of an astrolabe.

That was important, for I had, collected in various plastic bags, five or six very worn sections of a bronze circle that might have belonged to a broken astrolabe, or indeed almost anything. . . . But now the jigsaw was beginning to take shape. We had our second astrolabe, the world its twenty-eighth. By 1966, Lieutenant Commander David Waters, Director of the Department of Navigation and Astronomy at the National Maritime Museum in Greenwich, and the world expert on astrolabes, had indexed, measured, weighed and written up twenty-one, six of which were found in wrecks. Ours seemed to be identical to Waters's Numbers 9 and 10. Since, he has studied a few more, including two from the sea-bed, and a twenty-sixth was found recently in Bermuda on a Portuguese wreck of 1580–9.

The mariner's astrolabe was what made ocean navigation possible. The instrument enabled one to measure the height of the sun or the pole star above the horizon and work out what latitude the ship was in. It was the successor to the armillary sphere, used by the Greeks for many astronomical measurements, and the planispheric astrolabe that Arab astronomers and medieval astrologers used to forctell the movement of the heavenly bodics in order to know whether the time was right for embarking on a war, a journey or a marriage. The Portuguese navigators first used them at sea in the fifteenth century (the earliest time they are mentioned, according to Waters, is in 1481).

The instrument consisted of an evenly balanced brass circle suspended by a ring, and provided with a rotatable alidade or a diametrical rule with sights, turning within a circle of degrees, for measuring the altitude of stars or sun. (See plates 44–46.)

In 1673, at a time when the astrolabe was already being superseded by Davis's quadrant, which consists of a quarter of an astrolabe much enlarged, and by the cross-staff or Jacob's staff, an ecclesiastic, Abbot Denis, was instructing the pilots of Dieppe in the art of navigation:

> ... Navigation walks on two feet, latitude and longitude. ... to work out the latitude with an astrolabe, one must first take note of the roll of the ship and choose the spot where there is the least movement, near the mainmast. Then, slipping the ring over one's finger, one allows the astrolabe to hang free, lowering and raising the alidade until the rays of the sun align with the holes in the middle of the pinules.

In order to measure the height of the Pole Star at night, one lined the star up through the pinules by holding the instrument to one's eye, which one would never have been able to do in the case of the sun, without being blinded.

In new territory also, our methodical search led us this year to areas where we needed to use the large lifting balloons as often as previously we had used our crowbars.

In calm weather, the operation was a very simple one. One slipped a steel sling around the rock to be shifted, if its shape lent itself to such treatment (rocks with a concave middle were ideal, but alas, very rare). If the rock was round or egg-shaped, the only thing to do was to spin a whole web of cable round it. One then shackled the sling on to the lifting bag and inflated it with an aqualung tank. As the cable tightened, the rock would buck, waddle about a bit, hesitate and then go up, helped on its way by Archimedes, slowly at first, and then quicker and quicker until finally the balloon reached the surface. All that remained then was to tow the whole lot to an area that had already been excavated, and to sink the rock by pushing the deflater valve.

The weather on the north coast of Ireland might have been tropical in 1968 (the best summer of the century), but throughout the summer of 1969 it was absolutely normal, that is absolutely frightful. For weeks on end we kicked our heels in port. Northwest gales followed one after another. if it wasn't that, some distant storm around Iceland would be sending over a mountainous swell.

A swell complicates everything. First of all, one can hardly see,

227

because one is having to swim in a soup of stirred-up vegetable waste. Secondly, one must use one hand to hang on, to stay anywhere near the rock that is to be strapped. Strapping up a rock one-handed is not all that easy — try it! Then you have to try to pull or push the empty balloons from the boat to the rock, and nylon-lined neoprene balloons are heavy and extremely large. The sea pulls them forward, backward or anywhere that takes her fancy. You go and get help. With three of you pushing and pulling you eventually manage it. Out of breath, exhausted, pulse racing, finally you tighten up the last shackle of the last link. You ram the inflater tubes under the mouth of the first balloon, open the valve, and then try to get a look at what is happening, whenever the swell carries you anywhere near. As soon as it begins to lighten, the rocks goes quite mad. The coming and going of the waves drags the balloons, tearing out the tube, or else throwing eight tons of granite in your face, only to snatch it back a moment later. At this point your main concern is to avoid being squashed to a pulp. And yet you have to keep an eye on what is happening. But how can you possibly be expected to see anything, when the crazy rock is raising thick clouds of sand, when perspiration is running stinging into your eyes, and when with every other wave an algae frond sticks on to the face plate of your mask? The swell comes again, snatching at your hand hold, throwing you onto a jagged rock which catches the buckle of your lead belt. There you are, coming and going, holding the inflation cylinder under one arm, and with the other wrapped round a bit of seaweed while you fix your belt, with one eye on the buckle and the other on the rocky mass that is still hammering away at the sea bed, thudding dully like a rumbling earthquake.

Often, if the swell is persistent, it will shake the rock about long enough to split the steel cable with one cunning swipe against the jagged edge of a nearby rock, or else slip your careful arrangement of ropes. In that split second when your mask isn't obscured by seaweed, you get a brief glimpse of a bunch of balloons rising up to the surface like so many flares. Otherwise, if the cables hold, and the rock rises, you follow, towed by your uncontrollable team until you decide to sink it, or rather until you are left with no alternative other than being thrown ashore with it or dragged out to sea.

It was just such an exercise that earned Francis his only rest of the

228

season, a long convalescence at home nursing a bandaged hand and two crushed fingers.

One always finds something bigger than oneself. There were some super-monsters that were absolutely unassailable. When we couldn't lift them, we had to dig under them and crawl, and then, once underneath we would gradually undermine the supporting pillars, as a perfect fool would.

On 21 June, I was, as usual, doing something I ought not to have been, rather nervously chipping away at the support of a thirty-ton rock, under which I was following a trail of Neapolitan silver ducats in 'very fine' condition. I came out for a minute to fetch a bigger crowbar. Just as I got outside the trap, it collapsed. The slab literally brushed my flippers as it crashed down seven feet. When I had gathered my wits about me again, I saw just next to me a huge crab, unscathed, but lying on its back, being swept from side to side by the swell, dead but not crushed. Clearly it had died of shock. I have often wondered whether such a case of a crustacean being overcome by a heart attack might not open up a whole new field of marine biology.

All divers know from experience that whenever some gawper you meet by the harbour opens his mouth, it's always to ask the same question: 'What about sharks? Aren't you scared of sharks?' The Port Ballintrae summer visitors were no exception to the rule.

Our friends the salmon fishermen told us stories of having caught sharks in their nets, but we never caught sight of one. Once, way out to sea, we spotted a school of about a hundred killer whales. You could spot them easily by their large, black, tapering bodies, their pointed dorsal fin and large white patches. They moved forward in a group (like porpoises) from east to west and took not the slightest notice of us.

It was rather disappointing in a way. Days passed, then weeks, then months. The cameras were loaded. Already in my mind I had the plan for a chapter headed: 'We Grapple with the Maneaters' – and still nothing. The closest thing we met to a shark were some frightened little dogfish, no longer than your arm. It was disappointing, because after all there is *always* a shark scene in *real* treasure hunts, in the films and on television. Really we are doing it all wrong. No palm trees, no three-masted topsail schooner, no wreck, lying, sails torn, listing slightly, on the very edge of a reef, no captain's cabin door creaking open to reveal the chest and the regulation octopus, no typhoon, no traitors and no sensuous blondes in bikinis (two at least to keep up the psychological intrigue), not even the flash of knives at the sharing out.

Sadly we realise that we are the jobbing treasure hunters, the faceless figures with horny hands, the grey men. We are the artisans, with our coal shovels and pickle jars. Our work consists of shifting stones, under the quiet gaze of the cod, or sweeping sand with our hands for six hours a day, frozen to the marrow, and dying to pee in our neoprene pants. Last year we did have the pirates – a lucky break! Without that, who would have taken us seriously?

At the beginning of June we enjoyed another moment of glory. The *National Geographic Magazine* gave over thirty colour pages to my article. The first copy to arrive in Belfast, at the Public Library, was stolen three-quarters of an hour after being placed on the shelves, and the one in Queen's University half an hour later. The local press was busy paraphrasing the article. The typographers in the composing room had dug out the biggest type they could find from the back of their drawers – it had probably been lying there since V-E Day – to print GOLD right across the front page. The television people remembered us again, and once more there was the daily influx of curious visitors in the harbour and along the cliff path. But the pirates did not return. There was nothing to see this year. We were a disappointment to the tourists. By Sunday evening it was clear that the family parties were sorry they had come.

We had got a routine going. In theory it went something like this: up at 8 a.m., breakfast at the Manor Guest House at 8.30 a.m. for all; that is, except the one whose turn it was to refill the tanks. He went straight off to the compressor to finish filling the cylinders he hadn't managed to get done the previous evening. At 9 a.m., start loading; Francis brings the Zodiac round to the quay, we clamber aboard, squeezing in behind the parachutes, cylinders, sacks, weights, pump and everything else. . . . Louis meanwhile goes to fill up the petrol tanks. We dress: undergarments, first suit, second suit. Some last-minute preparations, then leave the harbour around 10.30 a.m. At 11 a.m. anchor at Lacada Point, on two grapples. By 11.15 or thereabouts we tumble into the water. Three hours' work on the sea-bed, long enough to get through one pair of cylinders (2 cubic metre tanks inflated to 200kg.), fifteen minutes on board, time for a cigarette while we change cylinders, followed by another three hours on the sea-bed, with a second pair of cylinders. Half an hour for the return journey if the weather is calm. If not, we have to take a more round-about route to avoid the dangerous 'one mile stone' where the swell and counter-currents stir the sea up until it is like a witch's cauldron. At 6 p.m., go ashore. An hour to unload, swallow a cup of hot coffee and undress. Ten minutes wait outside the bathroom door and then three minutes under a hot shower with the rest of the team drumming at the door. By 7.15 p.m. we are all showered and dry. For some of us, two hours' work breaking up the magma that we have brought back. Someone else must spend three hours filling cylinders. Maurice will spend the time repairing an engine or a compressor. The lucky ones get off lightly, cooking crabs and lobsters. For all of us there are some skilled gluing jobs to be done, mending the knees in our diving suits. And for me, finally, two or three hours at my desk, writing up the daily report, classifying what we have found, making a detailed inventory of all the objects, cleaning them in acid or carrying out the first stages of the preservation treatment, and sending off, posthaste, our most urgent administrative correspondence. At 10 p.m. or 10.30 we sit down to a supper of lobster, grilled salmon, or a leg of lamb, and at 11.30 p.m. Francis brings in the coffee and we roll out the green baize, put the bottle of Old Bushmills in the middle of the table, and lay out the bundles of notes. Louis shuffles the cards and the poker game gets under way.

At last one collapses into bed and then one tells oneself that underwater archaeology truly is a complete sport. And the proof is that one aches all over. One aches from having carried cylinders and motors, one aches from having pushed stones around like a human bulldozer, from having dug craters and built hills, shovelled sand and cleared it, one aches from having swum too much, from having towed enormous parachutes, pulled anchors or heaved aboard 120 lb. lead ingots.

The sea does not recognise weekends. Every season we lost between 12 lb. and 16 lb. each in weight. Right from the start we decided to rest only when the weather was bad, so when it kept

231

consistently calm for two weeks on end, or as once happened for six weeks, we all suffered strained backs, aching limbs, slipped discs or palpitations.

Two or three times, frozen, cold-ridden and dead tired, I did give up in calm weather after only one dive. The guilt that I felt in the evening was infinitely worse than the agony of diving again, and I didn't soon repeat the experiment.

When the bad weather did come, Maurice would announce: 'Equipment maintenance', or 'Dinghy cleaning'. Some of us would set to with scrubbing brushes, others with paint brushes and Francis, usually, would be given his own special task: his job was counting weighing, measuring and carefully classifying, one by one, all our lead bullets, including crushed ones, half ones and even quarter ones. He would also weigh and measure stone cannon balls and iron ones, then sort them out, checking them off, according to calibre, against the *Girona's* 8,166 balls for use with her fifty firing pieces of eight different types.

I would take our thousands of fragments of silver, pewter, bronze and pottery out of their boxes, spread them out on a table and sort them into little plastic bags, trying to fit the jigsaw together, or at least work out exactly how many different artifacts our various fragments must have made upon 26 October 1588, at midnight. How many gold-plated goblets, silver plates and forks, how many meat dishes, how many pewter pots and silver candlesticks, how many glazed clay bowls?

If the bad weather persisted I would get out my Nikon and go on with the photographic inventory of artifacts, or else I would make a trip to Belfast to take the jewels and gold coins to the bank and deliver the most fragile objects to the preservation laboratory for treatment.

The preservation laboratory, which operates under the combined auspices of Queen's University and the Ulster Museum, was of tremendous help to us. The Museum Curator, Mr W. A. Seaby, and the keeper, Lawrence N. W. Flanagan, had offered to help of their own accord, and Stephen Rees Jones, Director of the Laboratory, showed himself willing to put himself to any amount of trouble to solve the preservation problems posed by the thousands of impossible objects we would bring him, in the most daunting condition. Anything made of metal, other than gold or lead, that has spent a long period of time in the sea, requires very delicate preservation, as does anything made from an organic material (such as bone, leather or wood). Otherwise, as soon as they come into contact with the air, they are swiftly and totally destroyed. An iron cannon ball, for example, just out of its gangue of oxide and sand, looks as good as new, black and perfectly round. Once exposed to the air, it turns brown in a matter of minutes, red in an an hour, and after a few days the changes in temperature and humidity in the atmosphere cause it to crack and scale, and sweat great drops of brown liquid. After two weeks it begins to erupt in blisters and the whole of its outer layer flakes off. After another month or two all that will be left of the ball will be a shapeless little mound of rust. The same process occurs over a longer period with iron cannons and anchors.

Protected from erosion and borers by mud and sand, a wooden pulley block or figurehead may have remained in perfect condition. But without treatment the fibres of the wood will contract as it dries out. It will warp and crack, lose its shape and finally disappear to nothing. As the water seeps out, the destroyed cells of the wood collapse completely if they are left unsupported (briefly the treatment consists in replacing the water in the wood with polyethylene glycol to keep the fibres in shape). This is why bringing things like this up from a wreck, as souvenir hunting divers sometimes do, without having made any provisions for treating them, is effectively to destroy them. We took great care never to expose anything fragile that we found to the air. Depending on the object, we would either keep it under water, or else we would put the first stage of the treatment into operation immediately, ourselves.

For small objects, straightforward cleaning did not pose any problems. I did it myself in the evenings. My bedroom was cluttered with pots, filled with brownish, blue, green, murky liquids, bubbling away and filling the air with noxious smells and acrid fumes that used to make my eyes smart all night long. This was to dissolve the chalky encrustations or the black gangue that clogged some of the jewels.

But chemical, electro-chemical, or electrolytic preservation methods are long and complex. They require daily attention by a team of experts and a perfectly equipped laboratory. It had taken Stephen the whole winter to save some of the cannon balls, the anchor and about a hundred other metal objects. His masterpiece was the musket. He had let it stew over a long period, then rinsed it to remove the salt, and dehydrated it in alcohol before steeping it at heat in polyethylene glycol. The butt and stock of the gun were now like new. One could count the strokes made by the plane; the ramrod slipped in its hole better than on the night of the shipwreck. He returned to us in equally pristine condition the sycamore and soft wood (according to Queen's University botanists) sword pommels; a large lime-wood knife handle still bound with its original string; a penknife handle with copper flower-shaped rivets, carved from some exotic hardwood; a dagger handle, intricately decorated with plaited copper wire and its leather sheath; as well as a few oak and alder wood splinters of the galleass herself.

His assistants had patiently straightened out the pewter plates. They had glued the earthenware pots and the glazed plates together. They had rubbed the original animal oil back into the leather sandal straps and boot soles and made them supple once more, ready for wear.

By treating them with various complicated solutions, Stephen had also succeeded in saving the two bronze cannons, which were exuding a sort of white froth and threatening to lose their surface layer. This cleaning process had revealed a coat of arms embossed on one of the two firing pieces. The arms were clearly visible but undecipherable. They had weathered too many storms and suffered too much battering by stones and rocks. On the little breech loading cannon, I thought I recognised the arms of Spain. The four quarterings were there and the collar round it was certainly a Golden Fleece one. The breech blocks (*servidores*) had been given the same treatment, and inside Stephen had found intact the cotton match, the plug of powder and the popular wood stopper. (See plate 50.) We had also found two dozen miniature iron cannon balls (4·3 cm. calibre), so we were ready to fire. (See Appendix III for plan of the guns.)

It had taken lengthy correspondence on my part with sixteenth-century artillery experts, and many visits to museums and long research in books, to identify the gun (164·3 cm. long, calibre 4·5 cm.). The support pivot that held the trunnions was made of cast iron and had disappeared along with the *rabisa* (a 2 ft long stem that one rested on one's shoulder to aim) and the wooden chocks, or *cuñas* (put in through holes in the side to lock the powder chamber – the *servidor* or *recamara* – tightly).

I had called it quite incorrectly a 'falconete' because of its overall similarity to a fifteenth-century falconet. I had even toyed with the idea that it might be a 'pasavolante'. Finally, and without being quite sure of my ground yet, I decided 'esmeril'. (See plate 47.) I had lost one illusion along the way. Having been interested in antique Spanish naval ordnance for fifteen years, I had thought I knew something about it. My advice to those who share that illusion is never to open the masterly *Armada Guns*, by the late Professor Michael Lewis. They will need to do no more than flick quickly through it and the damage will be done. Not only will they realise right from the start that they know nothing about the subject, they will also realise that they never will know anything about it, unless like the author himself, they spend the best years of their lives going through all the contemporary literature, making an individual study of every gun in every museum, and taking apart every logbook, letter and list as well as the inventories of every fleet of every nation. Worse still, they will learn that the artillerists of the sixteenth century, who wrote treatises extending to many volumes, purely theoretical and full of mistakes, knew little or nothing about it either. First of all, the arts of building cannon, serving, laying and firing them were closely guarded secrets. Secondly, the technical vocabulary, dimensions and calibres, units of weights and measure, the whole terminology in fact, were subject to infinite variations. In the same way as happened with the names of ship types, for example, guns that were quite different in length, calibre, weight and appearance, would at different times and in different countries, or sometimes even at the same time and in the same country, be called by same names. (In the *Girona* inventory there were only eight named types of cannon, but we found shot for guns of at least eleven different calibres.)

Artillery first appeared in Spain in the fourteenth century. It developed rapidly in the fifteenth – which is when one finds it for the first time in ships – but it was not until the seventeenth century that Philip III first tried to standardise somewhat the manufacture of pieces of ordnance. Under Philip II, total anarchy still reigned in this area. The diversity of names used was infinite. It was not until I found (in Arantegui, the great Spanish expert) the following reference to some documents of 1547 in the National Archives in Simancas, that I found the answer to my particular problem: 'An octagonal esmeril [like ours], which fires a shot of ½ lb. [approximately the weight of ours], with the same weight of powder [about the weight of powder we found in our breech blocks] ... 38 calibres long from vent to muzzle [ours was about 36 calibres].' And: 'an octagonal esmeril firing 4-ounce shot [Ufano mentions 15-ounce shot for another esmeril] 24 calibres long.'

In 1587 Santa Cruz requested 'esmerils with two *servidores* each' for the galleasses. We found six of them. Spanish experts define the esmeril as 'a piece of light artillery, in use from the end of the fifteenth century to the first half of the seventeenth, falling somewhere between the *ribadoquin* and the musketoon, 38 calibres long'. Professor Lewis describes it as a small-calibre, short-range mankiller, breech loading and mounted on a universal joint pivot, used especially for defending a vessel in case of boarding by the enemy. F.F. Olesa Muñido concludes from his own research that 'it is a gun varying considerably in appearance, calibre and weight.'

But what finally disposed of any hesitation I might have had, was this providential quote from Lt Col Arantegui: 'Esmerils, like all other small guns, varied so much in weight and dimensions, that one could say that their features were whatever one wanted them to be.'

As for the other powder chambers, the big ones, that we found on Lacada Point without their guns, they belonged, I think to what the Marquis de Santa Cruz referred to in his inventories as a 'large esmeril'.

The other cannon – no possible doubt here – is a demi-saker. It has a calibre of 7·6 cm. and is 234 cm. long, or about 31 calibres (the expert, Lechuga, gives 32 calibres).

A demi-saker? Bronze? Once I had identified it, it began to remind me of something, that cannon. I dug about in the confusion of my files and out of the bale marked 'artillery' I pulled a note, scribbled down long ago in Madrid. 'In 1588, to arm the galleasses, the Duke of Medina Sidonia lent the Armada seven bronze demi-sakers from his personal arsenal at San Lucar.'

We had raised from a galleass a bronze demi-saker that was not a piece of naval ordnance (the Associate Curator of the Madrid Naval Museum confirmed this for me). Could it have been one of the seven pieces lent by the Duke himself? If only the arms were clearer! (See plate 49.)

39

A Bottle for Every Ten Gold Coins

Someone tapped me lightly on the shin.

I was digging in a deep cave, a long way under an enormous boulder, lying on the rock, flat on my stomach, my air cylinders scraping against the roof. I crawled out backwards.

I turned round: it was Louis. He was beaming. Behind his mask his eyes were shining. He was smiling broadly into his beard, and round his neck hung an enormous gold chain, three rows of gold chain – miles of gold chain.

The season had got off to rather a slow start. The inventories for the end of April and May were not remarkable, lists of fragments, nothing more. The first gold coin, a four escudo piece, did not come up until 11 May. It was Louis who found it. Then in June, Louis had a period of quite incredible luck. While the rest of us would work away staunchly in our corners and after five hours come up with one tiny, badly worn coin, he would be filling his bottomless green bag with a positive ballast of ducats and two-escudo pieces in perfect condition, plus twice as many pieces of eight and a few odd jewels, just for good measure.

Two miles from Port Ballintrae, the Irish distill the best whiskey in the world. During the lean days I had made a rash promise and thereby set a precedent: for every ten gold coins I would give the lucky diver a bottle of Old Bushmills.

It must be said that whisky is as necessary for divers on land as air is under water. It is a well established tradition in Ireland, and I had only been following the example of my predecessor, Sir George Carew, Master of the Ordnance, who used the same device in June 1589 to fire the enthusiasm of his men, when he was trying to raise some Spanish cannon off the West Coast. He gives a very good explanation for it in a letter to the Lord Deputy, dated 1 July:

> Yesterday we fastened our haullsers to a cannon of battery or basalyke as we supposed by the length, for they lie at four fathoms and a half of water, which was so huge that it broke our cables. Our diver was nearly drowned, but the Irish aqua vitae hath such virtue as I hope of his recovery.

Irish divers have not lost their faith in the old therapy and it is probably to that that they owe their resistance to the cold. Our friend John McLennan, for example, usually dives in a short neoprene suit, with bare arms, bare hands, bare legs and bare feet. Just to look at him, perfectly happy on the sea-bed in such a state of undress, is enough to make one shiver. I must admit though, he is a special case. John does actually make Old Bushmills whiskey. . . .

Anyway, by the time June came round, my rash promise was leading me into financial ruin and the rest of the team was falling into a drunken stupor. The day Louis came looking for me under the sea, wearing his triple gold necklace, I honestly saw the spectre of delirium tremens hovering in the algae.

His chain was as thick as a man's finger, 2·5 metres long and intact. Not one of its oval links had so much as a scratch on it. It was so heavy (1·8 kg.) that we couldn't help thinking of how some poor, rich nobleman must have been dragged down head first to the bottom under the weight of it.

In contemporary accounts, Spanish survivors often mention the chains that the English took from around their necks (sometimes they took the skin too). The English make markedly less mention of them in the minutes of their examination of prisoners, for not all of them went through the official channels which would have taken them to Her Majesty's chests. Among the questions laid down by the Lord Deputy for local authorities to ask Spanish prisoners before they cut their throats was 'whether any . . . have any chain, jewels or money of theirs in custody and who they be.' The question features in all the prescribed forms of examination without exception, and one David Gwyn, an interpreter who was said to have perjured himself and appropriated some gold chains taken from the Spaniards, found himself in very bad trouble.

One George Wadloke wrote to the Mayor of Waterford reporting that sixteen survivors had come ashore from a Spanish vessel run aground on the sand, wearing their gold chains around their necks. Medina Sidonia presented the Governor of Calais with a chain and noted the fact in his *diario*. Such chains were promised to French pilots, engaged in action in the Channel. They also came in handy for bribing traitors: in the autumn of 1588, in an attempt to buy off the English defence in Bergen Op Zoom, Parma promised Colonel Grimston 7,000 crowns, plus a gold chain for each officer.

In their portraits Renaissance gentlemen are invariably shown wearing such chains, which served as a necktie and an outward demonstration of wealth. A chain was also useful as the modern equivalent of the travellers' cheque: if he found himself short of cash a gentleman had only to open up a link with his teeth to pay for a horse, a meal or a girl.

Today, with a few exceptions, these chains have disappeared. Their value lay in the weight of the metal rather than in the workmanship and with changing fashions they were usually melted down. I knew of only one or two museums which still had examples. This is what made the ones found in wrecks absolutely priceless. (See plates xvi and 33.)

The sea is unpredictable. Next to the large chain, Louis had found another (76 cm. long), amazingly fine and light, a continuous chain, made in such a way – God alone knows how – that each of the flat links passed through three others: to cut it, one would have to cut not one but four links. This fragile masterpiece was all twisted, but complete, while other chains we found (a total of eight) had their links scattered all over the sea-bed. In 1967, for instance, as previously mentioned, the first gold object I found in front of the cave was a round link from a particular chain from which we kept finding more and more links every day for three summers, all over the site. They were everywhere, some open, some closed. By the end of 1968 we had 136 links, of five grams each, found either singly or in lengths of two, three or six. The chain then measured four feet. The following year it had grown to almost six feet. This chain is a plain one, identical to the one King Philip is shown wearing in an engraving done when he was nineteen, and similar to those depicted in other portraits painted by Rubens. I often wondered if it was actually possible that the sea should break a chain open and scatter such heavy, small objects so widely. Could not the owner have lost his chain, bit by bit, playing dice? And was it not more likely the links had been scattered along with the rest of the dead winners' possessions? But other small chains, like the figure-of-eight one, far too fine for anyone to have even thought of breaking them up, were scattered in the same way.... One splendidly worked, originally studded with pearls and other precious stones, had been similarly dispersed.

On the two-gold-chain day, Louis also found thirty gold pieces, but by that time we weren't even bothering to mention the escudos. Every day Louis used to find his dozen regularly, some days more. It had become an accepted pattern. When he came up we would ask: 'And what else have you found?'

What else? One day it was a gold signet ring, a large seal engraved with the letters IHS. (See plate 32.) IHS is the classical monogram for IHEOUS (Jesus in Greek). The H is stamped with a cross and underlined with a strange symbol: a nail from the cross and a sort of bracket, instead of the usual three nails. It was probably a Jesuit father's ring. Ignatius Loyola adopted the sigma IHS in 1541 in his seal as General of the Society of Jesus and it subsequently became the emblem of the institution (he is shown, in a famous portrait, wearing the same sigma on his breastplate). Alternatively the ring might have belonged to a Canon of the Order of the Holy Sepulchre, the religious order founded in Spain in the twelfth century, not the military order of knighthood of the same name. The nuns of the Order still wear the same seal, with the bracket instead of the nails.

Another day Louis fished up a Portuguese gold coin, the only one in the inventory, minted in the reign of John III (1521–57). On the reverse it had St Vincent with palm and ship and the inscription: 'Zelator Fidei usque ad Mortem'; on the obverse were the crowned arms of Portugal and 'Johannus III REX POTV ET AL' (King of Portugal and Algarve).

Another day it was a handful of gold buttons, little balls 0·5–1·5 cm. in diameter, engraved with stylised flowers and geometrical designs, with a ring to sew them on by. They were just like the ones seen on doublets in Spanish and Flemish portraits of the period. What amused me considerably was finding those same Spanish buttons, which we picked up by the dozen, on Sir Francis Drake's doublet and slashed sleeves in an engraving by Joss de Hondt. Did he get his off his prisoners' clothes?

And finally, another day, it was a gold book!

I was lifting myself on board and I saw that everyone was smiling. I knew what it meant. Louis had done it again? Of course! My eyes went straight to his little green bag and there was a block of gold. A block, exquisitely chased with flowers and scrolls. I took it in my hand – a little bible on a small double chain. It has a thick binding. On the cover, a saint, finely engraved, holds a staff in one hand and a book in the other. The engraved figure is framed by small pillars and a pediment. It must be St John the Baptist, for on closer inspection I can just see that the staff ends in a cross (half hidden by the frame) and has a banner on it. The oriflamme cross and the Holy Book (and often, but not always, a lamb, the Lamb of God) are the attributes of St John the Baptist in all religious iconography. The back cover, moulded into a now empty recess, must have contained a relic. The next day, a couple of yards away, Louis found the gold frame, like the one on the front cover, that must have held the protective crystal in place. The reliquary ($43 \times 32 \times 9$ mm.) opened like a real book, but the clasp had jammed when the cover got crushed by stones. We should have to wait until the evening to find out what marvels it contained.

That evening, very carefully, using jewellers tools, I removed the gold wire that had held the book closed for four hundred years and very slowly opened it. Inside lay neither diamonds nor emeralds, but a broken gold ring and two little columns with a hinge at the bottom (perhaps the broken pieces of some other jewel). Most important of all were five little round containers, five gold cylinders, fixed to the back cover. Two of them still contained a little tablet of red wax, all shrivelled up. What could they be? Pills? Incense? Poison? But there weren't any Borgias aboard. Some cosmetic concentrate? Rhinoceros horn aphrodisiacs, perhaps? In order to get the mystery cleared up, I sent off one of the wax-based tablets to the Chemistry Department of Queen's University in Belfast. The results of the analysis took some time to come through. At last I heard from the experts. In their

242

opinion it was without any doubt 'a tablet made from some wax-based substance'. (See plates xxvi–xxviii.)

Two months' later, after millions of viewers had seen the little book on British television, during a special fifty minute colour programme, I got my answer. It arrived from Miss Margaret Cronin along with an avalanche of other letters full of fantastic suggestions. The tablets were *Agnus Dei*.

Agnus Dei had been made in Rome since the ninth century, with the wax from the previous year's Easter candles, mixed with holy oil (the wax symbolised Christ's virgin flesh). They were votive objects, supposed to have miraculous, protective qualities, and were often worn hung round the neck. A highly complex ritual, modified several times over the centuries, accompanied each stage of their manufacture. In the sixteenth century there were specialist monks in Rome who made them in advance. On one side they stamped the image of the paschal lamb, the ancient symbol of Christ, the Lamb of God; of innocence; and St John the Baptist, God's servant, innocently suffering for his people. It was obvious that the image of St John would appear on a box made to hold *Agnus Dei*. The lamb stamped on the tablets carried a cross or a flag. On the reverse the monks impressed the image of a saint, or the name or arms of the reigning Pope. Nothing of that was visible any more on our red tablets, all cracked and shrivelled, and also somewhat smaller than usual.

The Pope would bless them all together, on the Wednesday of Holy Week in the first year of his reign and then every seven years after that. He dipped them in a mixture of holy water and oil over which he had said a few prayers. The distribution took place the following Saturday. During the Mass, after the *Agnus Dei*, the Pope would place packets of the wax tablets in the upturned mitres of bishops and cardinals who had come to receive them. The dignitaries of the Church, in their turn, would distribute them to those of their friends and acquaintances who in one way or another had shown themselves worthy of such a signal favour.

The counterfeiting of *Agnus Dei* was severely prohibited, and several Bulls were published forbidding the decoration or painting of them. These miraculous amulets were thought to protect their lucky owner from all evil forces, and particularly from fire and flood. Many examples are quoted of fires and serious floods being stopped in their tracks by an *Agnus Dei*. They also protected pregnant women from the perils of childbirth, and one of their prime functions was the protection of sailors from plague and storm.

At the time of the Armada, Queen Elizabeth had forbidden by law the importing of '*Agnus Dei* and other popish trumperies' into England.

The custom in Rome was that one was given, at the same time as the *Agnus Dei*, a little instruction book, a printed leaflet listing the amulet's many qualities. I wondered whether it was such a leaflet that was kept, carefully folded, in the deep recess in the back cover of our gold reliquary book. I also wondered about the fact that there were five gold containers in the box. Was it usual for an ordinary Catholic to carry not one but several *Agnus Dei*? Might the reliquary not have belonged to a bishop who had received his small supply in Rome and was parsimoniously distributing them (he still had two left out of five)? In which case it could possibly have belonged to the Bishop of Killaloe, who sailed with Don Alonzo on the *rata*.

Following Louis, I had my own period of plenty. I began by finding, around a small protruding rock, the ship's silver – gold plated, engraved and decorated, but smashed to smithereens. It made a silver jigsaw puzzle: broken knives and forks; fragments of dishes; plate or goblet rims; jug handles, samovar feet, chest hinges; ewer spouts, broken pieces of statuettes; bits of fruit or sugar bowls; candlesticks, flasks, inkpots or sauce boats. Then I struck a vein of four-escudo pieces that produced some six to twelve coins a day, as well as some small medallion or other, usually an empty frame, as a daily bonus. Some of these frames were originally parts of bracelets, others would have been badges, or held jewels sewn on to ribbons or doublets. Almost all of them had lost their central cameo, their miniature or their semi-precious stone. With exceptional luck, André found a pair of them intact, still set with bright pearls and a little central ruby. Bob found a very large one, but empty. Apart from that, bad luck dogged this tireless giant. Every day he moved underwater mountains, only to find nothing but half a lead bullet or a highly suspect bone. For a long time Francis shared his bad luck, while Maurice, a specialist since last year on Neapolitan ducats and scudis, used to bring back Charles v as a Roman Emperor one day, and Philip ii the next, crowned, bare-headed, or wreathed in laurels.

244

My record for 1969 was to be seventeen gold coins in one day of six hours' work on the sea-bed. I am the first to admit that compared to Maurice's twenty, and Louis's thirty coins, seventeen is not much But this time, I am pleased to report, no unfortunate incidents occurred while the coins were in my hands, and even though they were photographed, I did bring all seventeen ashore.

40

A History Lesson Under the Ocean

We found in all 405 gold coins, 756 silver and 115 copper coins, minted in six different countries – Spain, Portugal, the Kingdom of the Two Sicilies, the Republic of Genoa, Mexico and Peru; in eight different reigns – the Catholic Kings, Joan the Mad, Charles v and Philip II of Spain; Manuel I, John III and Sebastian of Portugal, and an unidentified doge of Genoa. They were struck in fourteen different mints: Seville, Toledo, Segovia, Madrid, Burgos, Cuenca, Granada, Corunna, Valladolid, Mexico, Lima, Potósi, Lisbon and Genoa, and were of sixty different denominations. (See plates 34–39 and xxi).

This seemingly extraordinary variety is easily explained. We did not bring up the contents of an official chest, but money that belonged to the many passengers who had come from far and wide to join the crusade. Some of the coins are very rare, two or three possibly previously unknown, and most of them at least 'very fine'. Some of them contain variations, anomalies, spelling mistakes, or inverted dates, such as to make the most sophisticated of numismatists jump from their seats.

As far as we are concerned they are quite simply beautiful objects that we love to look at and touch again and again, beautiful objects that set our minds wandering each time we see them, for as we found them, one by one, thirty feet under water, each one of those 1,276 coins gave us a fascinating history lesson.

Spain, united for the first time in the marriage of Isabella of Castile and Ferdinand of Aragon in 1469, became officially one nation ten years later. In 1492 the last territories were recaptured from the Moors. From the reign of the Catholic Kings, we found pieces of four and pieces of eight, bearing the yoke and the bundle of arrows intertwined, symbols of Ferdinand's and Isabella's respective states, and the arms of Spain (Castile, Leon, Aragon, Catalonia and the Balearic Islands) over the arms of Granada, marking the recent conquest of Granada and the end of the *Reconquista*. These coins would probably have been already 100 years old when the *Girona* went down.

Charles I of Spain (Charles V of the Holy Roman Empire) began his reign with his mother, Joan the Mad (widow of Archduke Philip of Austria) as Regent. We had about ten ducats from that period, found by Maurice, inscribed: CAROLUS ET JOHANA HISPANIARUM REGES ET SICILIAE. Charles was also King of the Two Sicilies, whose capital was Naples. It was at the mint in Naples that all our gold ducats and silver half ducats were struck, carrying his effigy as Holy Roman Emperor, wearing a Roman breastplate. These are inscribed CAROLUS V RO. IMP and on the reverse R. HISPAN. UTRIUS SICIL. (Charles V Emperor of the Romans, King of all the Spains and of the Two Sicilies). It was Naples that had armed the *Girona* and the three other galleasses of the squadron for Charles's son, her King, Philip II.

We have almost every coin of Philip's reign: one, two and four gold escudos, struck in almost every mint in Spain; one, two, four and eight silver reals (the famous pieces of eight); unfortunately we are still missing the half and quarter reals.

The Kings of Spain were also rulers of the West Indies and of the Americas. One look at the coins we found was sufficient to remind us of this fact: PHILIPPUS DEI GRATIA HISPANIARUM ET INDIARUM REX. Philip, like his father before him, had money minted in America. Many of our silver coins, pieces of eight, of four and two, bear the stamp of Mexico, Lima or Potósi (then in northern Peru, now in Bolivia). Some Mexican coins have the device PLUS ULTRA inscribed on a scroll stretched between two columns, Hercules' columns, representing the Straits of Gibraltar, against a background of waves. The ancients believed that the world ended at the Pillars of Hercules, and that beyond them lay nothing – *nil plus ultra*. Under the aegis of the Catholic Kings, Don Cristobal Colon proved that this was not so. The Spaniards were proud to recall it. *Plus ultra* – their empire stretched far beyond them.

In his youth Philip took as his second wife the Queen of England,

Mary Tudor. We found ducats dating from this period, bearing the name of Philip II, King of England, King of France and Naples, Prince of Spain, King of France (because of Calais, England's last stronghold and the last vestige of her claims in France). When the Queen, his wife, died childless in 1558, the King Consort lost all claims to the English throne. Identical half ducats say simply: 'Philip II, by the Grace of God, King of Aragon and the Two Sicilies.' Thus we know that the coins were minted after 1558.

Because the fleet assembled in Lisbon and there were some Portuguese units on board (Portugal had come under Philip's rule in 1580), we can explain why we found any number of Portuguese gold, silver and copper coins.

My acquaintance with numismatics is restricted to a limited period, from the sixteenth to the nineteenth century, of Spanish and colonial issues. I therefore had the greatest difficulty, and consequently the greatest pleasure, in identifying some partially effaced Neapolitan and Portuguese pieces. I would never have managed it without the help of Professor Michael Dolley, a brilliant and ebullient Irish numismatist, and Mr Wilfred A. Seaby, Director of the Ulster Museum in Belfast, whose reputation as a numismatist is worldwide and who was kind enough to allow me the run of his library.

But the coin that really stumped me was a small silver one that Louis found all by himself. On the reverse was a castle and a palm tree and the legend: DUX ET GUBER ... illegible ... ENU ... illegible ... and on the obverse was a cross, somewhere between a St George's cross and a Lusitanian cross and the inscription CONRADUS REX RO ... illegible ... A .. illegible.

A king, who was also duke *and* governor? Why didn't they throw in mayor for good measure? Who on earth could it be? I dug about in the history books and came across several highly improbable Conrads: a thirteenth-century Duke of Mazovia in Prussia; a Conrad von Jungingen and another von Wettin, who ruled over some obscure little states on the borders of Germany and Poland; and then some more who at least had the merit of being kings. A tenth-century Conrad I of Franconia: an eleventh-century Conrad II; a Conrad III of Hohenstauffen, who went to the Second Crusade; and a Conrad IV of Germany who died in 1254. But we were way off. In the sixteenth century there wasn't the ghost of a Conrad to be found in the whole

248

of Europe. Perhaps there was a collector of old coins on the *Girona*?

And then one evening, the Spanish Consul in Belfast introduced me to Professor Dolley. In the course of conversation I described our mystery coin to him. Dolley leapt out of his chair, exclaiming 'I know, I know.' He fell back, then sprung up again and immediately began to explain very fast and in great detail, that the coin was Genoese, probably contemporary with the Armada. It was a 'genovino', minted sometime between 1527 and 1557, modelled on a much older coin which had inspired such confidence in merchants and bankers all over Italy and the rest of Europe that it went on being minted until the eighteenth century. The Conrad in question had long been forgotten (in much the same way as Maria Theresa Austrian thalers are still minted in Vienna for the Yemen, where they are legal tender).

The Conradus in question, continued Professor Dolley, was probably Conrad ɪɪ, son of Conrad ɪ, who acceded to the throne of France after extinction of the Carolingians in 911. He was himself Emperor of the Franconians and had conquered Italy, where in 1027 he was crowned in Milan with the iron crown of the Kings of Lombardy. It was there too that he won the right to the title of King of the Romans, and Doge (Dux) and Governor of the ancient Roman province of Liguna, now the Republic of Genoa. This type of coin is famous in both gold and silver. Dolley showed me a picture of it, marked 'very rare'. Complete, the inscription reads: CONRADUS REX ROMA AS DUX ET GUBER RIPV. GEN.

The cameos, too, were proving something of an enigma. The previous year we had found eight very fine gold jewels, set with pearls, six of which still contained a lapis lazuli cameo, each bearing the profile of a different Roman Emperor wearing a laurel crown. This year Francis had been set to do nothing else for a month but look for the others. In May he found the ninth jewel. In September, Louis and André brought up the tenth and the eleventh. I think I know where the twelfth is – the last, maybe – but the equinoctial storms put us off and we left it behind.

I had assumed from the start that what we had there were the twelve Caesars. But in that case, who was who? The emperors celebrated by Suetonius in his *Lives of the Twelve Caesars*, were the twelve first: Julius Caesar, then Augustus, Tiberius, Caligula, Claudius, Nero, Galba, Otto, Vitellius, Vespasian, Titus and Domitian. Being the best known, these are the ones who have been portrayed most often by sculptors, miniaturists, engravers and the makers of cameos and medals, frequently using coins for the likenesses. With such a widespread iconography they ought to have been easy to recognise. In fact, the more portraits of Roman emperors I studied the more obvious it became to me that the special qualities of Renaissance artists, lay more in their powers of imagination and ease of style than in their concern for a good likeness of a Roman coin. Our cameos were not Roman but Renaissance ones and almost certainly Italian (or Spanish of Italian influence), like the jewels in which they were set. The experts were all agreed on that point. That they were all from the one workshop was obvious from the uniformity of medium and technique and also from the hair styles – the laurel crowns were identical. Glyptics, the art of eroding on hard stones, at which the Romans and the Egyptians excelled, had been enjoying a revival for 100 years already by the time of the Armada. This was due mainly to the patronage of the Medicis and Leo x. The best known artists of the sixteenth century (whose work, however, lacked the quality of the cameos produced in the studios of the previous century) were Domenico dei Camei and Valerio Vincentino (died 1546), who was particularly famous for his cameos depicting gods, mythological scenes, and emperors in the classical style. He might well have made ours.

My task was made that much more difficult by the fact that three of the profiles, while one could not deny that they were noble and pure, were utterly anonymous. Augustus, Tiberius, Domitian, one could give them any name one liked; they were interchangeable. I could, therefore, work only from the three faces with clearly defined features, which were easily identifiable. I immediately recognised, or so I thought, Julius Caesar, with his hollow cheeks and aquiline nose turning down to meet his hooked chin, and, possibly, Vitellius (or Vespasian) in the fat man with the double chin.

But it was the eleventh cameo that brought my theory crashing down. It was a young face, unusual, with a squashed boxer's nose, thick lips (the upper protruding above the lower) and a rounded chin with a deep dimple. That could not possibly be one of the twelve Caesars. But then, who was it?

It was a Renaissance piece so I looked through contemporary icon-ographies for portraits of figures considered important at the time – those same portraits that sixteenth-century cameo makers would have copied. And almost immediately I found my young Caesar with the boxer's nose. In a work dated 1544, 'Icones Imperatorum' by Jacobus Micylus, was a detailed engraving clearly showing every detail of his profile. It was Michael I, Rhangabe, crowned Emperor of the Romans in Byzantium in 811, when he was still very young. Within two years, as a result of his weakness and countless capitu-lations, he had become an object of ridicule. He abdicated and went to live out the last thirty-five years of his life in a monastery.

And what about the others? Were they just any old emperors, picked out at random from the twelve Caesars and others, or were they all Byzantine Caesars? By the time I had finished I was inclined to think that they were in fact all Byzantine emperors, for the one that I had originally called Julius Caesar was as like as two peas to Stauratius, who reigned for a short time in 811 just before Michael I, and my Vitellius/Vespasian could well have been Constantine the Younger (Constantine II) who after the death of Constantine I in 337 reigned jointly with Constantius for a short while.

And if in fact they were the Emperors of Constantinople, might the cameos not have belonged to Manuel Paleologus, a direct descendant of their successors, who, I knew, was on the expedition? What more appropriate for the victory Te Deum in London than that he should be wearing the portraits of his ancestors in a necklace on his breast? (See plates xxx and 42.)

41

Six Thousand Hours on the Sea Bed

September was drawing to a close. The faded algae were frayed like flags the evening after a battle.

Repeated gales finally drove us away for good. It was high time. The straps on our cylinders were covered with little green algae and shell-fish were thriving on our flippers. Our engines and compressors were giving up the ghost, the inflatable dinghies began to leak like sieves. Francis's knees had come through his two diving suits.

I handed Louis my second cylinder to inflate one last parachute. I wanted to feast my eyes one last time on the spot where I was leaving behind a little of my soul. It was raining. The clouds were low. I sat dreaming in the Zodiac as it rocked in the swell, anchored between two grapples.

I now knew everything that I wanted to know. I had proved what was just a guess. I had found the remains of a ship. It contained Spanish cannon, coins and seals from all over the Spanish Empire, and Spanish lead ingots. The name of the site perpetuates the tradition that it was a Spanish ship. The ship was connected in one way or another with Naples; the number of coins that we found from the Two Sicilies proves that. She sank at the end of the sixteenth century – the coins stop at Philip II and the last date is 1585. It was not a merchant ship; she was carrying too much shot and too much lead, plates, and ingots, for that. And besides the Spanish never traded with Northern Ireland. Therefore she must have been a Spanish warship. She must have come from the Armada. A great many Spanish and English documents contain accounts of the loss of the *Girona* somewhere in this area – none mentions any other Armada ship lost off Ulster. Spanish and English documents talk of jewels, gold and silver found on bodies and in the remains of the ship. We found 47 gold jewels, 8 chains, 1,256 coins, 2 insignia of knighthood, and any amount of gold table plate and silver, proof that there must have been many rich men aboard, and several noblemen. None of the ships lost, other than the *Girona* had a significantly large crew aboard. No other ship lost off Ireland would have contained cannon balls corresponding exactly to the *Girona*'s. And, finally, no other ship would have gone down with Captain Spinola's Order of Malta, or a ring belonging to Nicole de Champagney's grandson, drowned in the *Girona* and mourned on the spot by Captain Cuellar.

I watched the waves breaking off Lacada Point, 50 yds to the north-west. They catch on a reef there, a submerged mound, rising up in some 40 ft of water. At low tide the top of it is only about 12 ft below the surface. It was actually at the foot of this that Marc found the anchor and I found the astrolabe. It all seems clear.

That stormy night in October 1588, the *Girona* struck the top of the reef, or maybe she just rolled over it, caught athwartships by a breaker. As soon as the Spanish realised that they were about to go on the rocks they dropped anchor. It was near midnight. The pilot was standing on the deck holding his astrolabe at the ready, waiting for a break in the cloud to take a sighting on a star. As the galleass rolled his astrolabe slipped into the sea.

Between the reef and Lacada Point, I found the remains of a smaller anchor. Did they try to launch a boat? Did it capsize, losing its anchor?

The vessel had begun to turn round on herself, but the next moment she was being broken apart on Lacada Point. From her gaping hull spilled cannon balls and lead ingots along with all the kitchen equipment. A section of the hull, weighed down by the lead plates that had been nailed to it, stayed where it was. Some of the cannon were left high and dry, others rolled down the underwater slope until they reached the flat. Men came tumbling out of her, only to be drowned within minutes, scattered, thrown on to the cliffs or carried out to sea by the tide. Wave upon wave cast up on to the rock fragments of the dead ship and men with bulging pockets (and perhaps with their caskets, on which James McDonnell will have got his hands). The aftercastle broke away from the shattered hull and drifted eastwards. The Captain's cabin emptied out its treasures and its passengers, sprinkling the sea-bed with coins, jewels and a thousand more ephemeral things. It finally came up against a blind rock to the east of Lacada Point, crashed and split itself open underwater, disgorging its silver plate.

Another part of the *Girona* was carried along the west side of Lacada Point, leaving behind it a trail of perrier balls which we found, and men, whose possessions we also recovered. From there the swirling currents drove it on to a reef to the west of Spaniard Cave. It ended by running into the foot of it, together with all its cannon balls, ballast and débris. This was almost certainly part of the prow, containing the crew's quarters. We found only small coins there.

For 380 years, the sea churned it all up. Then along we came to undo what she had done.

And so the divers surfaced for the last time. I hoisted the neoprene lifting bags aboard. Maurice brought back the crowbars, the worn out shovels and the dented buckets.

For the last time we weighed the grappling anchors. As we headed into the swell the black sky broke, and the sun cast warm streaks of colour across the cliffs. On the rocky teeth of the reefs, spreadeagled, totem-like cormorants took advantage of the warmth and stretched out their wings to dry.

No one spoke. We were proud of our 6,000 hours of work underwater. The sea-bed we excavated is now gutted, broken up, overturned and unrecognisable. The rock, scraped to the quick for ten whole months, is gouged with deep wounds. The sea hid her secret well, but with patience we learned all her ruses, one by one, and snatched from her all she had been keeping to herself for 400 years.

Of course we did not cover every square inch. There are still a few gold coins scattered around at Port na Spaniagh and one or two cannon balls buried under stones and sand. But less and less of them, further and further apart, more and more difficult to find. We would not return to Port na Spaniagh. We had done a good job. We had fulfilled, maybe even surpassed, all reasonable expectations. Our consciences were clear.

The legal problems raised by my discoveries were without precedent and incredibly complicated. The artifacts recovered have no clear legal status and no owner. I am only the possessor of them.

My own wish was that rather than going under the hammer to the highest bidder and straight into the glass cases of a few American or Swiss millionaires, the entire collection from the finest jewel down to the humblest cannon ball should remain intact in a maritime or archaeological museum. There it could be permanently displayed with contemporary documents and together with our maps, charts and photographs that tell the complete story of those three long, marvellous years of work. After years of delays and negotiations with the Crown, I was to succeed. The Ulster Museum, Northern Ireland National Museum, was officially designated to house the collection, and the 'Girona Rooms' were opened on 22 June 1972.

And now, the most difficult part still remained to be done: from some 12,000 artifacts: jewels, coins, utensils, ship's remains, arms, shot, instruments, pot shards and other fragments, I must extract every bit of information they can still yield – about the galleass and her passengers, about life aboard, about the technical skills and the art of the period, and having done that I must publish it all.

After that we will all set off together to a new wreck.

One day, in the cave, I was trying to release the winged golden salamander from between three large stones. It was encrusted with rubies and engraved down to the tiniest scale. I did not want to scratch it. I thought I had been working at it for three quarters of an hour. When I had to go on to reserve, I realised that I had been there three hours, but at last I was holding the salamander in the palm of my hand, quite beautiful, and firmly set on its feet. Then, almost imperceptibly he beat his wings and wriggled. He looked up at me with his little dragon's eye, his turned up nose, and curled back his lip, showing his teeth. I smiled back at him and that day I knew that I was still a child and I swore to myself that I would remain a child for the rest of my life, that I would never stop enjoying the pastimes and simple delights of childhood. For I knew then that I was making good use of my life, every moment of it, because I knew that I was happy.

APPENDIX I

Alonzo Martinez De Leiva

'Our' Don Alonzo Martinez De Leiva must not be confused with:

—Don Sancho De Leiva, his father, Knight of Santiago, famous general of galleys and Viceroy of Naples.

—Don Sancho De Leiva, his brother, Knight of Santiago, who was not on the expedition.

—Don Pedro De Leiva, his younger brother, Knight of Alcantara, who served with his father and with his brother, Alonzo. No one knows whether he was on the expedition or not.

—Don Diego De Leiva (perhaps another brother) who sailed on the *rata* also, with his company of 145 soldiers (Tercio or Andalusia).

—Captain Antonio De Leiva, who had a company of 134 Castilians in the Armada.

—Don Francisco De Leiva, ex-admiral of the Plate Fleets, who was *cabo*, second in command of the squadron of Levant.

—Don Juan De Leyva, described simply as a 'knight adventurer'.

—Don Antonia Luis De Leiva, Prince of Ascoli, said to be the bastard son of Philip II, who sailed in the *San Martin* and who should not be confused with

—Don Antonio De Leiva, famous for his defence of Pavia against Francis I, favourite general of Charles V and first Prince of Ascoli (1480–1536). He was the uncle of Don Sancho, 'our' De Leiva's father.

There were two houses of De Leiva (or De Leyva; both spellings were used), the Castile one and the Murcia one. 'Our' Don Alonzo was 'Señor de la Casa De Leiva de Rioja' (Castile). His arms were sinoples, a tower with three open turrets or fretty gules, bordered gules charged with thirteen stars, three on the chief, four on the point, and three on each flank, one above another.

APPENDIX II

The Galleass

The name galleass was applied to large war galleys, in particular Venetian ones, but the real galleass was a large square-rigged vessel, a cross between a galley and a great ship, with an iron-covered beak. It was thought by its designers to combine the advantages of the two types of vessel, the free movement of the one with the firepower and solid bulk of the other.

Vittore Fausto built the first galleass in Venice in 1529, but at that stage it was no more than a large galley with lateen sails.

At the battle of Lepanto (1571) six Venetian galleasses, in the vanguard of the Christian galleys, destroyed the Turkish formation with the fire from their heavy prow batteries and managed to upset the enemy with their broadside perriers. Those particular galleasses, built by Frances Bressano, carried sixty pieces of ordnance – lombards, cannon, demi-cannon, culverins and perriers – in three heavy prow batteries and two poop batteries, the perriers between the thwarts, somewhat hindering their manœuvring. In the shelter of the castles were musketeers and arquebusiers. Those galleasses were 172 ft long by 22 ft wide. There were between thirteen and sixteen oars on each side. Chained to each of the twenty-six to thirty-two thwarts and protected by the upper deck, six to ten galley slaves pushed or pulled them, using grips fixed to the shafts. Two more oars reinforced the stern rudder.

In 1587, Santa Cruz had requested six for the Armada. He was expecting great things of them. And yet even at Lepanto the galleys had had to tow the galleasses into the battle and then position them for firing.

While the Venetian galleasses, Mediterranean vessels, were more like galleys than great ships, the ones that Bazan wanted for the Atlantic were closer to the great ship than to the galley.

There were never very many galleasses. The Channel encounters proved that in practice they combined the disadvantages of the galleys with those of the galleons, rather than their advantages. In normal conditions they moved under sail, using their oars only in absolutely calm, mill pond conditions. Even then, as soon as they were outclassed in fire power, the rowers became too vulnerable for the vessels to retain any worthwhile degree of mobility.

APPENDIX III

PLAN OF ORDNANCE SALVAGED

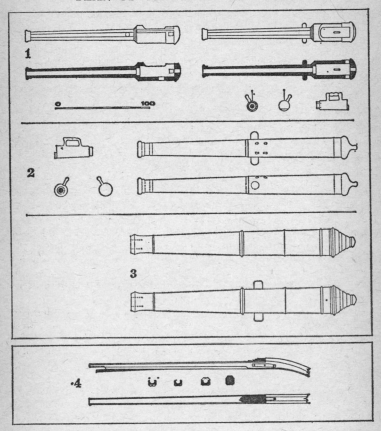

1. Esmeril with its *recamaras* (*Girona*, bronze)
2. Demi-saker with breech blocks of a gun not found (*Girona*, bronze)
3. Falcon recovered from the small island in Kiltoorish
    Lake (*Duquessa Santa Ana*, Iron)
4. Musket, not to the same scale (*Girona*)

APPENDIX IV

Family tree of the de Granvelles, showing the relation between Madame de Champagney and Don Tomas Perrenoto

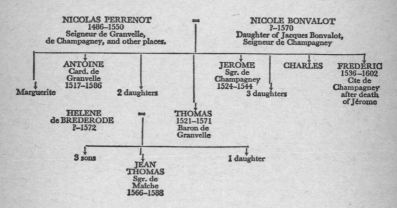

APPENDIX V

Summary Inventory of Artifacts Salvaged: 1967–9

Coins

Gold: 405
Silver: 756
Copper: 115

Jewellery

Important gold jewels: 35
Gold rings: 12
Gold chains: 8
Gold-plated chains: 1 (fragment)
Silver crucifixes: 2 (1 gold-plated)
plus several fragments

Medallions

Holy (made to be worn): 6
Round: 2

Nautical Instruments

Nautical dividers: 5
Astrolabes: 2
Sounding leads: 3
Unidentified: 1 (fragment)
Hour-glasses: 2 (doubtful, fragments of support)

Armaments

Bronze cannon: 2 (+ powder chamber of a third)
Small arms: 1 musket (stock only)
        2 flint locks (fragments)
        3 unidentified (fragments)
Sidearms: Swords or daggers: 4 (handles only)

Shot

Iron cannon balls: 61
Stone balls: 127
Lead bullets: 1,865

Lead

Ingots: 17 + 7 fragments
Plates: 23 + 3 fragments
Parts of Pulley blocks (square truncated pyramids, with a round central hole for the shaft): 32
Seals: 17
Steelyard weight: 1
Thin fragments of hull linings: several

Silver

Débris and fragments of
  Forks: 48
  Spoons: 22
  Ladles: 2
  Plates: 71 (one gold-plated)
  Small plates: 3
  Dishes: 41
  Gold-plated or decorated dishes: 10
  Sauce boats: 1
  Assorted spouts: 39
  Phials: 17
  Flasks: 4
  Bowls: 31
  Gold-plated or decorated bowls: 7
  Goblets and tankards: 27
  Covered pots: 27
  Candle snuffer: 1
  Sugar basin: 1
  Inkwells: 3 (doubtful)
  Candlesticks: 36
  Unidentified objects, moulded, gold-plated and chased: 26
  Chair decorations (?): 2
  Hilt-guard: 1
  plus many unidentified fragments

Pewter

Vases: 2
Bowls: 7
Dishes: 2
Soup plates: 3
Plates: 16
Small plate: 1
Capsules (?): 3
Pots: 2
Pots with handles: 2
Candlestick: 1
Jugs (or pitchers): 3
Hinge: 1

Bronze

Unidentified instruments: 11
Belt or strap buckles: 4
Feet from caskets, dishes, etc.: 3
Rod: 1
Decorated artifacts set on four feet: 1
Caslet on bronze feet: 1
Crucible: 1
Powder pestles: 2
Powder mortars: 2
Apothecary's pestle: 1
Nails: 19
Pins: 2

Copper

Dishes: 2
Circular container: 1
Cooking pot: 1
Knobs of cooking pot lids: 4
Cooking pot handles: 10
Feet off kitchen pots: 19
Stems and rods: 19
Unidentified hooks: 13
Unidentified tools and instruments: 7 (fragments)
Blade: 1
Ring: 1
Handle: 1 (from a knife or fork?)
plus many unidentified fragments

Pottery

Large pot with handle: 1
Other pots: 5
Small pot with spout: 1
Flat-bottomed vases: 2
Glazed pots: black: 3
             green: 8
             grey: 2
             yellow: 2
             white: 2
Decorated bowls: 4

Marble

Unidentified objects: egg-shaped, pierced from end to end: 4

Various

Knife: 1 (handle only)
Pen knives: 3 (handles and handle decorations)
Whetstone: 2
Rope: 3 bits
Sinkers: 13
Leather objects: straps: 2
                sole: 1
                Unidentified: 1
Glass bottle: 1 (fragment)
Window pane: 1 (bevelled corner fragment)
Bone: fragments (kitchen débris)
Anchor: 1
Anvil: 1
Small anchor: 1 (from a launch?)

INDEX

All Sphere Books are available at your bookshop or newsagent, or can be ordered from the following address:

Sphere Books, Cash Sales Department,
P.O. Box 11, Falmouth, Cornwall.

Please send cheque or postal order (no currency), and allow 7p per copy to cover the cost of postage and packing in U.K. or overseas.